MY HAVANA

The Musical City of Carlos Varela

For more than thirty years, musician Carlos Varela has been a guide to the heart, soul, and sound of Havana. One of the best known singer-songwriters to emerge out of the Cuban *nueva trova* movement, Varela has toured in North America, the Caribbean, Latin America, and Europe. In North America, Varela is "Cuba's Bob Dylan." In Cuba, he is the voice of the generation that came of age in the 1990s and for whom his songs are their generation's anthems. *My Havana* is a lyrical exploration of Varela's life and work, and of the vibrant musical, literary, and cinematic culture of his generation.

Popular both among Cubans on the island and in the diaspora, Varela is legendary for the intense political honesty of his lyrics. He is one of the most important musicians in the Cuban scene today. In *My Havana*, writers living in Canada, Cuba, the United States, and Great Britain use Varela's life and music to explore the history and cultural politics of contemporary Cuba. This book also includes an extended interview with Varela as well as the lyrics to all his recorded songs in Spanish and English, most of which are appearing in print for the very first time.

MARÍA CARIDAD CUMANÁ, formerly an adjunct professor in art history at Havana University, is a film critic and writer living in Miami.

KAREN DUBINSKY is a professor in the Department of History and the Department of Global Development Studies at Queen's University.

XENIA RELOBA DE LA CRUZ is the editor of the journal *Casa de las Américas*, published by the Casa de las Américas in Havana.

My Havana

The Musical City of Carlos Varela

Edited by María Caridad Cumaná,
Karen Dubinsky, and Xenia
Reloba de la Cruz

Translator: Ana Elena Arazoza

UNIVERSITY OF TORONTO PRESS
Toronto   Buffalo   London

© University of Toronto Press 2014
Toronto Buffalo London
www.utppublishing.com

ISBN 978-1-4426-4771-8 (cloth)
ISBN 978-1-4426-1578-6 (paper)

Library and Archives Canada Cataloguing in Publication

My Havana : the musical city of Carlos Varela / edited by María Caridad Cumaná, Karen Dubinsky, and Xenia Reloba de la Cruz ; translator, Ana Elena Arazoza.

Includes bibliographical references and index.
ISBN 978-1-4426-4771-8 (bound)   ISBN 978-1-4426-1578-6 (pbk.)

1. Varela, Carlos, 1963– – Criticism and interpretation. 2. Varela, Carlos, 1963– – Influence. 3. Popular music – Cuba – History and criticism. 4. Popular music – Political aspects – Cuba. 5. Songs, Spanish – Cuba – Texts – Translations into English. 1. Havana (Cuba) – Social life and customs. I. Dubinsky, Karen, editor II. Cumaná, María Caridad, 1964–, editor III. Reloba, Xenia, editor IV. Arazoza, Ana Elena, translator

ML420.V293M92 2014   782.42164092   C2014-902890-3

Cover Illustrations: (front) Carlos Varela in concert, Havana, 2013, photographed by Olivia Prendes D'Espaux; (back) Onelia López Ruiz, corner of Calle G and 17, Havana, from the installation, *The Wrinkles of the City – Havana, Cuba*, by JR and José Parlá/2012, Photographed by Mansoor Benham.

University of Toronto Press acknowledges the financial assistance to its publishing program of the Canada Council for the Arts and the Ontario Arts Council, an agency of the Ontario government.

 Canada Council for the Arts Conseil des Arts du Canada

 ONTARIO ARTS COUNCIL
CONSEIL DES ARTS DE L'ONTARIO
an Ontario government agency
un organisme du gouvernement de l'Ontario

University of Toronto Press acknowledges the financial support of the Government of Canada through the Canada Book Fund for its publishing activities.

Contents

Acknowledgments vii

Foreword xi
JACKSON BROWNE

Introduction: Varela's Musical City xiii
MARÍA CARIDAD CUMANÁ AND KAREN DUBINSKY

1 Carlos Varela: The Distinguished Son of William Tell 3
JOAQUÍN BORGES-TRIANA

2 The Persistence of "Memorias" 16
ROBERT NASATIR

3 "Politics Don't Fit in a Sugar Bowl": Cuba in the 1990s through the Music of Varela 35
XENIA RELOBA DE LA CRUZ

4 Carlos Varela and the Carousel of Cuban History 52
KAREN DUBINSKY

5 A Singer Who Uses the Guitar as a Camera: The Cinematic Quality of Carlos Varela's Songs 68
MARÍA CARIDAD CUMANÁ

6 Singing the Cityscape: Varela as Urban Chronicler   79
SUSAN THOMAS

7 Carlos Varela, Protest Song, and Cuban Music History   93
ROBIN MOORE

Epilogue. Carlos Varela: A Cuban Who Knows the Past but Can Also See the Future   101
PAUL WEBSTER HARE

Interview. Beginning a New Cuban Dream: An Interview with Carlos Varela   107
MARÍA CARIDAD CUMANÁ AND KAREN DUBINSKY

Appendix: Lyrics of Varela's Recorded Songs, in English and Spanish   125

Bibliography   263

Contributors' Biographies   271

Index   275

Acknowledgments

As we recount in these pages, this project began in Havana in 2004, when Havana film scholar María Caridad Cumaná advised Canadian researcher Karen Dubinsky, "If you want to know anything about the recent history of Cuba, you have to learn about Carlos Varela." It got a further stimulus in 2010 when the three editors found themselves (not completely by design) at the Latin American Studies Association conference in Toronto, presenting papers on Varela. Over the years, our mutual interest in contemporary Cuban music grew into a transnational, cross-cultural and cross-linguistic collaboration and friendship. The result is two versions of this book, in English and Spanish.

We are grateful that we found others who believed this book needed to exist and who shared our vision of what it could be. All of the contributors displayed both skill and patience as we progressed through the publication process. Robert Nasatir especially merits our gratitude for his editorial and translation skills and for his timely answers to countless e-mail questions. We also thank Queen's University's Senate Advisory Committee on Research (SARC) fund for providing a small grant that facilitated our editorial work and especially translation costs, as well as the Research Services office at Queen's for helping with other publication costs. Thanks to Rachel Abs, who compiled the bibliography, and Jaspreet Bal, who created the index.

A word about the translation: Ana Elena Arazoza, to whom we are enormously grateful, expertly translated most of the articles in Havana. Robert Nasatir translated his own article. The interview with Varela by Cumaná and Dubinsky was interpreted initially by Zaira Zarza in Havana, then transcribed and further translated by Vilma Vidal in Kingston. Translation of the song lyrics was truly a collaborative process, down to the last comma. The initial translation was done by Dubinsky, which was then edited and amplified by Raquel Martinez. Freddy Monasterio Barsó, Zaira Zarza, Robert Nasatir, and Paul Kelley provided additional invaluable translation advice. Carlos Varela's manager, Carlos Iglesias, also provided us with translations they had done for Varela's North American concert tours.

We would also like to thank Frances Mundy and Matthew Kudelka and the other talented people at University of Toronto Press for their enthusiasm for this project. We are very appreciative that acquisitions editor Len Husband had faith and was willing to take a chance on an unusual topic.

Finally, we collectively thank Carlos Iglesias and, of course, Carlos Varela. They supported this project from the beginning and offered remarkable assistance and encouragement. We hope they are as pleased to see this book as we are. Thanks also to Grettel Montes de Oca for her gracious hospitality.

Some words of individual gratitude:

Caridad Cumaná: I thank Mirta Carreras for her support in the development of this project, as well as my Cuban colleagues Xenia Reloba and Joaquín Borges-Triana for their enthusiasm in contributing to this book.

Xenia Reloba: To my sister Damaris Puñales Alpízar, without whose inspiration, insistence, and confidence I probably would not have written the original article for presentation at LASA in 2010. And thanks to Caridad Cumaná and Karen Dubinsky for their instant empathy and friendship and for inviting me with so much enthusiasm to this long-cherished project.

Karen Dubinsky: I would never be mistaken for either a Cubanist or a musicologist. But through this project, which has truly been a labour of love, I've learned a lot. My collaborators Caridad Cumaná and Xenia Reloba have been remarkable colleagues and teachers. I've also enjoyed working with Susan Lord, Cathie Krull, Jennifer Hosek, and Zaira Zarza, with whom I co-teach a Cuban culture course offered jointly by Queen's University and the University of Havana. I have also learned from the almost two hundred Canadian students (and counting) we've brought to Havana as part of this course, and the more than twenty Havana-based instructors who teach us, especially Professor Lourdes Pérez. Thanks to the Department of Global Development Studies at Queen's for supporting our work on this remarkable course, and the Facultad de

Filosofía y Historia at the University of Havana for hosting us. One conversation with my brilliant young friend Dairon Luis Morejón Pérez about the music of his country is worth at least the last three academic books I've read. Conversations with other friends around dinner tables in Kingston and Havana always help me see the world in a different way; thanks to Scott Rutherford and Sayyida Jaffer, Mary Caesar, Freddy Monasterio Barsó and Zaira Zarza, Paul Kelly and Susan Lord, Geoff Smith and Roberta Hamilton, Ruth Warner, Cynthia Wright, Vivian Rocaberti, the Rodríguez and Pérez families, Aldo Peña Morejón and Vanessa Chicóla, Dannys Montes de Oca, Mirta Carreras, Julio César González Pagés, and the luminous Emilia Fernández. And thanks to my inspirations, the singers, drummers, dancers, bass players, and piano players of the future: Fadzai, Kurt, Wilson, Oscar, Mauricio, Daniel, David, Lia, Lis, Oscar, and my sunshine, Jordi Arturo. Susan Belyea truly knows the meaning of *No es el fin*.

Foreword

JACKSON BROWNE

On a trip I made to Cuba in 2002, I met Carlos Varela and heard his songs for the first time. I went there with a delegation of politicians and political consultants from California, both Democrat and Republican, who were making the journey to find out for themselves if the situation there held any hope for an end to the impasse that has defined US–Cuba relations for fifty years. As a requirement of our visa, there was an agenda of meetings with various citizens' organizations and government figures, as well as some time for sightseeing and cultural discovery.

Friends who had been to Cuba told me that if I was to go there, one person I had to meet was Carlos Varela, and they attempted to explain to me what he means to the Cuban music scene. My knowledge of Cuban music was, and still is, somewhat limited. Most of what they told me was lacking context, and it took my travelling to Cuba and meeting people there to begin to understand what the songs of Carlos Varela mean to the Cubans living in Cuba, and also to the Cubans who have left.

Carlos was away singing in Venezuela when I arrived. Upon his return he very graciously arranged for a party with his musicians and his family and friends, but before it could happen it was postponed due to a speech in the same neighbourhood by Fidel Castro, which necessitated shutting down access to the whole area. So Carlos and I bought a bottle of rum and went to my hotel room, and with the help of our bilingual friends, began singing our songs to each other. As word got out that he was in the hotel, the room filled up with Cubans and Americans, all striving to translate his lyrics to me, and mine to him, and provide them with context, with footnotes and asides, nimbly stepping over the barriers of the past several hundred years of cultural misunderstandings, geopolitical brinksmanship, and strategic manoeuvring. Occasionally Carlos would address the (rumoured) surveillance system beyond or inside the hotel room walls, and joke with the (presumed) government agents listening in.

What is contained in a song? How many truths and universally felt human needs and emotions can be expressed in rhythms and melodies and words? When songs are good, they speak to everyone who hears them.

Cuban musicianship is universally hailed as taking place on a superior plane. Fuelled by passion and the combustion of historic forces, it has happened at the pivotal juncture of European and African cultures. Add to this elevated plane of Cuban music the voice of a person whose expression springs from a shared experience, and who brings a sense of a shared destiny to the stories and songs of his generation, and whose generation has embraced the same rock and roll that the rest of the world has been listening to.

Carlos sings of those who have stayed. And he sings of those who left. I have accompanied Carlos on two US tours and have seen Cubans jump to their feet with tears in their eyes as he sings of the experiences and to the concerns of those born into the choices his generation has been faced with. In Cuba he is a figure known by all for his willingness to speak the truths that everyone knows but are not always willing to speak. He is adored by the youth and respected by all, even by those who consider his truthfulness to be "unhelpful" to the Revolution.

I am happy that there is a book now that translates and discusses the songs of Carlos Varela for those of us who want to know them better, and for those who have yet to hear them. In the words of Carlos Varela, "From the beginning of time there have always been those who build walls, and those who build doors." May this book be a door through which this and future generations pass.

Introduction: Varela's Musical City

MARÍA CARIDAD CUMANÁ AND
KAREN DUBINSKY

Ian Padrón's *Havanastation* (2011) is a film about two schoolchildren from different sides of Cuba's growing class divide. In an early scene, their teacher leads a discussion about the leaders of the independence movement of the nineteenth century. "Who was the man who taught us how to think?" she asks the class, a clear reference to the philosopher, abolitionist, and independence advocate Félix Varela. "Carlos Varela," responds one of her students. The class erupts in laughter, and another student jumps to his feet to perform an enthusiastic air guitar rendition of "Siete," one of Carlos Varela's well-known hits. "Sorry, teacher, I mean Félix," the dejected student responds. The scene, and the shamefaced apology, takes place under the eye of none other than Fidel Castro, from his perch aerie in a poster on the classroom wall. (We might pause here to recall Carlos Varela's observation, in his song "Robinson": "religion starts within the walls of the school.") There is more than a humorous case of mistaken identity – rock star versus nineteenth-century philosopher – at work in this scene. The moment could be interpreted as a summary of the thirty-year career of Carlos Varela: the man who taught Cubans how to think, sing, play the guitar, and challenge authority, all with great dramatic flair.

This book brings together musicologists, historians, international relations experts, film scholars, and journalists from Cuba, Canada, Britain, and the United States to explore, assess, and appreciate the impact – local, national, and international – of Carlos Varela's work. We write from inside and outside Cuba, and from inside and outside academia. While all of us have written individually about various aspects of Cuban society, our combination of voices is not often heard. Barriers to conversations, particularly between Americans and Cubans, make collaborations like this one complicated and rare. Ours is a book about music, but it is also about many other things: immigration, generations, cinema, the city of Havana, political power, and the history and future of the Cuban Revolution. It really could not be otherwise, since music, as Ned Sublette has written, is so essential to the Cuban character that "you can't disentangle it from the history of the nation."[1]

What do a British diplomat, an American rock star, a Canadian historian, several American musicologists, and a variety of Cuban writers have in common? The artistic production of one individual is at the centre of this book, but this is not primarily a biography. Rather, because he has been a protagonist and observer of Cuban cultural and social life of the past several decades, Varela provides us with a lens through which to understand recent Cuban history – in particular, Havanese history. He is a gifted musician and lyricist who can, as Joaquín Borges-Triana puts it here, "find poetry in even the most derelict corner of Havana." But his influence and his engagement extend beyond the clubs and theatres of Havana. As the *New York Times* recently noted, "when one of the best-known musicians in Cuba landed in the United States, his first appearance was not on stage but in the Capitol."[2] Varela's December 2009 visit to the United States was significant in many respects, especially given that he – like most Cuban artists and intellectuals – had been denied the opportunity to visit during the Bush years. Walking through the Capitol buildings, guitar in hand, Varela lobbied Members of Congress to lift economic and travel restrictions, had lunch with senior White House officials, held a panel discussion with journalists, and gave a concert in the House Budget Committee meeting room. Several months later, Varela's hugely attended multi-city concert tour was cited by Western Hemispheric Affairs Assistant Secretary Arturo Valenzuela – in an address to the Cuban American National Foundation – as an example of the increased artistic and cultural exchanges between Cuba and the United States favoured by President Obama. This was a remarkable reversal of the situation in 1994, when an MTV Latino employee lost her job after a Miami exile group (ironically, the same the CANF) complained about her involvement in organizing a group of Americans to visit Havana for a Carlos Varela concert.[3]

In these instances and countless others, Varela has been both commentator and protagonist, moving from observer to participant. His ability to generate controversy is matched by his skill at mediating political tensions through music – something he has been doing since the 1980s. During his recent tours of Cuba, the United States, Canada, and many Latin American countries with his 2009 disk *No Es El Fin*, singing

Carlos Varela and Silvio Rodríguez, 1986. Courtesy of Carlos Varela Archives

songs such as "El viejo sueño acabo" (The Old Dream Is Over), Varela's status as one of Cuba's foremost poets and political commentators has continued. The intense political honesty of his lyrics, and his ongoing popularity among Cubans in the diaspora and on the island alike, makes Varela an illustrative figure for those interested in the politics of popular music – in any country – and in the history and future of Cuba.

Varela emerged from the Nueva Trova movement of Cuban singer/songwriters, one of the heirs to the musical tradition forged by Silvio Rodríguez and Pablo Milanés in the 1960s. He graduated from the Instituto Superior del Arte (ISA) in 1990 and formed his first band in 1986. Parochially, if accurately, known in North America as "Cuba's Bob Dylan," he has produced eight CDs and has toured Europe, the United Kingdom, Latin America, the Caribbean, and North America. He has shared the stage with many of the world's musicians, including the Americans Jackson Browne and Bonnie Raitt, Spain's Joaquín Sabina and Miguel Bosé, and Brazil's Ivan Lins. He helped organize, and appeared at, the mammoth Concierto por la Paz, a peace concert in Havana in September 2009 that brought together musicians from the United States, Puerto Rico, Spain, and other countries for a remarkably non-sectarian celebration. That more than one million Cubans stood in Havana's Revolution Square (in thirty-degree heat for five hours) at this concert is yet one more example of the centrality of music as a cultural form – and political language – in contemporary Cuba.

The problems confronting Cuban artists are well known. Leonardo Padura Fuentes has identified a number of contradictory forces that are shaping contemporary Cuban cultural expression. As he puts it, the "rigors of censorship, the effects of being marginalized, [and] the current presence of a voracious marketplace for these talents" have combined in powerful ways to set the terms of that expression today, for all artists.[4] And the work of musicians specifically is shaped by the fact that Cuba has a musically literate and tremendously receptive population. As British musicologist Geoffrey Baker noted in his recent exploration of hip hop and *reggaetón*, when he arrived to do research in Havana, "people were talking about music a lot."[5] Varela himself has observed that because Cuba does not have music stores every hundred metres, listeners really pay attention to his lyrics.[6] Also, there is little access to the Internet, and little in the way of print media, and iPods are few. Yet there *is* music – everywhere. Music of all genres has become increasingly available through an vast network of CD "pirates" – self-employed vendors who operate above and below ground, selling a huge variety of burned CDs on city streets (including those of outspoken Miami-based critics such as Willy Chirino). Cubans have developed a tremendous capacity for transcending difficulties, and music, as Robin Moore has argued, provides daily opportunities for both release and reflection.[7] In recent years especially, as Cuba ponders its future, some of the most challenging political conversations in the country are being conducted through music in a wide range of styles.

The politics of music extend beyond the incredibly daring lyrics of many contemporary Cuban musicians, Varela being only one example. The ability of musicians to move across to "the other shore" and breach the US/Cuba divide has been a source of controversy for many years. When high-profile Cuban musicians, such as Paquito D'Rivera or Arturo Sandoval, decide to immigrate, their choices are as well known (and strongly felt) as those by other Cuban musicians to stay put.[8] Only in Cuba would a musician the stature of Pablo Milanés record "Yo me quedo" (I'm Staying) in the aftermath of the mass emigration controversies of the early 1980s. Musicians resident in Cuba who have crossed the divide to perform in the United States have sometimes been met with hostility, as was the case in 1999, when around 3,500 protesters

Carlos Varela and Pablo Milanés, circa 1990. Courtesy of Carlos Varela Archives

gathered in Miami to protest the presence of Los Van Van, even hurling rocks and eggs at those trying to enter the venue where they were performing. Also, the presence – or absence – of Cuban musicians has been a political hot potato for the Latin Grammys. That awards ceremony was once relocated from Miami over fears that the nomination of resident Cuban musicians would cause protests, and award-winning Cuban musicians such as Ibrahim Ferrer and the hip hop group Orishas have been denied US visas to attend.[9] And the controversies don't go in just one direction, as US superstars Jay-Z and Beyonce learned in 2013 when their anniversary vacation in Havana generated outrage from prominent Cuban American politicians. More significantly perhaps, it also generated significant musical questions about American policy towards Cuba. As Jay-Z wrote in "Open Letter," after his visit:

> I'm in Cuba, I love Cubans.
> This communist talk is so confusing.
> When it's from China, the very mic that I'm using.[10]

"Generation of Moles." Frank Delgado, Carlos Varela, Gerardo Alfonso and Santiago Feliú. Havana, circa 1988. Courtesy of Carlos Varela Archives

The controversies generated by popular musicians both inside and outside Cuba all point to one of our central conclusions in this book: in Cuba, music matters, and so do musicians.

Varela is part of what Sujatha Fernandes has recently termed the "artistic public sphere" of Cuban society, where people "evaluate competing political alternatives, rethink the basic values of the revolution and reformulate visions for the future."[11] Clearly, Varela shares this perspective with many others. As Robert Nasatir notes here, Varela's own generation is inseparable from the history of Cuba, and his closest contemporaries – most notably, Santiago Feliú, Gerardo Alfonso, and Frank Delgado – merit their own studies. Cuban musicians share this artistic public sphere with other cultural producers, including filmmakers – recently analysed by Ann Marie Stock and Cristina Venegas – and a host of others of all ages, who have recounted their stories to John Kirk and Leonardo Padura Fuentes.[12] This sort of contemporary cultural work reflects on national identity and on what it means to be

Cuban from the perspective of those who have inherited the Cuban Revolution rather than those who built it.

Given the cataclysmic changes ushered in by the 1959 revolution and its aftermath, "generation" is a social category of tremendous significance in Cuba. Varela is perceived as – and understands himself to be – the voice of the generation raised within the promise of a revolution that, after the collapse of the Soviet Union and the beginning of the "Special Period" in 1991, seemed to be collapsing. For example, in one of his most popular metaphorical works, "Guillermo Tell," he sings:

> Guillermo Tell, tu hijo creció
> quiere tirar la fleche.
> le toca a él probar su valor
> usando tu ballesta
>
> William Tell, your son grew up
> He wants to shoot the arrow.
> It's his turn to show his valor
> Using your arrow

Clearly, the father–son conflict expressed here is also a piercing commentary on how Cuban political power has been arranged. Joaquín Borges-Triana points out in this book that Varela is at once a part of, and apart from, the Cuban Revolution. This is perhaps what Varela had in mind when he wrote in "El leñador sin bosque" (The Woodcutter without a Forest, 1995) that he prefers to live "far from the throne and the dragon." Yet at the same time, his observations about the problems and contradictions of Cuban daily life emerge from values created by the revolution itself – a paradox also apparent in contemporary Cuban hip hop.[13] *Trovadores de la herejía* (Troubadors of Heresy), an important anthology of interviews with Varela and his contemporaries published recently in Havana, also captures this double-edged spirit of Varela's generation:

> We consider them *trovadores* of heresy because they are loyal to the *trova* tradition and sing what they have seen, suffered and dreamed with their voices, both individual and universal ... Honesty is the best way to be committed to their land, which is why they are *trovadores*, heretics and at the same time they are sons who testify to the great heresy that is the Cuba we make for the good of all.[14]

Many others have explored the ways in which the upheavals of the late 1980s and 1990s transformed Cuban cultural life. In a recent anthology, Ariana Hernandez-Reguant asks whether one can speak of a "Special Period culture." Her answer, echoed by others who have studied this period, is to emphasize an "increasingly deterritorialized notion of Cuban culture." Thanks to increasing migration, tourism, and economic and cultural flows, since the early 1990s being Cuban has meant "being cosmopolitan."[15] If the Special Period had a soundtrack, Varela's music would feature prominently. Owing to both the spirit of his lyrics and, as several contributors explore here, the diversity of his sound – a mix of rock, folk, jazz, and more, with individual influences that range globally – studying Varela's work adds important musical texture to analyses of new trajectories in Cuban cultural history and identity.

Varela may be the voice of his generation, but he is also a singular figure whose lyrics have endeared him to several generations of fans, musicians, scholars, and other commentators the world over. As both Joaquín Borges-Triana and Paul Webster Hare note here, Varela's music is so well known, in Cuba and in the diaspora, that it often seems as if his band is accompanying the audience at his concerts. And this despite a long history of censorship, which he summed up laconically in verse in "Memorias": "sometimes they play me on the radio / sometimes they don't." Press coverage of his career is extensive and global, and scholarly analyses of his work have appeared in leading musicology and Cuban Studies journals.[16] His songs have been reprinted in Cuban Studies textbooks, and he has been invited to speak at universities throughout North America. He also regularly addresses North American delegations of students, policy makers, musicians, and others visiting Havana. As former UK ambassador Paul Webster Hare recounts here, Varela's international influence extends widely, touching US schoolchildren and foreign diplomatic missions alike.

It is sometimes difficult for an artist – or anyone, really – who attains the status of generational icon to stay relevant. Indeed, that is the ultimate message of "Guillermo Tell": icons, be they artists or revolutionaries, grow up. Varela seems to have maintained his ability to connect across musical styles and generations. His work has been sampled by Los Aldeanos, one of the more politically daring hip hop groups (of a challenging genre); and one of his earliest songs, "Apenas abro los ojos" (As I Open My Eyes), a melodic tribute to the power of dreams, has recently been remixed by the hip hop group Doble Filo. Along with a generation of Cubans now in middle age, Varela would no doubt find much truth in the words of the youthful Los Aldeanos rapper El B: "I'm not a problem / I'm the result of your experiment."[17]

The contributors to this anthology have come together from different countries writing in different languages and from different political and disciplinary perspectives. We also use different styles of writing. For the Cubans in this anthology (Borges-Triana, Reloba, Cumaná), Varela's work resonates as – to apply Robert Nasatir's felicitous phrasing – the soundtrack to their lives. There is a different tone to the writings of the Cuban contributors, one that is inevitable (and itself illustrative) as they explore and recall the profound emotional legacy of Varela's work. In *The Art of Protest*, T.V. Reed notes how music can deliver an emotional charge that politicians and others can only dream of. "It is one thing," he writes, "to hear a political speech and remember an idea or two. It is quite another to sing a song and have its politically charged verses become emblazoned on your memory."[18] This seems an especially apt insight for Cuba, where no one is a stranger to political speeches. The contributors from Britain and North America (Nasatir, Dubinsky, Thomas, Hare, Moore) have found in Varela's compositions a guide through the history of Havana, Cuban culture, musical generations, and the Cuban heart. We all share the conviction that Varela's work merits widespread critical attention because he, like all artists, takes us places that only the poets can go. For that reason this book includes an extensive appendix in which Varela's recorded songs are translated into English for the first time. Throughout his career, Varela has consistently told journalists that he prefers to "let his music speak for itself." However, we also include, as an epilogue, an interview with him, conducted by Cumaná and Dubinsky, in order to amplify his perspective on the issues this book explores.

We hope this book will help desimplify a country that is often understood in one-dimensional terms, perhaps especially in North America. José Quiroga has observed that the Cuban exile community does not divide neatly into two categories, Miami and Havana. There are, in his words, "Cuban exiles in Havana."[19] We are not sure that Varela would choose a word as polemical as "exile" to describe himself. But through his work one can appreciate the banality of simply contrasting "Miami" and "Havana" perspectives on the world. Varela has repeatedly referred to himself as a "bridge" between Cubans on and off the island, and he has been insistent that his music not be used to "sanctify one kind of Cuba or another."[20] We hope the international conversation in this book about the impact of Varela's music inside and outside Cuba will add clarity to a complex history.

Carlos Varela and Jackson Browne, Havana, 2013. Photographed by Olivia Prendes D'Espaux

In the foreword to this book, the American musician Jackson Browne reflects on his experiences with Varela on tours through the United States and Europe as well as during many visits to Cuba. After this introduction, we offer a chapter by the well-known Cuban musicologist and journalist Joaquín Borges-Triana, translated into English here for the first time. Borges-Triana provides a general overview of the emergence of Varela and his peers (the underground "generation of moles," as he christened them in print many years ago), in the context of the cultural and intellectual fermentation of 1980s Cuba. Borges-Triana emphasizes the influence of post-structuralist philosophies on Cuban artists from this generation, and how those musicians and other artists departed from traditional orthodox Marxist understandings of Cuban society. Borges-Triana, who was shaped by the same era, also offers personal reflections on what Varela has meant to his generation, and recounts the artistic challenges that generation faced, such as censorship and inadequate recording and concert facilities. He also provides an introduction to each of Varela's recordings.

In his chapter "The Persistence of 'Memorias,'" US-based musicologist Robert Nasatir locates Varela's work in the larger orbit of *trova* singers, beginning with the first generation of the 1960s, in particular Varela's mentor Silvio Rodriguez. Nasatir uses the 2010 re-release of Varela's classic 1989 composition "Memorias" to explore a critical perspective that has been persistent over decades of Cuban *trova*. He also helps define and explore the "stylistic quirks and thematic preoccupations" that characterize Varela's songbook: "short and enigmatic phrases, plays on words implying multiple meanings, the tension between simplicity and ambiguity, and, most of all, the relations between generations and between families." Thus, besides analysing Varela, Nasatir rethinks the general history of Cuban *trova* through Varela's generation.

The song "La política no cabe en la azucarera" (Politics Doesn't Fit in a Sugar Bowl), from Varela's fourth album *Como los peces* (Like Fish; 1994), provides Cuban journalist Xenia Reloba de la Cruz with an entry point for a guided tour of the economic crises that Cuba confronted in the 1990s. Her article places Varela's musical description of Cuba's devastating Special Period in the context of the cinema, painting, and other artistic expressions of that era; it also provides a sustained analysis of what many consider Varela's most powerful work. Two decades later, Reloba sees reflected in Varela's work some of the same emotional and psychic survival strategies – or as she puts it, processes of "emotional restoration" – that Cubans employed during what was a chaotic and painful period. According to her, Varela's texts are parables full of complex codes that can be difficult to decipher for those unfamiliar with Cuba. Yet when one considers his use of a wide variety of international rhythms, and his emotionally sympathetic characters, his work – even when it emerges from particular historical events such as Cuba's Special Period – becomes not only intelligible but universal.

After these overviews of Varela and his times, past and present, we move on to chapters that spotlight particular themes in his work. Karen Dubinsky considers how Varela positions himself as both participant observer and self-conscious historian of his times. Songs like "Memorias" and "Jalisco Park," which employ complex images of Cuba in the 1960s and 1970s, are concise history lessons (evoking Springsteen's formulation, "we learned more from a three minute record baby than we ever did in school.") This chapter considers various historical themes and images in Varela's work, topics such as the Cold War, immigration, and political leadership. It also considers how Varela's music has helped create new forms of Cuban political citizenship. As the voice of the person on the street or in the neighbourhood, or on Havana's sprawling seawall, the Malecón, Varela is the historian of those who observe, experience, and feel dramatic historical change but never seem to *make* it.

Caridad Cumaná, a Cuban film scholar, analyses how Varela's early training as a student of theatre is reflected in his musical production and performance. This chapter also explores the many cinematic references in Varela's work, how filmmakers have used his music, and how a wide array of cinematic concepts can be employed to describe and understand his artistic production. Above all, Cumaná underscores the profound *visuality* of Varela's work, particularly in his many songs about Havana. For Varela, she argues, Havana is like a stage, "where people travel to the music of his songs."

Susan Thomas, a US-based musicologist, focuses on Varela's considerable contribution to the genre of "Havana music." Musicians, especially those born after the revolution, have created an aural map of the city, retelling and redrawing the city for listeners on and off the island. Perhaps more than any other songwriter, Varela is intensely associated with what Thomas calls the "painful beauty" of Havana, and his work uses the cityscape as a catalyst for exposés of longing and disillusionment. Havana is of course a place of immense cultural resonance the world over, but as Thomas argues here, some of the city's most powerful representations have been *heard* rather than read or seen. What, asks Thomas, does Varela's nostalgia for Havana *sound* like?

Finally, Robin Moore, a leading scholar of Cuban music in North America, takes a panoramic view of Cuban musical history in order to show how Varela builds on and communicates with generations of Cuban musicians since the nineteenth century. Especially in terms of the political and socially engaged aspects of his song lyrics, Varela can be viewed as continuing well-established Cuban traditions.

We end with a brief epilogue by Paul Webster Hare, former British Ambassador to Cuba and now a lecturer in international relations at Boston University. Hare writes a personal reflection on what Varela has to say to foreign observers. Why, he asks, would a British diplomat take his family to a concert – at Havana's Karl Marx theatre, no less – to hear someone whose songs were still largely unknown in Europe? Varela could be seen as an example of what some call "cultural diplomacy." Yet unlike, for example, the American jazz musicians sent by their government to tour the Soviet Union as cultural emissaries during the

Cold War, Varela emphatically represents no one.[21] As Hare puts it, he sings of "the mysteries and mixtures of real life which is never so one-dimensional as politicians like to imagine."

A variety of perspectives – on Cuba, music, politics, and history – are represented in these pages. We certainly do not always agree with one another, but all of the contributors to this book would echo the assessment made in an earlier anthology of Cuban and non-Cuban commentators on Cuban music, that "with the possible exception of certain former colonial powers, there is probably no country on earth whose music has had such extensive foreign impact, relative to its size, as has that of Cuba."[22] The international significance of Varela's work is undeniable, but he has also earned the title – noted here by Susan Thomas – that *Beat* magazine once bestowed on him: the poet of Havana. We hope this book – and Varela's lyrics, of course – will show our readers and his listeners the truth of that claim. Varela's profound impact on Havana exists in the symbolic register of music, but it has also sometimes taken a more concrete form. Before moving to our musical analysis, we end with two illustrative moments from Havana's geographic and cultural history.

In 1990, the well-known Afro-Cuban musical group Sintesis organized a concert in Havana to pay tribute to John Lennon on the tenth anniversary of his death. They had wanted – following Beatles tradition – to perform on the roof of a building in the heart of Vedado, near the Coppelia and the Hotel Havana Libre. But the authorities deemed this location too disruptive to the city's traffic flow. Instead they were granted permission to use a relatively out-of-the-way park, in the residential neighbourhood of Vedado. The concert, held in December 1990, was nevertheless a tremendous success. As thousands of people gathered to enjoy the music, one of the performers, Carlos Varela, took the mike. "I don't know what this park was called before," he declared, "but from now on it should be called John Lennon Park." The name stuck, and the park now boasts a well-known (and often visited) statue of John Lennon himself.[23]

A few blocks from John Lennon park lies Jalisco Park, near the busy corner of 23rd and 12th streets, in the neighbourhood where Varela grew up. Varela's "Jalisco Park" recounts Cuban history from the perspective of a child growing up in the turbulent 1960s and 1970s. The song is one of Varela's signatures, but the park itself had become derelict and been abandoned, like many parts of Havana, during the lean years of the 1990s. After the song became popular, however, the park – the "paradise of metal" Varela recalled from his youth – was suddenly and almost magically repaired. Varela explains this transition more fully in the epilogue to this book. It continues to be a popular, functioning children's park in residential Vedado, far beyond the well-maintained tourist areas of town.

In her contribution here about how Varela set Special Period traumas to music, Xenia Reloba cites Cuban music critic Roberto Zurbano's view that "music, by itself, does not explain anything." Rather, music provides a "spark, or a reflection" of what might be occurring at a given time.[24] It's an insight worth considering as we prepare to consider the impact of one singer at one historical moment. One doesn't want to overestimate music's authority, of course. But at the same time, as these stories from Havana's urban landscape suggest, it is difficult to find a better example of music's power to inspire change.

NOTES

1 Ned Sublette, *Cuba and Its Music from the First Drums to the Mambo* (Chicago: Chicago Review Press, 2004), p. 19.
2 Ginger Thompson, "Trying to Sway America's Cuba Policy with Song," *New York Times*, 28 December 2009, p. A4.
3 Anya Landau French, "Carlos Varela Unplugged at New America," *The Havana Note.com*, 18 December 2009, http://www.thehavananote.com (accessed 5 January 2010); "Remarks by WHA Assistant Secretary Arturo Valenzuela to the Cuban American National Foundation," 20 May 2010 (in author's possession); Larry Rother, "MTV Worker Dismissed Over Cuba Concert," *New York Times*, 9 June 1994.
4 John M. Kirk and Leonardo Padura Fuentes, *Culture and the Cuban Revolution: Conversations in Havana* (Gainesville: University Press of Florida, 2001), p. 186.
5 Geoffrey Baker, *Buena Vista in the Club: Rap, Reggaetón, and Revolution in Havana* (Durham, NC: Duke University Press, 2011), p. 29.
6 French, "Carlos Varela Unplugged."
7 Robin D. Moore, *Music and Revolution: Cultural Change in Socialist Cuba* (Berkeley: University of California Press, 2006), p. 260.
8 See, for example, Ian Michael James, *Ninety Miles: Cuban Journeys in the Age of Castro* (Lanham, MD: Rowman and Littlefield, 2006).
9 Miguel de la Torre, *La Lucha for Cuba: Religion and Politics on the Streets of Miami* (Berkeley: University of California Press, 2003), pp. 132–5; Daniel P. Erickson, *The Cuba Wars* (New York: Bloomsbury Press, 2008), pp. 218–21.

10 Cheryl Contee, "Jay-Z's Open Letter on Cuba Trip Kicks a Brick out of a Cold War Wall," *The Guardian*, 12 April 2013, http://www.theguardian.com/uk (accessed 17 April 2013); William M. LeoGrande, "The Cuba Lobby," *Foreign Policy*, 17 April 2013.

11 Sujatha Fernandes, *Cuba, Represent! Cuban Arts, State Power, and the Making of New Revolutionary Cultures* (Durham, NC: Duke University Press, 2007), p. 3.

12 Ann Marie Stock, *On Location in Cuba: Street Filmmaking during Times of Transition* (Chapel Hill: University of North Carolina Press, 2009); Christina Venegas, *Digital Dilemmas: The State, the Individual, and Digital Media in Cuba* (New Brunswick, NJ: Rutgers University Press, 2010); Kirk and Padura Fuentes, *Culture and the Cuban Revolution*.

13 Baker, *Buena Vista*, p. 45; Roberto Zurbano, "El Rap Cubano: Can't Stop, Won't Stop the Movement!," in *Cuba in the Special Period: Culture and Ideology in the 1990s*, ed. Ariana Hernandez-Reguant (New York: Palgrave Macmillan, 2009), pp. 143–59.

14 Bladimir Zamora and Fidel Díaz, *Trovadores de la herejía* (La Habana: Casa Editorial Abril, 2012), p. 11. Here the authors are evoking a well-known speech by Jose Martí, "Con todos y para el bien de todos" (With and For the Good of All).

15 Hernandez-Reguant, "Writing The Special Period: An Introduction," in *Cuba in the Special Period*, p. 10.

16 Reflections on Varela's music can be found in English in Moore, *Music and Revolution*; Susan Thomas, "Did Nobody Pass the Girls the Guitar? Queer Appropriations in Contemporary Cuban Popular Song," *Journal of Popular Music Studies* 18, no. 2 (2006): 124–43; Thomas, "Musical Cartographies of the Transnational City: Mapping Havana in Song," *Latin American Music Review* 31, no. 2 (Fall–Winter 2010): 222–6; Robert Nasatir, "El hijo de Guillermo Tell: Carlos Varela Confronts the Special Period," *Cuban Studies* 39 (2008): 44–59, Vincenzo Perna, *Timba: The Sound of the Cuban Crisis* (Aldershot: Ashgate, 2005); Jose Quiroga, *Cuban Palimpsests* (Minneapolis: University of Minnesota Press, 2005); and Lauren E. Shaw, "Los Novísimos and Cultural Institutions," in *A Changing Cuba in a Changing World*, compiled by Mauricio A. Font (New York: Bildner Centre for Western Hemispheric Studies Graduate Centre, 2008), pp. 578–89. Spanish-language commentaries include Antonio López Sánchez, *La canción de la Nueva Trova* (La Habana: Atril, 2001); Juan Pin Vilar: *Carlos Varela* (Madrid: Fundación Autor, 2004); Radamés Giro and Isabel Gonzáles Sauto, *Cincuenta canciones en años de Revolución* (La Habana: Editorial José Martí, 2008); Joaquin Borges-Triana, *La luz, bróder, la luz: Canción Cubana contemporánea* (La

Habana: Centro Cultural Pablo de la Torriente Brau, 2009); and Zamora and Díaz, *Trovadores de la herejía*.
17 Baker, *Buena Vista*, p. 50.
18 T.V. Reed, *The Art of Protest: Culture and Activism from the Civil Rights Movement to the Streets of Seattle* (Minneapolis: University of Minnesota Press, 2005), p. 28.
19 Quiroga, *Cuban Palimpsests*, p. 23. For another complex view of Cubans outside Cuba, see also Ruth Behar and Lucía M. Suárez, eds., *The Portable Island: Cubans at Home in the World* (New York: Palgrave Macmillan, 2008).
20 Jordan Levin, "Cuban's Songs Bring Message," *Miami Herald*, 6 March 1998.
21 See, for example, Penny von Eschen, *Satchmo Blows Up the World: Jazz Ambassadors Play the Cold War* (Cambridge: Harvard University Press, 2004).
22 Peter Manuel, "Introduction," in *Essays on Cuban Music: North American and Cuban Perspectives*, ed. Manuel (Lanham, MD: University Press of America, 1991), p. viii.
23 Ernesto Juan Castellanos, *John Lennon en la Habana: With a little help from my friends* (La Habana: Ediciones Union, 2005) p. 142.
24 Roberto Zurbano, "La música popular como espejo social," Sección Controversia, *Temas* 29 (April–June 2002): 63.

MY HAVANA

The Musical City of Carlos Varela

Chapter One

Carlos Varela: The Distinguished Son of William Tell

JOAQUÍN BORGES-TRIANA

I am a person who believes in the concept of generation. Perhaps because of this, I admit I am a man from the 1980s, shaped, intellectually, by the influx of the ideas in fashion back then. In those years, Cuba was a whirlwind of unprecedented artistic activities. In ways that had not existed before, artists and writers placed intellectual creativity above any formal innovation to express reality. In this sense, I share the opinion of Iván de la Nuez Carrillo, who declared, in 1989:

> Another mode of intellectual and ontological creation is becoming dominant, and it bases its dominance precisely on the cultural individual, in contradiction with the "must be" which reigned (with its alternatives) since the sixties ... The eighties have produced a culture I call discordant, and that has not been consequently explained from the theoretical, historical or political points of view. If the sixties seemed to be sailing through a homogeneous universe, the eighties have exposed important underlying and seriously conflicting problems. This new intellectual production is being shaped as a cultural system with its own life within Cuban culture. Its various levels of representation suggest an interest in building hegemony.[1]

The second half of the 1980s turned out to be favourable for renewed artistic expression in Cuba. Thus, after almost twenty years, outstanding painter Umberto Peña returned to one of the exhibition halls of the National Museum of Fine Arts with a comprehensive retrospective of his work. Literature also displayed thematic and formal transgressions. In 1988, the award for fiction of the tabloid *El Caimán Barbudo* was presented to Sergio Cevedo Sosa for his book *Rapsodia Bohemia*, inspired by Cuba's so-called *freakies* (a sort of hippy). In the same contest the award for poetry was presented to a collection of poems by Norge Espinosa titled *Las pequeñas tribulaciones* (The Small Tribulations). The collection included the famous poem "Vestido de novia" (Wedding Gown), a text that – together with the short story "¿Por qué llora Leslie Caron?" (Why Is Leslie Caron Crying?), by Roberto Urías – reclaims a homoerotic tradition in the country. The fourth wall in a play of the same title written by Víctor Varela knocked down other walls. Young visual artists burst onto the streets of Vedado with ideas that revitalized arts on the island, and in a memorable performance urged us to "Meditar" (Meditate) at the base of the José Martí Monument in Revolution Square. These were all part of a greater movement, of which music also formed a part, born as a result of all that tremendous creative energy.

Problems over the relationship between artists and artistic institutions, never before discussed in Cuba, were aired publicly in the 1980s. A new generation, educated by the Revolution, arrived with their own ideas about creativity. This generation adopted a new attitude. Their curse would no longer be that of original sin; they were the Revolution itself. They would find their own space and provide their own answers. The Ernesto Che Guevara's wish would come true: we had not created simple, docile yes-men who would follow official thought unquestioningly.[2]

This is the context in which the work of Carlos Varela began. Varela is undoubtedly one of the major voices of contemporary Cuban song, a logical continuation of the so-called Renaissance in Cuban Art (as coined by Uruguayan Luis Camnitzer) that emerged as a result of the New Sociocultural Thought of the 1980s. Certainly, from 1986 on, many things were said – some in favour, some against – about what was known as the second generation of the Nueva Trova. In 1988, at the request of my friend, journalism professor Ángel Tomás, then director of the cultural section of the Cuban daily *Juventud Rebelde*, I published an article titled "La generación de los topos" (The Generation of Moles), in which I discussed key aspects of the work of the country's singer/songwriters.[3] The article sparked heated debate about my argument, which was that "Nueva Trova" constituted a "generation of moles" – my term for the underground artistic life of the creators. In trying to explain the same phenomenon, others coined a new term: "innovative *trova*."

Both labels pointed to the emergence, in 1978, of a group of singer/songwriters whose fame would grow in the 1980s. This group's music was very different from that of their predecessors. Creators like Santiago

Feliú, Donato Poveda, Alberto Tosca, Carlos Varela, Gerardo Alfonso, and Frank Delgado were the bearers of new ideas. They also shared a commitment to transforming Cubans' daily realities. With their sharp, witty texts – which the illustrious representatives of closed bureaucracy and ideological inflexibility did not like at all – these young creators compelled reflection in ways that recall something Haydée Santamaría once said: "The issue is not to write committed songs, but to write songs that make us committed."

The songs of Carlos Varela can be placed in this sociocultural context. He speaks for the thoughts and feelings of a whole generation: those of us who were born in Cuba in the early 1960s. One way or another, I have always identified with the artistic perspective of this creator.

Varela began, as Caridad Cumaná elaborates in this book, by studying theatre. The idea of telling stories, fables, parables, and so on inspired him to write lyrics with a moral ending. Unlike most popular singers, he is influenced more by narrative than by poetry. His enrolment in the School of Performing Arts of the Instituto Superior de Arte (ISA) was critical to his development; so was the influence of Cuban *trovador* Pedro Luis Ferrer, mostly with regard to his use of the six-string guitar as accompaniment. Varela stood out not just because he sang with a guitar, but also because of what he made that guitar do.

Varela's time in ISA was extremely important for his aesthetic vision. The artistic and literary trends of 1980s Cuba were launched by students in the arts and humanities, who found themselves embedded in the unique environment then prevailing in the country's universities and especially at the University of Havana. All of these young people in their twenties (who were just at the stage of provocation and transgression, if we accept that every age plays its own role in culture) understood and embraced postulates of the artistic avant-garde. For example, they were drawn to the radical aesthetic precept that art, above all, must have social legitimacy. In this way, artistic creativity would serve a social function, or a sort of sociology of art.

Varela shares this perspective with an entire movement of painters, writers, musicians, filmmakers, and playwrights, all of whom confronted, in one way or another, the social conditions of 1980s Cuba (especially the second half of that decade). In their creative discourse, they addressed the crisis of values and rethought taken-for-granted strategies and social policies. This generation denounced bureaucratism, the dogmatism of Cuban cultural policy, and the lack of aesthetic pluralism in the country. They rebuked the timid, inward-looking discourse that had dominated Cuban cultural production in the 1970s – a discourse that had paralysed Cuban intellectual life in that decade.[4]

Varela is clearly a product of his time and generation, but another important aspect of his artistic development was the time he spent working alongside Santiago Feliú, Frank Delgado, and Gerardo Alfonso. Together, they were inseparable – "our Beatles," as I have called them elsewhere.[5] Each blended his own skills with the others, and their time together benefited all four greatly in terms of their future individual development. Unfortunately, EGREM – the only recording label in the country at that time – was not interested in their work, so it was not professionally recorded. Only a few takes recorded during live concerts have been preserved.

It was in 1983, I remember well, that a sort of music club called "Trobar" came together at the pool of the Hotel Nacional. At these Sunday gatherings, Gerardo Alfonso and Xiomara Laugart sang "Madrugué" – a song I liked a lot – while Santiago Feliú interpreted "Para Bárbara." You could also hear Carlos Varela singing "Tijeras" and "Crucigrama" – which I have never heard again – while Frank Delgado offered "Son de la suerte," with accompaniment by *tres* player Candelita.

Little by little they learned one another's music, discovering when a voice or a guitar should come in to enhance the harmony. In this way was founded the beautiful and fondly remembered quartet known as "Los Cabecipelaos" (literally "scalped heads"), as they were named by officials of the Culture Department of the Union of Communist Youth. The high points for this group were the concerts given by Carlos, Gerardo, and Frank at the Teatro Nacional de Guiñol in 1985, with guests such as the well-known Cuban writer Eduardo del Llano, and the concerts at the la Casa del Joven Creador (Young Creators House) and the Cuban Cinematheque in 1986. In truth, not many people attended these concerts; most of the time the theatre was half empty. And because advertising and promotion methods do not favour ensembles, the four went their separate ways in search of their own paths.

In 1994, Carlos Varela talked to Cuban journalist Mario Vizcaíno Serrat about what caused the separation:

> The time in which we lived ultimately separated us and destroyed everyone: the old and the new. When Nueva Trova collapsed as a movement, everything else dispersed also. There were attempts to resuscitate it, but these were so loaded with bureaucracy that the movement landed in the hands of people who were not representative as artists. The musicians

realized it was necessary to record, and to obtain instruments, and there was no longer a movement to organize things. Each one began to find ways to continue, and then in 1986 or 1987 we drifted apart. We began to travel abroad, a lot. Santiago, Gerardo, Frank, and myself, each of us separately, not together [...] But those years were important for us to understand how powerful it was to be together on the stage, and much more today, when we can show what we did, and how much we learned.[6]

In the second half of the 1980s, Carlos Varela was branded as a "troublemaker," mostly because the criticism he expressed in his songs was timely and necessary. It is odd that some people question an artist's right – indeed, duty – to discuss real problems. A work of art cannot solve problems – everybody knows that – but it does not try to. If a work of art could do that, they would be few problems left. Yet how can we question music's legitimacy? Songs like "Tropicollage" and "Jalisco Park" inevitably dealt with some of the ugly things that at that time reigned among us (and that still do reign – although under a different guise now, essentially they are the same). Whether or not the intent of such songs was to help change things, Varela always plainly and simply expressed his disagreement, his nonconformity, and his own point of view.

Towards the end of the 1980s, new subjects and new (as well as old) contradictions marked Cuban intellectual life. The young writers and artists of that time quickly established a distinct cultural identity for themselves. In them, as Ernesto Hernández Busto and Víctor Fowler Calzada have said, the exotic, the thirst for freedom, and the search for national origins all blended in a unique alchemy.[7] It was a time when new philosophical trends were circulating in Cuba and huge transformations were occurring on the Cuban cultural scene. As Fowler Calzada has stated:

> The word postmodernity could be heard in any conversation, just as much as post-structuralism, Joseph Beuys, Habermas, Lyotard, Foucault, Lezama, Borges and a hundred other names that were mentioned, sometimes in a chaotic manner and as part of an equally chaotic knowledge. It was, nevertheless, an exceptional time because, in spite of all the criticism it could receive, a younger generation was acting within the intellectual world to remove the heavy burden of prohibitions and official censure, which was, in the seventies, imposed on the country's media, education and culture.[8]

To understand the vision of the 1980s generation, of which Carlos Varela was one of the most prominent artists, one must understand how it emerged and was nurtured. Its roots were manifestations of the historic left *and* right wings of philosophy. The need to find other currents of thought arose because the Marxist idea that "all men are equal" was not enough to support a theory of culture. Specifically through Leninism (not Marxism) – and, after Lenin's death, Stalinism – the socialist world was encouraged to believe that addressing cultural issues seriously meant ignoring the more pressing problems of the people. Historically conservative positions in politics and philosophy had created an environment inclined towards criticism of culture.

So it made sense to refer to philosophers such as Nietzsche, Schopenhauer, and Ortega y Gasset; to Freudian psychoanalysis; to the scientific mysticism of Swiss psychiatrist Carl Gustav Jung; to the theories of Austrian physician, sexologist, and psychoanalyst Wilhelm Reich; and to the sociology of Erich Fromm's *The Fear of Freedom*. At the same time, young Cubans were encountering the writings of Antonio Gramsci, Theodor Adorno, Michel Foucault, Peter Sloterdijk, Gilles Deleuze, Giorgio Agamben, Maurice Blanchot, Richard Rorty, Pierre Bourdieu, Jean-François Lyotard, Jean Baudrillard, Jacques Derrida, Omar Calabrese, Félix Guattari, and the Hungarian reformist, literary critic, aestheticist, and philosopher György Lukács. In the theatre, followers of Jerzy Grotowski, Eugenio Barba, and our own Vicente Revuelta (and his "Group of Twelve") were grappling with the unfathomable contemporary metaphycisist George Ivanovitch Gurdjieff. Influenced by these thinkers, young Cuban artists and intellectuals of the second half of the 1980s analysed power in their own unique way, a way that diverged from the Marxist orthodoxy under which they had been raised. Many of them were attracted to the study of the "end of the great emancipating stories," stories that aimed to desecrate those who were still standing.

By 1986, the difficulties faced by musicians like Varela were not only practical (in bureaucratic terms, they were not *emplantillado*, that is, officially employed by an enterprise), but also institutional.[9] Government technocrats were trying somehow to decide the future of musicians. It mattered nothing to these people that many of Cuba's singer/songwriters were hugely talented. Indeed, talent usually leads to conflict with authorities, especially when the social environment lacks a genuine music culture that can appreciate what is truly good and that offers avenues for artistic growth.

One example of the consequences of this involved Varela's first big concert, held on Saturday, 29 April 1989, at the Charles Chaplin Theatre of the Cuban Institute of Cinematographic Art and Industry (ICAIC). This now legendary performance could be described as an urban chronicle:

> The common thread of his influences is the last hurrah of the vanguard of the 1960s (Dylan, Lennon, Simon, Silvio), but his work uses more commonplace and familiar references. If the first group forms the center of his formation, "peripheral" (but no less crucial) correlations foster the development of this unusual character in the details he selects and which appear in his last and, perhaps, most important productions. These *resources* (I intentionally emphasize the term) can appear in Sting's impressive syntheses but also in certain works of Cindy Lauper, Phil Collins, or Peter Gabriel. It also is impossible to deny the influence from the south: from there he incorporates the best of Argentine rock and the conceptual experiments of Leo Masliah.[10]

By 1989, Varela had expanded his repertoire. He was then a young man of strong social commitments, and his songs were completely in tune with the values of his contemporaries. Just as had happened when he was playing with Feliú, Delgado, and Alfonso, the growing acceptance of his songs in small venues gave Carlos confidence in his own direction. So, in his case, did the repeated broadcast of song of his songs on Radio Ciudad de La Habana. Yet he was still anxious: Would he be able to find and fill larger and better venues? As his artistry grew, he fought for better places to play his music. It was then that, without losing an inch of his "love for the lyre," as an experienced singer would say (according to my friend Bladimir Zamora), Varela invited six young musicians to form a band, called Señal en el Asfalto (Sign on the Asphalt), even though they were unable to obtain musical instruments of their own.

Audiences identified with Varela's lyrics in songs that articulated their everyday lives from the perspective of values created by the Revolution itself. Carlos declared in an interview in the literary tabloid *El Caimán Barbudo*:

> That's why it hurts so much when someone underestimates us or does not prompt dialogue, when someone behaves as if it would be better we were passively stupid. The truth is that, thanks to the Revolution, this

generation has studied enough to think and reason, and make proposals worthy of consideration. We act as any other authentic young person educated by the Revolution would act.[11]

Varela at the time was writing songs like "Tropicollage" (a foresighted critique of the tourist economy), "Jalisco Park" (a nostalgic account of the once famous amusement park, serving as a simile for Cuban history), and of course "Guillermo Tell," which he sang for the first time at the 1989 Chaplin concert. Because of the strong conjunction of significance and signifier, this song about the legendary crossbowman, his son, and the apple became one of Varela's most popular, for it captured the mood of a whole generation. As Dubinsky also explores in this book, the Chaplin concert proved that Varela was already a mobilizing force in Cuban culture. That 1,700 Cubans attended the concert, with 200 turned away at the door, testifies to his early cultural importance. Now there was no good reason to deprive Varela of radio and television primetime or to refuse him access to recording time at EGREM. Yet still he was denied these things.

The importance of "Guillermo Tell" cannot be overstated. In its own unique language, it synthesized perfectly the conclusions of generational studies that had been carried out in the second half of the 1980s, which found that twenty-year-olds felt barred from participation in multiple areas of social life and decision making. This conjuncture of song and social reality is not at all a surprise, for as Gregorio Marañón has said, "in science and in art all roads lead to the same place: truth."[12] "Guillermo Tell" corroborates what Uruguay's Julio Brum said in an interview with his compatriot researcher Ernesto Donas: that we must understand the singer/songwriter "not only as a creator of songs, but also as a source of theory and reflection."[13]

For the generation of artists and intellectuals to which Carlos Varela belonged, their bedside philosopher was Michel Foucault, especially his *Microphysics of Power*. According to Foucault's new concept of power, multiple techniques and tactics of domination had replaced the concepts of State and sovereignty. This idea captivated the generation of Cuban creators born in the 1970s and the early 1960s. According to Ernesto Hernández Busto, Foucault's popularity reflected the fact that "Foucault had written about our major preoccupation as emerging intellectuals: the issue of power and its relation with the State on the one hand, and knowledge on the other hand."[14] Post-structuralism favoured a new type of state, a network of open communities fragmented into micro-polities. This new concept provided an opening for Cuba to communicate under equal conditions with the avant-garde of Western thought. For the 1980s generation of Cuban artists and intellectuals, postmodernism explained their political realities through its analysis of legitimating strategies, something that the exhausted theoretical environment of Western democracies could not do. The idea that power is not held but is exercised was intellectually highly attractive to creators of Carlos Varela's generation.

In 1989, during a tour in the Canary Islands, Varela was offered the chance to record his first album. That is how *Jalisco Park* was born. However, he did not record it with Señal en el Asfalto, the band that had been accompanying him, but rather with musicians from the Canary Islands and with synthesizers and keyboards. For these reasons, in terms of vitality and dynamism, one cannot compare that album with the music he made with Señal, however well-intentioned the effort. *Jalisco Park* reflects a period, but it does not suggest the energy the songs generated when Varela played them in Havana before that album was made. That is why *Carlos Varela en vivo* was recorded, with all the advantages and disadvantages of doing so in Cuba. *Carlos Varela en vivo* was produced in 1990, by which time the audiences knew all of his songs by heart, so that he and his band were practically accompanying the public during concerts. This live album had some mixing problems. Overall, Varela was very unlucky with his first albums, not only with regard to technology, but also in terms of recording contracts and distribution. The CDs were like phantoms: they appeared in a few venues, disappeared in others.

His third recording project, *Monedas al aire* (Coins in the Air), produced in 1992, can be described as a transition halfway to folk-rock language. The song on that album that opened the road for what he would do in his next project was "Robinson," which works as a photograph, capturing an instant of Cuban reality. Robinson – a man alone on an island – invokes the desperate neglect and isolation felt in Cuba at the beginning of the 1990s as a result the collapse of the Soviet Union and the subsequent economic crisis.

Two years later, Varela produced his fourth album, *Como los peces* (Like Fish), which had a distinctive folk sound. This album, like the previous one, includes lively, uptempo songs. Some, such as "Solo tú puedes traer el sol" (Only You Can Bring the Sun), evoke Irish rhythms, mixed with the sound of a gypsy who sings something like an Arab chant. At the same time, the album includes songs in the style of "Como un angel," (Like an Angel) a folk-pop ballad, making the production, in a way, a pop CD.

In my opinion, of all Varela's recordings, *Como los peces* has had the greatest impact, for reasons that Xenia Reloba explores in this book. This CD and *Trovatur* by Frank Delgado are productions of fundamental importance to recent Cuban discography, for they address all of the multitude of problems Cubans faced in the 1990s. These works painstakingly analyse our environment and comment intelligently on the social challenges every individual confronts, especially those born in the 1960s.

Varela's next album, *Nubes* (Clouds; 2000), was a "concept album" about emigration. According to Cuban critic Frank Padrón Nodarse, in this album Carlos uses the leitmotif of Havana, "its obsession with exile, [and] the incursions into the remotest corners of the self [the other exile]." For Varela, he continues, "the remotest corners [of Havana] live inside the human being."[15] An outstanding song on this album is "Sequía del alma" (Longings of the Soul), dedicated to the poet Ramón Fernández-Larrea. This piece makes one shiver, reminding us of friends who are no longer here. The excellence of Varela's guitar playing and that of his colleague Amed Medina cannot be overlooked.

Siete (Seven) was released in 2003. On this album, Varela again worked with excellent musicians. According to Bladimir Zamora, *Siete*, like many of Varela's previous discs, is structured as a cantata: "Each piece has its own particular predicate and at the same time it revolves around an axis, in this case the number seven, with its infinite capacity for analogies."[16] Its twelve songs, recorded with guests musicians like the American singer Bonnie Raitt and Cuba's own Juan Formell and Los Van Van, again illustrate that Varela has always been able to express himself in multiple genres. In *Siete*, he resorts to synthesizers and electronic instruments, but this does not obscure his creative identity. His perennial themes and his musical personality are always audible in his tunes, his harmonies, and his singing and guitar playing.

After *Siete* was released, Varela's international stature rose. In 2004, he worked with American musician Jackson Browne (who has since become his great friend), performing in England and other European countries. A year later, the Mexican filmmaker Alejandro González Iñárritu used "Una palabra" (A Word) as the theme for a short film, *The Hire: Powder Keg*, launching that song's international success. The same song was used by the director Tony Scott for the final scene of *Man on Fire*.

Varela's next album, released in 2004, was the first volume of *Los hijos de Guillermo Tell* (The Sons of William Tell), a compilation of sixteen pieces and one of his most successful works. Cuban music critic Bladimir Zamora offered this assessment in 2004:

> *Los hijos de Guillermo Tell* proves you can be loyal to the essence of the *trovador* and at the same time interact with other modalities of Cuban and foreign music, especially rock and jazz. This anthology shows he is not tied to one or another format, or specific sound, but rather he circulates, guided by motivations that most times go beyond music itself.[17]

With his most recent album *No es el fin* (It's Not the End; 2009), Varela has reinvented himself. In this production, jazz elements acquire an importance they had not in previous works. This can be heard in songs like "Telón de fondo" (Backdrop) and "Bendita lluvia" (Blessed Rain). We also find a marked lyricism – something that Varela has employed since his very first works in the early 1980s. Such is the case with "Todo será distinto" (Everything Will Be Different), "El viejo sueño acabó" (The Old Dream Is Over), and the wonderful "De vuelta a casa" (Coming Home).

While Varela's fans in Cuba and abroad wait for new albums, I want to end by noting that the many scholars who have studied his music – including all of the contributors to this book – have described him as a unique urban storyteller who can find poetry in the most derelict corners of Havana. As Susan Thomas writes, his songs stand out for being tributes to the Cuban capital. "Bulevar" and "Habáname" are only two examples of this.

For Cubans of my generation, two phrases became embedded in our culture in the 1980s: "You have to wait," and "It takes time." Literary and artistic history offers plenty of cases when artists found themselves frustrated and marginalized by their own environment. Varela has avoided this fate, not by luck but because he understands that one is born in a specific place to bear witness to it. He is sentimentally attached to Havana, so he is faithful to the *trovaholics* of the bohemian Parnassus, to the parks and street corners, and to his friends in a country that is constantly renewing itself (even when it doesn't seem to be). Varela is a musician who understands being Cuban ("lo cubano") as working in an intermediary space, as creatively appropriating universal ideas, as fostering dynamic relationships instead of absolutes. In that sense, *Cubanidad* is universal.

NOTES

1 Iván de la Nuez Carrillo, "El cóndor pasa," *La Gaceta de Cuba*, June 1989, pp. 11–12.
2 "Official thought" should be understood as the thought that meets the following requirements: it comes from those institutions that dictate or suggest policies, it legitimizes in the theoretical field the political agreements that have been previously established, and, at the same time, it legitimizes itself through such agreements and through the practices resulting from them. On Guevara's concept of the "New Man," see Ernesto Che Guevera, "El socialismo y el hombre en Cuba," in *Obras*, t. II (La Habana: Casa de las Américas, 1970), pp. 367–86.
3 Joaquín Borges-Triana, "La generación de los topos," *Juventud Rebelde*, 28 August 1988, p. 9.
4 This period has become known as the "five grey years" of Cuban culture, as described by Ambrosio Fornet, "A propósito de Las iniciales de la tierra," *Casa de las Américas* 164 (1987): 148–53. For more information about this period and the repercussions for Cuban culture, see the following, all presented at Conferencia del Ciclo "La política cultural de la Revolución: memoria y reflexión," available at *Criterios* (website of the Centro Teórico-Cultural Criterios): Arturo Arango, "Con tantos palos que te dio la vida: poesía, censura y persistencia," http://www.criterios.es/pdf/arangotantospalos.pdf (accessed 18 June 2007); Mario Coyula, "El Trinquenio Amargo y la ciudad distópica: autopsia de una utopia," http://www.criterios.es/pdf/coyulatrinquenio.pdf (accessed 3 April 2007); Ambrosio Fornet, "El Quinquenio Gris: Revisitando el término," http://www.criterios.es/pdf/fornetquinqueniogris.pdf (accessed 7 February 2007); Eduardo Heras León, "El Quinquenio Gris: testimonio de una lealtad," http://www.criterios.es/pdf/erasleonquinquenio.pdf (accessed 18 May 2007); and Desiderio Navarro, "Introducción al ciclo," http://www.criterios.es/cicloquinqueniogris.htm (2007).
5 Joaquín Borges-Triana, *La Luz, bróder, la luz: Canción Cubana Contemporánea* (La Habana: Centro Cultural Pablo de la Torriente Brau, 2009), p. 36.
6 Mario Vizcaíno Serrat, "Carlos Varela: el gnomo y el guerrero," *La Gaceta de Cuba*, January–February 1994, pp. 20–2.
7 Ernesto Hernández Busto, "Recuerdos (cubanos) de una vida dañada," *Cubista Magazine* 1 (Spring 2004), accessed 10 July 2005, http://www.cubistamagazine.com/010101.html; Víctor Fowler Calzada, "Limones partidos," *Cubista Magazine* 5 (Summer 2006), http://www.cubistamagazine.com/050108.html (accessed 10 November 2006).

8 Fowler Calzada, "Limones partidos."
9 For an explanation of the development of the Cuban music industry since the Revolution, see Robin Moore, *Music and Revolution: Cultural Change in Socialist Cuba* (Berkeley: University of California Press, 2006); and various essays in Peter Manuel, ed., *Essays on Cuban Music: North American and Cuban Perspectives* (Lanham, MD: University Press of America, 1991).
10 Iván de la Nuez, "La canción como laberinto hacia una totalidad otra," *La Gaceta de Cuba*, July 1989, p. 5.
11 Bladimir Zamora, "Carlos Varela. Una huella en el asfalto," *El Caimán Barbudo* 22, no. 255 (February 1989): 20–1.
12 Gregorio Marañón, "Frases y pensamientos," *Revista Cultura* 1 (2005), Centro Bibliográfico y Cultural de la ONCE, Madrid, pp. 45–8.
13 Ernesto Donas, "Problematizando la canción popular: un abordaje comparativo (y sonoro) de la canción latinoamericana comprometida desde los años 1960," Actas del V Congreso Latinoamericano de la Asociación Internacional para el Estudio de la Música Popular (IASPM-AL), 2008, http://www.hist.puc.cl/iaspm/rio/Anais2004%20(PDF)/ErnestoDonas.pdf (accessed 20 May 2008).
14 Hernández Busto, "Recuerdos (cubanos) de una vida dañada."
15 Frank Padrón, "Aunque sea gris la tarde," *Revolución y Cultura* 1 (2002): 64–5.
16 Bladimir Zamora, "La gente siempre sueña," *La Jiribilla* 107 (2003), http://www.lajiribilla.cu/2003/n107_05/aprende.html (accessed 20 June 2006).
17 Bladimir Zamora, "Los más pegados al pantalón," *La Jiribilla* 182 (2004), http://www.lajiribilla.cu/2004/n182_10/aprende.html (accessed 15 January 2005).

Chapter Two

The Persistence of "Memorias"

ROBERT NASATIR

For Curline Parker Meriwether

At the Festival de la Nueva Trova held on the Isla de la Juventud on 27 October 1984, Silvio Rodríguez dedicated his song "La canción de las sillas" (The Chair Song) to "los jóvenes de la Nueva Trova" (the youth of Nueva Trova).[1] That song was already fifteen years old – he had written it in 1969. This concert was a moment of transition and change, of cooperation and incorporation, between generations of the *trova*. Silvio's dedication did more than suggest that the older *trovador* supported the newer ones; it also served as a caution to budding singer/songwriters. The first-generation artist sang:

> El que tenga una canción tendrá tormenta,
> el que tenga compañía, soledad.
> El que siga un buen camino tendrá sillas
> peligrosas que lo inviten a parar.
>
> Whosoever has a song will also have tempests,
> whosoever has company, solitude.
> Whosoever follows a just path will face dangerous
> chairs that invite him to stop and rest.

Carlitos Varela, then only twenty-one years old, also performed at that festival as one of the new, second-generation voices now attracting attention and acclaim. One of the songs he performed, never recorded and now forgotten, "Hijo del fuego" ("Son of Fire"), resonated with the older *trovador*. It also pointed to many of the style hallmarks and thematic preoccupations that would come to define Varela's songbook: short and enigmatic phrases, plays on words implying multiple meanings, a tension between simplicity and ambiguity, and, most of all, a focus on relations between generations and between families. The central idea,

> El humo es hijo del fuego
> Y sin embargo es bastante sucio
>
> Smoke is the son of fire
> And, nonetheless, is still pretty dirty

summarizes metaphorically Varela's position as a singer/songwriter and that of many of his contemporaries who were born after the Cuban Revolution of 1959. They are the smoke that results from fire; yet instead of being purified by the process, they are, as the song expresses it, dirty.

The metaphor of "Hijo del fuego," like many that Varela has developed throughout his career to understand distinct generations, does not allude solely to his personal position within the *trova* or to the role of the *trova* in the Revolution; it also underscores his generation's place in Cuban history. Indeed, these things are inseparable. From his earliest songs, Varela has shown that he understands the *trovador*'s role in Cuban society, and he uses to advantage his identification with his audience: he and that audience are analogous to various sociopolitical relationships within the revolutionary project. Varela sees himself as part of a long tradition of *trovadores*, as part of a multi-generational discourse that parallels the Revolution's historic development. Put another way, to understand his place on the trajectory of the Nueva Trova – which is the intention of this chapter – is to confront a problem that has preoccupied Varela himself throughout his career. This study implies a desire to understand an aesthetic process through historical events, as well as the opposite – that is, a desire to comprehend historical events through an aesthetic process. Both processes, the aesthetic and the historical, the *trova* and the Revolution, emphasize progress that more often than not manifests itself as cyclical and repetitive. This reality, both contradictory and commonplace, is ultimately what defines the work of Carlos Varela.

According to Joaquín Borges-Triana, studying the Nueva Trova and Canción Cubana Contemporánea requires at least two approaches:

The analysis must begin from a double perspective: [*trova*] as an expression of the cultural context in which it is produced, but also as a crucial factor in the construction of cultural identities, a dialectical approach which facilitates the study of music "in" and "as" culture, which opens doors to unlimited interdisciplinary and methodological possibilities.[2]

This observation underscores the multiple roles embraced by the *trovadores* and specifically by Carlos Varela. He is observer and participant, singer and composer, critic and agent. As with many singer/songwriters, his principal subject from the beginning has been his place in the unfolding history of revolutionary Cuba. That place, that context, offers him and his contemporaries both unusual perspectives and unique ways of communicating them.

As is readily apparent with other members of the so-called Novísima Trova, that is, the second generation of the Nueva Trova – Frank Delgado, Gerardo Alfonso, and Santiago Feliú, certainly the most famous, along with Alberto Tosca, Adrián Morales, Arturo Arango, Marilyn Bobes, Alex Fleites, and Xiomara Laugart – artists of this generation are highly diverse in their styles and influences. All, though, have as their foundation the acoustic guitar and the music of the first generation of the Nueva Trova. In addition, their music reflects the influence of the Vieja Trova, that is, the *son*, the *bolero*, the *habanera*, the *cha cha chá*, and the *guajira*, which together comprise the soundtrack for the lives of all Cubans from childhood. But at the same time, each of the second-generation *trovadores* has his own identity, his own "persona trovadoresca": the *choteo* of Frank Delgado and his bittersweet songs like "Embajadora de sexo" (Sex Ambassador), "Cuando te vi" (When I Saw You), "La otra orilla" (The Other Shore), "Carta de un niño cubano a Harry Potter" (A Cuban Child's Letter to Harry Potter), and "Carta a Santa Claus" (Letter to Santa Claus); the polyrhythmic games and explorations into Afro-Cuba of Gerardo Alfonso with songs like "Espiritual," "Tetas africanas" (African Breasts), "El ilustrado caballero de París" (The Illustrious Gentleman of Paris), "Habana llena de gente" (Havana Full of People), and "Sábanas blancas" (White Sheets); and the inspired guitar playing of Santiago Feliú and his harmonica-accented stream-of-consciousness meditations in "Vida" (Life), "Batallas sobre mí" (Battles Over Me), "Las seis menos cuarto" (The Six Fifteen), "Solo arcoiris" (Only a Rainbow), and "Para Bárbara" (For Barbara). Of course, these observations are superficial. Each of these artists deserves a longer study.

For Carlos Varela, as for his contemporaries, identity is malleable. He assumes the role of the rocker who observes, catalogues, and criticizes. But at the same time, in many of his songs, especially his earliest, he makes a strong effort to identify his diverse influences. With regard to Cuban music, Varela celebrates Bola de Nieve, the "negro pianoman" in an eponymous song. A few years later, in "Como los peces," he borrows a verse from "Lágrimas negras" (Black Tears) by Miguel Matamoros. He also pays attention to international music; examples are his well-known tribute to the Beatles in "Memorias" and, more recently, his allusion to another important influence in "Todo será distinto" (Everything Will Be Different):

> Hay una lluvia que va a caer
> dijo el viejo Bob Dylan,
> a nadie le gusta perder
> digan lo que digan
>
> A hard rain is going to fall
> Said old Bob Dylan
> No one likes to lose
> No matter what they say

These references underscore the tensions between different generations of artists, but also his identification with them, as well as his position as part of their legacy. They also emphasize the interplay in his songs between continuity and rupture.

Setting aside these direct allusions in his lyrics, many musical influences are easily recognizable in his songs. In them, we can hear the British rockers of the 1960s and 1970s, including The Rolling Stones, Genesis, and The Clash; the North American folk-rock of Paul Simon and Neil Young; the Argentine rock of Charly García and León Gieco; and the Spanish pop songs of Joan Manuel Serrat. However, the most important influence on Varela has been the Cuban Nueva Trova of those decades, the works of the so-called first generation. Obvious influences here include Pablo Milanés, Noel Nicola, Amaury Pérez, and Vicente Feliú, but undoubtedly, the most important *trovador* in Carlos Varela's development as a young artist was Silvio Rodríguez.

Although it is impossible to state definitively when the Nueva Trova began, its development is commonly associated with the second half of the 1960s, with the energy and ambience of the Cuban Revolution and with those young artists who wanted to celebrate and, importantly, question early aspects of its implementation. A common misconception outside the island is that the *trova* artists supported the Revolution blindly without questioning their government's policies. Actually, the young artists who began to gather and give concerts at the Casa de las Américas, thanks to the efforts of then President Haydée Santamaría, who organized the Centro de la Canción Protesta in 1967, often expressed criticisms. In 1969, Alfredo Guevara, Director of the Instituto Cubano de Arte e Industria Cinematográficos (ICAIC), asked Santamaría to recommend artists to work with the ICAIC on soundtracks. In April of the same year, the Grupo de Experimentación Sonora del ICAIC (GES) was founded. Led by classical guitarist and composer Leo Brouwer, artists such as Pablo Milanés, Silvio Rodríguez, Noel Nicola, Sergio Vitier, Sara González, and Eduardo Ramos participated in intensive training in music theory, composition, and arrangements, with the emphasis on classical, jazz, and popular music. For many of the participants, it was the first and only musical education they received. In December 1972, the Movimiento de la Nueva Trova (MNT) was founded under the auspices of the Unión de Jóvenes Comunistas. Besides incorporating many GES veterans – Milanés, Rodríguez, Nicola – the MNT offered recognition, approval, help, and space for the growing waves of *trovadores* on the island, many of whom had been inspired by the GES sound. The MNT imposed a certain level of control over both the quality and the message of the young artists – often a difficult task. Until it was dissolved in 1986, the MNT developed and promoted these artists, while also moulding and controlling them.[3]

To understand the importance of the first generation of the Nueva Trova, and specifically of Silvio Rodríguez, in the development of Carlos Varela, it is worth reviewing the lyrics for "Jalisco Park," where Varela cites and describes the *trovador*:

> Un día jugando, no supe por qué
> en el 67 mataron al Che
> y así giró su historia, como el carrusel
> y la soñada idea de ser como él.
> Después el pelo largo, la moda y la confusión
> llegaban al 70 con el sueño del millón
> y así surgió aquel loco que primero nadie entendió
> diciendo cosas raras como en aquella canción:
> "La era está pariendo un corazón
> no puede más se muere de dolor.

> One day in 1967, I didn't know why
> they killed Che
> And just like that his history turned
> Like a carousel
> And the dream to be like him was born
> Afterwards, long hair, style and confusion
> The 1970s arrived, with the dream of a million
> And in the midst of this that crazy guy arrived,
>   who at first no one understood,
> Saying weird things like in that song:
> "The age is giving birth to a heart
> It can't do anything more, it's dying of pain ..."

There is much worth noting in these lyrics. They begin with the death of Che Guevara, an incalculably important event in Cuban history and for the direction of the country in the following decades. However, Varela manipulates the verb *girar*, as he does in the previous verses and will again in the one that follows, thus emphasizing repetition. Che's death and the disasters of the 1970s – "el pelo largo, la moda y la confusión" (the long hair, style and confusion) – are part of a historical process that introduces "aquel loco," Silvio Rodríguez, and his strange songs. And, as with any good prophet, no Cuban understands what he is saying. In addition, as Dubinsky notes later in this book, Varela compares Guevara's history with a carousel – a curious image that occupies a prominent position in these lyrics. The comparison is shocking in the context of Che's life and death. And, still more troubling, instead of repeating the refrain of the first two verses – "Todo daba vueltas como el carrusel" (Everything spins in circles like a carousel) – Varela cites directly the song Rodríguez wrote when he heard about Che's death: "La era está pariendo un corazón" (The age is giving birth to a heart). The appropriation of the earlier text is significant, because it implies that Varela is participating in a tradition he shares with Rodríguez, a tradition that has placed Varela in the generation that is continuing what Rodríguez began. Put more simply, Varela is identifying with Rodríguez, with his music, with his struggle, and with the contradictions of his experience.

But it is important to note as well the use of the word "loco." An audience familiar with the Nueva Trova will recognize another important allusion. At this point, it is worth remembering that many songs of the Nueva Trova are well-known even though they have never been recorded because their lyrics are critical of the government, and sometimes because the *trovador* is too confrontational. In the case of Rodríguez, the songs that most inspired the young artists of the Nueva Trova – not just Carlos Varela – were the polemical songs, the ones with the most critical lyrics. The Silvio they loved was the one who had to cut sugarcane to "aclarar sus ideas" (clarify his ideas) after he named the then-prohibited Beatles as the most important musical group of the day; their Silvio was the one who said of Pablo Milanés when he could not appear on a television program, "Pablo isn't here today not because he doesn't want to be, but because others don't want him to be."[4] Instead of the Silvio of clouds and unicorns, they preferred the Silvio of "Nunca he creído que alguien me odia" (I've Never Believed Anyone Hates Me), of "Debo partirme en dos" (I Must Split Myself in Two), and of his many unrecorded pieces, one of the most problematic of these being "Oda a mi generación" (Ode to My Generation):

> A los veintisiete días de mayo del año setenta
> un hombre se sube sobre sus derrotas,
> pide la palabra momentos antes de volverse loco.
> No es un hombre, es un malabarista de una generación.
> No es un hombre, es quizás un objeto de la diversión,
> un juguete común de la historia
> con un monograma que dice bufón.
> Ese hombre soy yo.
>
> Pero debo decir que me tocó nacer en el pasado
> y que no volveré.
> Es por eso que un día me vi en el presente,
> con un pie allá, donde vive la muerte,
> y otro pie suspendido en el aire, buscando un lugar,
> reclamando tierra de futuro para descansar.
> Así estamos yo y mis hermanos,
> con un precipicio en el equilibrio
> y con ojos de vidrio.
>
> Ahora quiero hablar de poetas,
> de poetas muertos y poetas vivos,
> de tantos muchachos hijos de esta fiesta
> y de la tortura de ser ellos mismos,
> porque hay que decir que hay quien muere

sobre su papel,
que vivirle a la vida su talla tiene que doler.
Nuestra vida es tan alta, tan alta
que para tocarla casi hay que morir,
para luego vivir.

Yo no reniego de lo que me toca,
yo no me arrepiento pues no tengo culpas,
pero hubiera querido poderme jugar
toda la muerte allá, en el pasado,
o toda la vida en el porvenir
que no puedo alcanzar.
Y con esto no quiero decir que me pongo a llorar.
Sé que hay que seguir navegando,
sigan exigiéndome cada vez más
hasta poder seguir o reventar.[5]

On the twenty-seventh day of May in 1970
a man rises before the defeated,
asks to say a word moments before going mad.
He is not a man, he is the juggler of a generation.
He is not a man, he is, perhaps, a diversion,
A common plaything of history
With a monogram that reads, "Buffoon."
I am that man.

But I should say that it was my luck to be born in the past
And I won't go back.
But because of that, one day I saw myself in the present
with one foot there, where death lives,
and the other foot suspended in the air, looking for a place,
Seeking a place in the future to rest.
That's how my brothers and I are:
tottering on a cliff in the equilibrium,
And with glass eyes.

Now I want to talk about poets
dead poets and living poets
so many young children of this party
and of the torture of their existence,

because it must be said that there are those who die
doing their job,
that living life to its fullest has to hurt.
Our life is so high, so high
that to touch it you nearly have to die,
So that you can live, later.

I don't reject what I have to do,
I don't repent because I'm not guilty,
but I would have preferred either everything
in the past, where death lives,
or life in the future
that I can't reach.
By saying this, I don't mean that I'm going to cry.
I know that I have to keep navigating,
let them keep asking more and more from me
For as long as I can continue, or until I explode.

The reference to "aquel loco" in "Jalisco Park" does not merely allude to the song Varela cites, "La era está pariendo un corazón"; it also makes the listener think of the protagonist of "Oda a mi generación," the man who "pide la palabra momentos antes de volverse loco" (asks to speak moments before going mad). It is notable that the song begins on 27 May 1970, days after the public announcement of the failure of the Zafra de los Diez Millones (Harvest of Ten Million), the unrealized "sueño del millón" sugar harvest that Varela mentions in "Jalisco Park." The year also marks the beginning of the Grey Years, the repressive 1970s, when the Cuban government followed the Soviet model and reorganized the economy. As often occurred, artists participated in concerts and events to motivate the public to complete the harvest. However, the disappointment and frustration expressed by Silvio Rodríguez in the lyric suggests a much broader and deeper disappointment, one that speaks to his situation and that of his generation. His self-description is sad and brutal: he is not a man, he is "un juguete" (a toy). Also, the metaphor of having one foot in the past and the other in the air "reclamando tierra del future para descansar" (demanding a place in the future to rest) is striking, although completely appropriate. Truly, his situation resonates and will resonate with Varela a few years later. In both cases, the singer/songwriter would have preferred living either in the past or in the future, not in the uncertain present. It is worth noting as well that Rodríguez insists he is innocent – that is, he stresses his position in a reality that he did not create.

In 1996, some twenty-five years after Rodríguez wrote "Oda a mi generación," Carlos Varela and Santiago Feliú participated in a tribute concert for Joan Manuel Serrat and Silvio Rodríguez at the Teatro Nacional in Havana. The concert was a celebration of the influence of the two older artists on the younger *trovadores*. Varela and Feliú performed together and separately, alternating between the honorees' songs and their own – which were often inspired by the works of Rodríguez and Serrat. This was an important moment in the revolutionary project. As a result of the austerity measures imposed during the "período especial en tiempo de paz" – the euphemistic Special Period of the 1990s – the tentative idealism and optimism of the 1980s had disappeared, replaced by an uncomfortable sense of déjà vu amidst the return of what the Revolution was supposed to have eliminated, that is, the indignities of a tourism-based economy. It was also a key moment in Varela's artistic development. After beginning his career with *Jalisco Park* (1989), *En vivo* (1991), and *Monedas al aire* (1992), he had just released *Como los peces* (1994), marking his creative peak as a *trovador*, as a singer/songwriter, critic, observer, and interpreter of his historic reality. In hindsight, that album was the culmination of the first part of his songbook with its unforgettable songs such as "La política no cabe en la azucarera," "Pequeños sueños," "Foto de familia," and "Como los peces."

In an introspective moment during the tribute concert, Varela performed an impassioned version of "Oda a mi generación." Then he told the audience: "That was the ode that Silvio sang to his generation. That was Silvio's, this is mine."[6] He then sang "Guillermo Tell," the song that continues to define him, his contemporaries, and his audience.

Although the lyric refers to the Swiss hero who shot an arrow at an apple placed on his son's head, naturally, the story connects with many of the *trovador*'s obsessions, such as family, legacy, and generations. An ideal metaphor for the situation of those who were born in the years immediately after the Cuban Revolution, the lyric illustrates the conflict between those who supported and participated in the process and those who received it as an inheritance they never asked for. Varela wrote it in 1989, at the beginning of the economic crisis that would be the defining experience of his generation, and it has became an anthem for the harshest years of the 1990s, a symbol of the suffering of those Cubans who lived through and survived that decade. The songwriter himself has written: "I wrote it in twenty minutes, but I suppose it had been cooking for a long time in my head. I used what in theatrical terms is called the magic 'if.' Imagine; what would have happened if William Tell grew up and told his father it was his turn to shoot the arrow?"[7]

Doubtless, "Guillermo Tell" is the song that summarizes all of the obsessions and preoccupations of Varela and his contemporaries. The idea of the son who rejects his father's game – an obvious metaphor for the young Cubans of the Special Period – continues to resonate with many Cubans, both those who experienced the 1990s first-hand and those who were born after the collapse of the Soviet Union and who never knew a world under Soviet patronage. Reflecting as it does a specific historic moment, it is appropriate that this song also stresses the problems of legacy and inheritance, of generational conflict, and it is especially notable that Varela identifies this song as his version of an earlier lyric by Silvio Rodríguez. That is, "Guillermo Tell" both records and results from a specific historic moment that is also cyclical. The tension between father and son is constant, even though – citing Wordsworth – the child is the father of the man. Or, if one prefers paraphrasing Martí, afraid of everything, the father seeks refuge in the son. As Varela puts it, "wherever there is a father and a son, wherever there are two generations, the ghosts of William Tell and his father will appear."[8]

Considering that this was watershed moment in Varela's career, it is surprising that between *Como los peces* and his next album there was a gap of six years. It is noteworthy that those were significant years in the development of the *trova* and of Cuban music in general. Even setting aside the explosion brought about by the Ry Cooder production *Buena Vista Social Club* and all the spin-offs from that project, the years since the second half of the 1990s have been exceedingly rich with regard to musical composition and production on the island. Borges-Triana refers to the legacy of the *trova*, after the first two generations, as Canción Cubana Contemporánea.[9] In other words, after the Novísima Trova, the dissolution of the MNT in 1986, and the subsequent proliferation of the *trova* style through many channels – including the Asociación Hermanos Saíz and the Centro Cultural Pablo de la Torriente Brau – *trova* grew and developed in many directions. As an inevitable consequence, the discussion of generations has become too facile and superficial. The 1990s saw the arrival on the scene of the celebrated Peña de 13 y 8; they also marked the first appearance of important projects such as the duo Gema y Pavel and Habana Oculta, as well as the early contributions of Kelvis Ochoa, Luis Alberto Barbería, Pepe del Valle, Carlos Santos, Boris Larramendi, Andy Villalón, and the group Superávit.

Then in the new millennium another group of young artists appeared, associated with the Centro Pablo de la Torriente Brau and the *A guitarra limpia* program, among them Ariel Díaz, Fernando Bécquer, Diego Cano, Samuel Águila, Heidi Igualada, Silvio Alejandro, Pavel Poveda, el dúo Karma, and, from other places, Buena Fe, Tony Ávila, Raúl Marchena, Diego Gutiérrez, Yaima Orozco, and the duos Aire y Madera and Janet y Quincoso. Ariel Díaz recalls:

> The new century brought new combinations of forces and interests. We have the fruitful and interesting metamorphosis of the duo Buena Fe, the badly promoted CD *Trov@nónima.cu*, the contradictory *Acabo de soñar*, with poems by José Martí, the nomination of the *A guitarra limpia* CDs in the Cubadisco festival, the take-off of William Vivanco, projects such as Interactivo and Aceituna sin hueso, the video of the duo Karma competing and winning in faraway lands, Yusa in the Ronnie Scott, the noisy return of Habana Abierta, some of us in European festivals, the return of Karel y Carlos from their separation, the help of the Tropa Cósmica y Trovacub, young *trovadores* in the jungles of Guatemala, Haití, and Belice, cooperating with medical brigadas, the vitality of our closest artistic parents, Frank, for example, surrounded by youth, Santiago with Symphony, without Julieta, Varela in Hollywood, and twenty five years of the songs of Gerardo.[10]

These were productive years during which artists of the second generation of the *trova* became heroes to a younger generation. Without realizing it, the most recognized *trovadores* of the Novísima Trova had become "padres." Ariel Díaz remembers that when Fernando Bécquer attended a concert by Carlos Varela and Gerardo Alfonso, "we heard them sing 'Tropicollage' together, and after that he wouldn't stop until he learned to play the guitar."[11] Indeed, these were important years for many artists of the Novísima Trova, especially Frank Delgado with his discs *Trovatur* and *Pero qué dice el coro* and the prolific Gerardo Alfonso with his concerts as well as his albums *Recuento* and *Cuarto del siglo*. Varela found himself faced with new styles and new artists, and with a new role as "padre" of a generation of *trovadores*. All of this, and the generational conflicts that had always preoccupied him, resulted in a more intimate and introspective style on his long-awaited next album, *Nubes* (2000).

Even a casual listen makes it clear that *Nubes* marks a new direction for Varela. It is the only completely acoustic album in his catalogue. It is also one of his most important albums – certainly his most important work after *Como los peces* – and it is difficult to understand his subsequent albums without understanding how they relate to *Nubes*. The guitar playing is simple and smooth, the lyrics minimalist and humble. Instead of observing and describing his world, which had been his earlier approach, and instead of donning the rocker-rebel persona, Varela on *Nubes* is pensive and tentative, modest and soft-spoken, and his observations reflect his disappointment and confusion as he confronts himself and his art as part of a process, one step of many. Like Silvio Rodríguez in "Oda a mi generación," more than ever Varela finds himself with one foot in the past and the other in the air seeking the future. This idea resonates with the first words of "Será sol" (It Will Be Sun):

> En vano fue cerrar los ojos
> y no saber dónde mirar.
> En vano fue quedarnos solos
> frente a la colina de los tontos
> viendo pasar el mundo
> en silencio.
>
> In vain we closed our eyes,
> Not knowing where to look.
> In vain we remained on our own,
> Facing a hill of fools,
> Watching the world go by,
> In silence

The disappointment continues in the chorus, where he emphasizes his faith in the cycles of nature, that good will become evil and that evil will in turn become good:

> Mirando cómo caen las hojas
> tratando de encontrar a Dios,
> lo que hoy es luz, mañana es sombra,
> lo que fue lluvia será Sol,
> será Sol.

> Looking at how the leaves fall,
> Trying to find God,
> What is light today, is shadow tomorrow,
> What was rain will be sun
> It will be sun.

Also, good and evil never completely vanish: they remain as alternating parts of the process. This idea is expressed most strongly in the chorus of the album's title song, "Nubes":

> No jures por la tempestad
> aunque tu Luna se está apagando,
> las nubes no se irán, no se irán, no se irán,
> no se irán,
> solo se quedan adentro y llorando.

> Don't swear by the storm,
> Although your moon is burning out,
> The clouds won't go away, won't go away, won't go away,
> won't go away,
> They only stay inside and cry.

It is tempting to think of the tempest as an allusion to the classic Cuban poem "En una tempestad" (In a Storm) by José María Heredia. One should place one's trust in the tempest – that is, one should not swear by what seems all-powerful or inevitable in the moment. Rather, one should trust the constancy of the process: the clouds never really vanish.

In his next album, *Siete* (2003), he reverts to his earlier rock sound, yet the ideas and the persona of the *trovador* are the same as on *Nubes*. More than ever, Varela sees himself as part of a cyclic process that also implies a linear and historical progression. This contradiction lies at the heart of the album, as the title track illustrates. The numbers seven and seventeen – themselves indivisible – play with the even numbers seventy, ten, and eighty. This reflects a chronological progression, with the divisible numbers representing a history that repeats itself. Appropriately, the repetition of divisible numbers emphasizes the repetition of family divisions. All of this also relates to ideas' presence and absence, being and not being, *ser* and *parecer*. In "Estás," another song from *Siete*,

Varela sings of searching for a person who is not there and of how that absence makes the person seem all the more present. The manipulation of presence, absence, and permanence continues throughout the album.

The effort to reconcile two contradictory realities is also prominent in Varela's most recent album, *No es el fin* (2009), especially in songs like "El viejo sueño acabó," "Todo será distinto," and "La marea." Appropriately, he stresses this idea at the end of both albums: on *Siete*, the chorus of "Estás" repeats itself as a piano-and-voice ghost track; and on *No es el fin*, the disc begins and ends with a music box playing "Send in the Clowns." At the start of the album, the listener hears the winding of the box and then the music; at the end, the song's last notes are heard as the music box runs down. In both cases, the effect is unsettling: an unexpected repetition leaves listeners disconcerted, dizzy, and alternating between linear and circular, just like the composer himself.

Varela began his career as part of the Novísima Trova, itself a legacy of the singer/songwriters of the Nueva Trova like Pablo Milanés, Noel Nicola and, of course, Silvio Rodríguez. The problem with youth movements is that as artists grow older, younger generations always follow. Thus, artists who continue practising their art find they eventually outgrow their youthful personae. In Varela's case, there are several recent examples of how he views his own place in the development of the *trova*. The title of his 2005 album, *Los hijos de Guillermo Tell vol. 1*, an anthology of previous releases, implies that he recognizes his audience as William Tell's children, that is, as children of a Revolution and heirs to a history unique to the twentieth and twenty-first centuries. This shared experience pertains to a specific group that lived through key events of the 1990s (a moment that Xenia Reloba explores in detail in this book). The songs he has selected for this album suggest a need to preserve a musical tradition so that it can be shared with those who came afterwards. In this sense, *Los hijos de Guillermo Tell vol. 1* serves two purposes (as does *Carlos Varela: All His Greatest Hits* – a similar collection released in support of his 2009 tour of the United States). First, Varela's act of organizing diverse songs into a representative collection reflects his attempt to control and celebrate his own public persona. This resonates with his older fans' nostalgia. But equally important is a second purpose, which is to reach and educate a new audience – sometimes the grandchildren of William Tell, sometimes *trova* fans more generally.

With the passage of time, the two contradictory characteristics of the Revolution, its linear and its cyclical movements, and their implications for the Nueva Trova, have become the subtext of Carlos Varela's songbook. The "hijo del fuego" heralded the "hijo de Guillermo Tell." But now, who is he? It is curious that to promote his recent tour, Varela produced a video of a new version of "Memorias" from his first album. It would be easy to assume that he simply wanted to generate publicity with a song that many of his fans would recognize – out of nostalgia or dedication. In reality, though, the song and the video constitute an entirely new version of "Memorias."

One of his best and most beloved songs, "Memorias" deals with the experience of those who were born after the Cuban Revolution and who grew up during the difficult years of the 1960s and 1970s, the years of the Bay of Pigs, the Cuban Missile Crisis, the death of Che Guevara, the Harvest of Ten Million, and the "Quinquenio Gris" – that is, the Grey Years that culminated in the Mariel Boatlift of 1980. Yet despite its historical references, the song has a quality that places it outside of chronological time – more precisely, it is *indifferent* to time. The first words underscore the inevitability of a history that repeats itself. The *trovador* is seated "como hace un siglo atrás," as though it was a century ago. Time passes, but nothing changes, not even the relevance of the film *Memorias del subdesarrollo* by Tomás Gutiérrez Alea, about the perpetual struggle between staying on the island and leaving it. That movie is already twenty years old, and thus, Varela and his song are its heirs and reflect its continuity. Also, like the film, the *trovador*'s song records and preserves – perhaps perpetuates – a historic moment and at the same time is a witness to its passage. In 1989, "Memorias" served as the touchstone for a generation. It was a way for a specific generation to identify and define itself. In 2011, the song meant even more.

There are only a few differences between the two versions of "Memorias," but they are important. The most obvious change has to do with the line that mentions *Memorias del subdesarrollo*. Instead of

> es extraño que a los veinte años
> no se apagó su luz
>
> It's strange that after twenty years
> Its light has not gone out.

Varela sings "a los cuarenta años." It is a small change – easy to miss if one does not listen closely – but it implies a great deal. If Varela had not changed the number of years, the song would be in the past, a work of nostalgia. The change insists that the audience recognize how the world Varela described in 1989 still exists. The movie is now forty years old, but its conflicts have not disappeared. Specific situations may have changed, but the general collective experience is equivalent. Some references are dated – Superman and Elpidio Valdés – but others maintain their currency (Santa Claus, Christmas Tree, The Beatles). The new version of "Memorias" culminates in several lines that were not part of the original lyric and that serve as a coda to the new version:

> Voy a pedir un minuto de silencio,
> voy a pedirle al sol de los desiertos,
> por esas madres que me enseñaron
> que existe vida después de muerto.
> Voy a pedir un minuto de silencio,
> voy a pedirle a Dios y al mar abierto,
> por los muchachos que nos dejaron
> y no llegaron nunca a ningún puerto,
> a ningún puerto,
> no.[26]

> I'm going to ask for a moment of silence
> I'm going to ask the sun of the deserted
> For those mothers who taught me
> That life exists after death
> I'm going to ask for a moment of silence
> I'm going to ask it from God and the open sea
> For those kids who left us
> And never arrived at any port
> At any port
> No

These sad and moving lines at the end of the song summarize the most important themes in the songbook of Carlos Varela. He asks for a silence he will never receive, and he wants the silence for the mothers who taught him that "existe vida después de muerto" (life exists after death) and for the young people who "nunca llegaron a ningún puerto" (never arrived at any port). Those young people died in transit, and because of that, they remain forever young in memories of the past. Once again the *trovador* emphasizes familial relations and, at the same time, the presence of a great beyond towards which we are all moving.

The journey is difficult, and we may never arrive at any port. Yet we move forward continually and never stop; despite the passage of time, the present is the same as the past. In recent years, Carlos Varela has come to understand himself as a point on a line and also as part of a circle. The effort of reconciling this contradiction produces a dissonance that is both inevitable and painful. Achieving this reconciliation is impossible, yet it is also impossible to stop singing about the need for it, because ultimately this is what it means to be a *trovador*, in the same way that, for his public, living and dying in the attempt to reconcile two contradictory realities is what it means to be Cuban. What the *trovador* wants more than anything else, for his public and for himself, and what Carlos Varela asks for from the cacophony of his reality, is, ironically, a moment of silence.

NOTES

1. Silvio Rodríguez, "La canción de las sillas," *Kubamusica Festival de la Nueva Trova* (Matxitxa, TX, 059–CD I, 1996).
2. Joaquín Borges-Triana, *La luz, bróder, la luz: Canción Cubana Contemporánea* (La Habana: Ediciones la Memoria, 2009), p. 8.
3. For more information on the GES del ICAIC, see Jaime Sarusky, *Una leyenda de la música cubana. Grupo de experimentación sonora del ICAIC* (La Habana: Editorial Letras Cubanas, 2005). For more on the MNT, see Antonio López Sánchez, *La canción de la nueva trova* (La Habana: Ediciones Musicales Atril, 2001).
4. Pablo Milanés had been in one of the infamous Unidades Militares de Ayuda a la Producción (UMAP) and had encountered problems because of his appearance – an afro associated with the controversial Black Power movement in the United States. Joseba Sanz, *Silvio: Memoria trovada de una revolución* (Bilbao: Guazapa Liburuak, 1992), p. 108.
5. Thanks to Nelson Cárdenas for giving me a cassette of these songs many years ago. More recently, after thirty-six years, Silvio Rodríguez recorded the tune for a collection of unreleased songs from the late 1960s and early 1970s. See Silvio Rodríguez, *Érase que se era* (Ojalá 8869 700507-2, 2006).
6. The concert "Cantores de fin de siglo" with Carlos Varela and Santiago Feliú, in honor of Silvio Rodríguez y Joan Manuel Serrat, was held in 1996 at the Teatro Nacional. Thanks to Caridad Cumaná for giving me a copy of the concert.
7. Varela, notes, *Los hijos de Guillermo Tell vol. I* (Graffiti Music Group, 2005).

8 Varela, notes, *Los hijos de Guillermo Tell vol. I*.
9 Borges-Triana, *La luz, bróder, la luz*, pp. 6–8.
10 Ariel Diaz, *La primera piedra* (La Habana: Ediciones la Memoria, 2009), p. 41.
11 Diaz, *La primera piedra*, p. 16.

Chapter Three

"Politics Don't Fit in a Sugar Bowl" Cuba in the 1990s through the Music of Varela

XENIA RELOBA DE LA CRUZ

In "La política no cabe en la azucarera" (Politics Don't Fit in a Sugar Bowl) from his 1994 album *Como los peces,* Carlos Varela offers an inventory of the crisis that Cuba was undergoing at the time. The relationship between the two main terms in the song's title, while not strictly antagonistic, implies a certain opposition. Politics represents all that is established, the conventions of the authorities; the sugar bowl, in the literal sense, is the container for a foodstuff valued for its energy-giving properties. The song is a reference to the people's daily struggle for survival. But there is another connotation: in Cuba, sugar could be considered a national essence; thus, the sugar bowl symbolizes a state that until very recently based its economic development on the cultivation and export of sugar. Why can't politics fit into a sugar bowl? Just what doesn't fit? On these questions Varela is uncharacteristically explicit.

Composed in the traditional rhythm of the *cha cha chá*, this song – one of the last on the album – sets aside Varela's usual impressionism. In other songs, his discourse is ambivalent, his narrative fable-like, and the message can be interpreted in various ways. In "La política no cabe en la azucarera," however, his point is much clearer: politics is failing to solve the crisis, and as a result, Cuban families are being shattered. One by one, he recounts the most popular strategies for coping with the situation: individualism ("someone yelled: each man for himself!"); immigration ("at the table on Sunday there are two empty chairs, they are 90 miles away from mine); corruption, even in circles that have traditionally been furthest removed from it ("a worker sees me, he calls me an artist, and nobly I raise his status,[1] he goes around trading in tourist money, he has four children and life is hard"); and prostitution and pimping ("women are a good business, some walk around alone and some have a partner"). And he alludes to the fuel shortage that constantly makes itself felt in Cuban households in the form of blackouts ("today for sure they'll cut the lights").

Besides describing daily realities, Varela reiterates the need for change and the frustrations of living with stagnation: "the people are waiting for something, but here nothing happens." The climate has aggravated the crisis, in addition to the circumstance that Cuba is an island: "It's really hot in old Havana, the tide gets higher with every passing day." Obviously, he is not just referring to geological features: the social temperature is also rising, and he feels uneasy about it. Yet he declares, almost apologetically:

> ¡pero entiéndeme brother!
> -dijo tómalo como quieras,
> la política no cabe en la azucarera,
>
> But understand me, brother,
> Take it as you'd like,
> Politics doesn't fit in a sugar bowl.

Como los peces was produced four years after the fall of the Berlin Wall and three years after the collapse of the Soviet Union. Thousands of miles from these events, Havana and Cuba were in chaos.[2] In 1993, Cuba's gross nation product crashed to $1.26 billion, from an average high of $8.5 billion during the 1980s. Per capita income on the island fell from third place in Latin America (after Chile and Colombia) to twenty-third.[3]

Cuba's economic decline was clearly visible by the early 1990s, but it had actually started some five years earlier. Between 1985 and 1990, signs of unrest had begun to appear in the Eastern European countries that had been part of the Council for Mutual Economic Assistance – a body to which Cuba had belonged since 1972 (with most favoured nation status). In the mid-1980s, the socialist countries' model of development, which emphasized quantity over quality of products, entered a crisis, even while economic relations with the capitalist West were noticeably deteriorating. In 1986, the Cuban government declared a moratorium foreign debt payments. The West responded by suspending credit, which led to a 30 per cent decrease in imports.[4]

September 1990 marked the beginning of the "Special Period" in Cuba. Daily life came to mean nothing more than endurance – Cubans faced shortages of food and clothing as well as deteriorating transportation. Blackouts became more frequent and prolonged, and many factories closed or limited their production hours, which meant that significant numbers of workers had to stay at home on truncated pay or accept work for which they had no training or experience.[5] The lack of supplies (including medicines) for hospitals and for schools at all levels meant that the two pillars of social development in Cuba were beginning to crumble. As they had done in past hard times, Cubans looked to the north, to the ocean. The year 1994 saw the "raft crisis," the most dramatic emigration by sea from Cuba since the Mariel Boatlift of 1980. Meanwhile, the government struggled to solve the crisis. Between 1993 and 1995, it began a highly controlled experiment in opening the island's economy to foreign investment; it also decriminalized the possession and circulation of hard currency. This included allowing US dollar bank accounts.[6]

The economic crisis had a strong impact on families as several generations struggled to live under the same roof and sometimes in the same room. Economic hardships and scarcities triggered daily clashes and were often unbearable.

All the while, the government avoided acknowledging these deteriorating daily realities. It was as if the country's media had been stunned into silence: the number of newspapers shrank, and those still publishing printed fewer pages; many other publications, both general and specialized, closed their doors; and radio and television broadcasting hours were reduced. No attempts were made to use non-traditional means to disseminate information. During this period, significant national and foreign events affecting the country were described briefly at best. As a consequence, the media faced a decline in their traditional role on the island. Rarely was information provided that might help people understand the political and economic challenges facing the country, which obviously had not arisen overnight. In "La política no cabe," Varela was expressing the rising cynicism about Cuba's superficial discourse:

> Todos quieren vivir en el noticiero
> Allí no falta nada y no hace falta el dinero
>
> Everyone wants to live on the news,
> there nothing's lacking and money isn't short.

In this informational void in which debate barely survived, artistic and literary production took on tremendous importance as a form of compensation. Conditions for criticism were favourable in 1986, at a time when Communist Party of Cuba was calling for the revamping of the socialist system through "rectification of mistakes and negative trends." However, this process was set back by the shock of the late 1980s. The trend was reversed; the doors were closed. Apparently, criticism was not such a good idea after all: arguments, even when expressed creatively, were now possible weapons for the enemy to wield. And those weapons were especially dangerous now, when the Cuban economy was on the verge of being asphyxiated.[7]

I will mention two examples of art that found ways to connect with the daily realities of ordinary Cubans. Cuban cinema, which had built a tradition based on the aesthetic principles of 1950s Italian neorealism, attempted to depict reality by means of an art that depends heavily on its own industrial nature: no money, no cinema. In this context, mention should be made of two films with very different aesthetics: *Strawberry and Chocolate* (1993) by Tomás Gutiérrez Alea and Juan Carlos Tabío, and *Madagascar* (1994) by Fernando Pérez, then an "emerging" filmmaker. *Strawberry and Chocolate* is the film version of the short story "El lobo, el bosque and el hombre nuevo" (The Wolf, the Wood, and the New Man) by Cuban writer Senel Paz. It is a plea for tolerance and understanding of "the different." In the closed Cuban society of the time, this theme was both necessary and highly commendable. *Madagascar*, released the following year, is one of the bleakest works of recent Cuban cinema. Through this film one can reconstruct very closely the bleak spirit of the times and how individuals survived in it.

Cuban theatre arrived late to the vibrant 1980s. Even so, several important plays were produced in that decade that commented on daily realities. Others rewrote the classics as a means to restore Cubans' self-image as a people. Discussing the production of *Manteca* by Alberto Pedro, Cuban theatre critic Omar Valiño noted that "the symbolic connotation in this production appeared to be closely related to the heroic existence/resistance of ordinary Cubans."[8] He added that

> *Manteca* provides a two-level modified image of the Island: on the one hand, the accumulation of a culture of things, global and integrating, which goes down to the rice plate set on the table; on the other hand, the crisis of the system, triggered by the transformations occurred in the

world. Thus, the island is understood and interiorized as an Island, as an isolated reality within the globalizing configuration.[9]

Music is of course a powerful vehicle for social commentary, and it too made a contribution in this decade. The songs created by Carlos Varela, a prominent member of what Borges-Triana has famously termed the "generation of moles," provide a complex and multifaceted look at this period. In 2002 the Cuban journal *Temas* published a debate on popular music as a mirror of society.[10] In it, Joaquín Borges-Triana argued that

> Throughout history, Cuban music has always encouraged self-reflection. Through music we look to ourselves as well as various events of daily life, both social and intimate ... [Music] sheds light on certain problem areas, especially those of daily life. Sometimes, it hits a raw nerve.

Like his colleagues, Varela was directly influenced by his predecessors, who made it their responsibility to critically analyse the problems of the society they were building. And like their predecessors, Varela's Nueva Trova generation struggled against the many institutions and officials who had misgivings about this "weird" way of seeing and expressing our society.

Borges-Triana has also commented that while most of this generation tended to write complicated lyrics, those lyrics later became more "readable."[11] They abandoned the rhetorical complexities that had made their messages hard to digest. Some wrote in more intimate registers, with touches of rock, pop, and other Anglo-Saxon genres (Santiago Feliú, Carlos Varela); others resorted more to humour and maintained Cuban musical traditions (Frank Delgado); still others inflected their songs with Afro-Caribbean and Brazilian traditions (Gerardo Alfonso).

The 1990s took Varela's generation – and almost everyone else – by surprise. These musicians had by then attracted significant numbers of fans, and despite the strictures they faced with regard to state radio and television broadcast policies, some of their songs received airplay.

Varela and the rest of his generation set out to recount the reality around them and to tell stories through their music. As many in this book have pointed out, Varela is a chronicler of urban life. But at the same time, he has developed a universal sensibility by integrating foreign rhythms and interpretations. His lyrics are parables that rely on complex codes that can be difficult to understand for listeners who do not grasp the Cuban references. Even so, it is possible for non-Cubans to understand his work. He creates sympathetic characters and immerses us in their emotional realities. When he lectures us, he does not do so openly. For him, the individual is central. Varela's followers often identify with him, for he has established himself as someone with common problems, dreams, and hopes. At times, though, his vision of the world becomes blunter, and his lyrics become declarations of principles emerging from the place and time in which he lives. Cuban art critic Roberto Zurbano has stated that

> music, by itself, does not explain anything; it does not offer a lofty academic lesson about an event or a sociohistorical experience. Rather, it presents a *tableau vivant*, a chronicle, a spark, a reflection – sometimes very brief, other times momentous – of what is happening in a certain time. As the artist expresses authentically his or her social, ethno-social origins, gender, political position, religious commitment, she or he becomes a reflection of the person who is living in a certain time and in a certain place.[12]

The songs on *Como los peces* vividly describe some of the survival strategies of the Special Period. They are tinted with their creator's experiences of that era in ways that help us reconstruct what we were at the time: fragile beings, buffeted by sudden changes to social structures that had long seemed impregnable. Although it may not have been his intention, his songs reveal that we were on the brink of chaos and afraid of what it portended. We had taken our daily lives for granted, as something natural and obvious. From birth we had found reality "constructed, objectivated, and pervaded with meanings that become such in and during the socialization process."[13] Thus, when that reality was suddenly destroyed – despite the widely heralded promises of "real socialism" – we were knocked completely out of place:

> In a situation of crisis, independently of the level in question – personal, familiar, community, social – the old and the habitually known do not occur, thus do not offer a response. The new realities demand new referents through which to understand them. Such uncertainty creates anguish and anxiety precisely because of the lack of these referents. Therefore, daily life and behavior is ruptured in countless ways, because the old referents just don't work anymore.[14]

The search for meaning compelled by the crisis of the Special Period is the thread that runs through *Como los peces*. Most of the album's twelve songs have intimate lyrics. All are fables imparting lessons.

The album's title song offers an interesting perspective on disillusionment. How do we react to being disillusioned? Just like fish do. Confusion turns us mute: "people pray and asks for things in silence" (just like fish), "the parents don't want to talk about the situation," "prisoners survive and learn to keep quiet" (like fish); and meanwhile, "the news speaks of resignation," "people swallow and look at each other" (just like fish), the "kids speak of disillusionment and in silence they go to the sea and swim off" (like fish). This song, like many of Varela's, highlights the ocean and Piñera's "damned circumstance of the water everywhere around."[15] Varela also uses religious symbols repeatedly, although neither churches, nor prayers, nor the "black tears" of the virgin,[16] nor the tears that fall down Jesus's face, offer a credible escape from the confusion the song recounts. Disillusionment brings about impotence. The individual is alone, and his/her condition is intensely felt (musically so as well), but the narrator is distant. The crisis is experienced by others: "people pray," "the kids swim off," "the mother cries," "the parents do not want to talk." The only appearance by the *trovador* we might consider "explicit" is when he quotes a well-known passage from "Lágrimas negras" (Black Tears):

> Aunque tú me has echado en el abandono,
> aunque ya han muerto todas mis ilusiones,
> lloro sin que sepas que este llanto mío
> tiene lágrimas negras
>
> Even though you have abandoned me
> Although all my illusions have died
> I cry without you knowing
> That I am crying black tears

Here, we can implicitly identify the author with his characters, yet there is still a certain distance. This suggests that he does not agree with the passive attitude with which the story's protagonists live their present.

That the album is thematically framed by the search for meaning is confirmed in its very first song. In "Como un angel" (Like an Angel), the themes of loneliness and lovelessness predominate; the story shifts between loss of faith and isolation as a survival strategy. Religious symbols abound: God, the Virgin, a cross, an angel. Varela is reminding us that religious faith is a common response to times of crisis. This is more than a simple sociological observation about Cuba in the 1990s. He is suggesting here that although religious faith became more socially acceptable on the island in that decade, it continued to be viewed as subversive. The protagonist of "Como un angel" has "a tattoo of a cross on her back, where it can't be seen." This in fact is doubly subversive, for tattoos were socially unacceptable at that time. "Como un angel" expresses a social trend: the search for refuge in religion (whatever the denomination), which many hoped would protect us.

But the search for meanings is not related solely to religious faith. It is also associated with the pursuit of utopia, which, given the unsurmountable problems of the 1990s, seems to have halted in those years. The new meaning of utopia in that era allows us to reconstruct ourselves as individuals and social beings, and at the same time to try to restore or establish new social values. The ongoing desire for utopia and for the defence of individual aspirations is addressed by Varela in "Pequeños sueños" (Little Dreams), whose protagonists include a truck driver fascinated by a *Playboy* pin-up, a young women in love with a *trovador* and thus rejected by her father, a mother placing flowers in front of the photograph of her deceased husband, and a singer and his guitar. All of these people cling to personal fantasies that make them momentarily happy. The "smallness" of these dreams contrasts with Varela's strong vindication of the need to have them (observe the recurrence of the possessive pronoun "their") – that is, of the right to dream. In the story, the characters' loneliness is undoubtedly relevant. Loneliness makes them even more visible as individuals, with hopes that are not necessarily transcendent but that *are* their own and therefore valid. In such "small dreams," one can read a certain contrast with those "great dreams" that were being dispersed throughout the era. Now that the great dreams have became much less clear, individuals must learn to understand themselves.

Como los peces defends the importance of the individual as the core of change, in terms of both the self and society. In "Solo tú (puedes traer el sol)" (Only You Can Bring the Sun), Varela establishes a dialogue with the protagonist, who is called to elevate herself and overcome winter ("it was harder than others"). He uses the language of the weather to construct a threatening landscape ("When the wind hits your eyes hard"; "Save your soul from the storm / The hurricane is nearing"), and he calls for optimism – a slight divergence from the general tone of the album. The call to "save your soul," while not explicitly religious or mystical, seems to confirm the vitality of faith. In this song, Varela includes an uncharacteristic reference to himself, both as a creator and as a person:

> Hace mucho tiempo que se dicen cosas
> y aún se sigue hablando de mí.
> Yo sé que es el precio de cuidar la rosa,
> yo sé que es el precio de quedarme aquí

> They have been saying things about me for a long time
> and they are still talking about me.
> I know what it takes to care for a rose,[17]
> I know the price of staying here.

In the last two verses, he slips in, as if by chance, a dilemma that had an enormous impact on Cuban society in the 1990s (a dilemma that continues): Do we want to live our "Cubanidad" inside or outside Cuba? Where is it easier or more comfortable to offer our vision of our identity, and how relative is that comfort?

The right to express individuality in the face of social restrictions is the theme of "Graffiti de amor" (Love Graffiti). Varela chooses darkness as the backdrop for this tale of individual self-expression: the protagonist arrives "under the light of dawn." It is also significant that the character's means of expression are personal: her lipstick and, in a dramatic ending, a tattoo. Furthermore, Varela uses the verb *rayar* (scratch) instead of something more subtle to explain the decision of the woman, who, having been prevented from painting coloured fish on the city walls, has chosen to "scratch" her own body "with a tattoo of love." Varela doesn't specify the meanings of the symbols she wants to draw. What is important here is the intense need to draw – a desire that, when socially suppressed, results in the self-aggression represented by the tattoo. In the verses

> desde entonces prohibieron
> dibujar lo que sentía el alma,
> para cuidar y encadenar la calma

> from then on it was forbidden
> to draw what one feels in the soul,
> to protect and shackle the peace

the opposition established between the verbs *cuidar* and *encadenar* is perhaps a comment on official discourse: in times of crisis, it's healthier to keep quiet.

"Hombre de silicona" (Silicon Man) is another defence of individual freedom. It explores a theme rarely encountered in Cuban music of the 1990s: homosexuality, bisexuality, and transvestism. From today's perspective, the text is rather naive. In his attempt to represent the protagonist's desire to escape from an unwanted physical appearance and become someone else ("he dreamed of having the breasts of Madonna ... the legs of Cher"), the singer appeals to some already obsolete clichés ("He was a man, he was a man, but he had a heart of a woman"). In the lines

> Estaba preso dentro de su mismo cuerpo
> sin poder escapar del dolor,
> su sexo que importaba si era falso o cierto
> si ya moría con la ilusión.
> El era libre, era libre
> pero soñaba con dejar la prisión.
>
> He was a prisoner of his own body
> Without the power to escape his pain,
> What did it matter if his sex was true or false
> If he lived with the illusion.
> He was free, he was free
> But he dreamed of leaving the prison,

Varela explores the paradox of individual choice and the social perception of that choice. As he continues the story:

> En el barrio lo miraban de una forma extraña
> por eso apenas se asomaba a su balcón.
> Sus amantes le decían: la mujer araña,
> pero en la calle le gritaban: maricón.
>
> In the neighbourhood they looked at him funny,
> That's why he hardly went on to his balcony
> his lovers called him spiderwoman,
> But in the streets they yelled "fag."

One of most significant songs in *Como los peces* appears in the middle of the album: "Foto de familia" (Family Photo). In the imaginary of the many Cubans, the song is controversial, for it dissects – from my very committed perspective – emigration and its impact on the family and on society as a whole. It is not surprising that shortly after this album came out, "Foto de familia" was used as the theme song for (and inspired the title of) the very successful 2001 Cuban film *Video de familia* by Humberto Padrón.[18] In this song, Varela emphasizes the passing of time and the shared yearning for "something that never came back." Words such as loneliness, nostalgia, lies, betrayal, distance, separation, governments, borders, and religion all become negative as they interact with the constantly repeated "family." This time, Varela is writing in the first person plural, thus involving himself more actively in the story. A few lines of the text merit particular attention. When Varela sings that we are "trying to live inside the same bubble, alone," he is perhaps suggesting something about the coexistence and contradictions of loneliness. Later in the song, he borrows a well-known line from Silvio Rodríguez's "Pequeña serenata diurnal" (Small Daytime Serenade): "o casi nada, que no es lo mismo pero es igual" (or almost nothing, which isn't the same, but is just like it).[19] This line contributes little to the song; even so, it is suggestive due to its origins. This song's happy tone, its meaning, and its expression of a sharp historical memory, are in sharp contrast to that of Varela's.

One of the more intimate songs on *Como los peces* is "Grettel." The melancholic mood and highly lyrical text make this one of the warmest songs on the album. In "Grettel," the search for meaning focuses on a couple and explores how one's partner provides meaning in a world in crisis. Varela includes here some of his usual references – Jim Morrison's poetry and Tarot cards, both of which recur in later songs. Another of Varela's recurring references, the city of Havana, here acquires a distinct meaning. In "Grettel," the city becomes "even more difficult, even darker, more alone." This occurs specifically when the woman to whom the song is sung is not there: her absence makes everything disappear, even things that should fade naturally ("the day does not break, at least not for me"). It is especially suggestive that Varela confesses that his presence in the city, and indeed in the country, is directly associated with the presence of his partner.

In "El niño, los sueños y el reloj de arena" (The Child, the Dreams, and the Hourglass), Varela returns to the convention of the fable to tell the story of a boy who dreams of "seeing a day that never dawns." As the song progresses, the dream is shared, but only to a certain extent (the singer "dreams songs and others prefer to keep quiet"). It is significant that such dreams are described, elsewhere in the song, as "cursed." Words such as solitude, distrust, silence, disappointment, and pain predominate. The desire for change contrasts with the absence of signs of change, and this reinforces the despair that permeates the song. Also remarkable is that the one who dreams is essentially an individual, although sometimes that one person turns into a collective character. The collectivity, the community, seems dispersed, haunted by fears ("it is not that no one trusts, but it is difficult to trust," "people live in fear, fear of hoping").

"El leñador sin bosque" (The Woodcutter without a Forest) continues Varela's meditation on the loss of hope. In this song, the religious referents are negative:

> la Inquisición
> quemó mi bosque con fuego, mi bosque.
>
> the Inquisition
> burned my forest with fire, my forest

It is important to emphasize again that at the time *Como los peces* was being produced, Carlos Varela was a well-known singer/songwriter in some circles, but his music was not regularly broadcast on Cuban radio and TV. As Borges-Triana and Nasatir have noted in this book, renowned *trova* singers like Pablo Milanés and Silvio Rodríguez supported Varela and others of the same generation; yet in some quarters there was still a great deal of ambivalence about his work and his opinions on issues of the day. These opinions were not openly expressed by him, but they *were* circulated *sotto voce,* and they formed part of the myth that nourished his image among his followers. "El leñador sin bosque" has some of Varela's most explicitly anti-authoritarian lyrics. In what might be considered his declaration of principles, he sings:

> Por eso vivo alejado
> del trono y el dragón,
> prefiero ser olvidado
> antes que hacer de bufón.

> That's why I live far away
> from the throne and the dragon,
> I prefer to be forgotten
> rather than being the jester.

The optimistic ending brings us back to the ambience of the fable:

> Soy leñador desde mi niñez
> y aunque no tengo bosque
> sueño con árboles
>
> I've been a woodcutter since childhood
> and although I don't have a forest
> I dream of trees.

Como los Peces is steeped in disillusionment and the search for meaning. It ends with what has become one of Varela's – and Havana's – classic songs: "Habáname." As Thomas also explores in this book, in this song Varela personifies the city and laments its deterioration; he explicitly blames its physical ailments on the passage of time but also on the indifference of its inhabitants. And he subtly blames them on the authorities.[20] It is a painful song, its mournful message and haunting melody serving as a beautiful tribute to the Cuban capital as well as an excellent means of understanding it – at least emotionally – from the perspective of the 1990s.

In 1994, another of the "generation of the moles," Santiago Feliú, sang about one of the most common strategies individuals used to survive in a divided and crisis-ridden Cuba:

> De escudo quiero el corazón desnudo,
> volverme sabio para divertirme,
> buscarte siempre y no perderte siempre
> sentir sintiendo para no entenderlo más

or, in other words:

> Bailemos juntos, solo hay una fiesta,
> somos estatuas olvidadas de mañana,
> dame un abrazo y no tengamos frío,

> Like a shield, I want to bare my heart,
> to act wise if only to amuse myself,
> to look for you always, not always lose you,
> to feel, and by feeling, not have to understand anymore
>
> Let's dance together, there is only one party,
> we are forgotten statues in the morning,
> embrace me so we won't be cold.[21]

Whether sardonic or melancholic, rebellious or seemingly abject, the songs analysed in this chapter serve as a comprehensive overview of the multiple readings that the Cuba of the 1990s deserves. These songs do not tell stories with clear endings. The 1990s were a time of demolition and reconstruction, although for those living through those years, the latter seemed a remote possibility.

Twenty years later, *Como los peces* remains one of Varela's most popular albums. Its songs express moods that were a product of the years when they were written, and they have contributed significantly to the effort of emotional restoration we Cubans started twenty years ago.

NOTES

1. Varela quotes and recontextualizes two lines of the song "Llover sobre mojado," included in Silvio Rodríguez's 1984 production *Tríptico*, vol. 2. While in Silvio's song the worker expresses his admiration for artists and reflects on their place in society, in Varela's song the meaning, although not completely subverted, has been given a subtle twist. The artist is still admired by the worker, and, perhaps this is why the worker needs the understanding (or the approval) of the creator, since "la vida está muy dura" (life is so hard) and he is forced to be corrupt.
2. *Webster's Random House Dictionary* gives as definitions of "chaos" (among others), "A state of utter confusion or disorder," and "The infinity of space or formless matter supposed to have preceded the creation of the Universe." In any case, in 1990s Cuba, some of the seemingly immutable myths of the social system we had been creating for almost four decades were changing or disappearing. In my view, in many sectors of Cuban society there was a generalized impression that we were on the brink of an abyss or chaos. We needed to either regenerate ourselves, as if by magic, or disappear.
3. Mareelén Díaz Tenorio, "La familia cubana ante la crisis de los 90,"

http://bibliotecavirtual.clacso.org.ar/ar/libros/cuba/cips/caudales05/
Caudales/ARTICULOS/ArticulosPDF/1118D019.pdf (accessed 25 March
2010).
4 Ernesto Chávez Negrín, "Población y crisis económica en Cuba: la familia
y la dinámica demográfica del Período Especial," paper presented at the
symposium "Población y pobreza en América Latina," Buenos Aires, 9–11
November 2000, http://bibliotecavirtual.clacso.org.ar/ar/libros/cuba/
cips/caudales05/Caudales/ARTICULOS/ArticulosPDF/1819C021.pdf
(accessed 25 March 2010). The author argues that the principal reasons for
the deterioration of the economy were as follows: the strengthening of the
US embargo, falling oil prices (Cuba was re-exporting fuel that had been
sold to it at preferential prices by the former Soviet Union), the reduction
in sugar production due to climatological events, diminished efficiency in
the internal economy, and the increased debt with the West due to the high
level of imports.
5 Negrín, "Población y crisis económica en Cuba."
6 Negrín, "Población y crisis económica en Cuba."
7 In 1992, the US Congress approved the Torricelli Act – more formally, the
Cuban Democracy Act. Among other things, this act prohibited subsidiaries of US companies in third countries from engaging in commerce with
Cuba and established that ships calling on Cuban ports for commercial
purposes could not enter the United States within 180 days following the
date they left Cuba. In 1996, the Helms-Burton Act – more formally, the
Cuban Freedom and Democratic Solidarity Act – was approved. This act
provided that any non-US company that had commercial dealings with
Cuba could be the object of legal sanctions and that its officials would be
barred from entering the United States. The same act set conditions on economic aid to Russia and the emerging Eurasian nations so that they would
contribute to "ending the Communist regime in Cuba." Both acts are still
in effect.
8 Omar Valiño, "Trazados en el agua. Para una geografía ideológica del
teatro cubano de los años noventa," *Temas* 15 (July–September 1998): 116.
9 Valiño, "Trazados en el agua."
10 "La música popular como espejo social," Sección Controversia, *Temas* 29
(April–June 2002): 61–80.
11 Borges-Triana, in "La música popular como espejo social," 18.
12 Zurbano, in "La música popular como espejo social," 63.
13 Consuelo Martín Fernández, Maricela Perera Pérez, and Maiky Díaz Pérez,
"La vida cotidiana en Cuba. Una mirada psicosocial," *Temas* 7 (July–
September 1996): 93.
14 Fernández et al., "La vida cotidiana en Cuba."

15 In his 1942 poem "La isla en peso," the Cuban writer and playwright Virgilio Piñera (1912–1979) wrote: "La maldita circunstancia del agua por todas partes/ me obliga a sentarme enlamesa del café./ Si no pensara que el agua me rodea como un cáncer/ hubiera podido dormir a pierna suelta" (This damned circumstance of water everywhere around / makes me sit at the coffee table / If I didn't think that the water surrounded me like a cancer/ I could have slept like a baby). Here we see the idea that Cuban identity is always associated with the condition of being an island – that is, isolated – and the degree to which this "damned circumstance" affects the development of our being. This recurring theme has been evident recently with the resurgence of interest in the life and works of Virgilio Piñera in Cuba.

16 It is fairly common for Cuban songs of this period to make intertextual references to popular music. Here, Carlos Varela's text is "talking to" the famous *Lágrimas negras* by the Cuban songwriter Miguel Matamoros (1894–1971).

17 A reference to Saint-Exupéry's *The Little Prince*, which for generations of Cubans has a significance that has not been supplanted by later interpretations.

18 The film was Padrón's thesis at the School of Audiovisual Media at ISA. According to the Cuban critic Juan Antonio García Borrero, this film "is a continuation of the dialogue initiated in *Memorias del subdesarrollo* (Memories of Underdevelopment) regarding exile, uprootedness, and other emotionally charged topics that are common to all contemporary Cubans." García Borrero, "La utopía confiscada. De la gravedad del sueño a la ligereza del realismo," *Temas* 27 (October–December 2001): 25–6.

19 The phrase from Silvio Rodriguez's song appears in the following context:

> Amo a una mujer clara
> que amo and me ama
> sin pedir nada
> – o casi nada,
> que no es lo mismo
> pero es igual
>
> I love an honest woman,
> that I love, and who loves me,
> who asks for nothing,
> or almost nothing,

>   which is not the same,
>   but is just like it.

20 Note that at that time, this singular declaration of love for the city was extra-officially censored in some of the Cuban broadcast media.
21 From "De escudo" on the CD *Náuseas de fin de siglo* (1994) by Santiago Feliú.

Chapter Four

Carlos Varela and the Carousel of Cuban History[1]

KAREN DUBINSKY

Musicians are underappreciated historians. One scholar who recognizes this, cultural critic George Lipsitz, describes popular music as a "vital repository for collective memory," because songwriters help create "alternative archives of history" out of the experiences, dreams, and memories of people who rarely appear in traditional archives.[2] Lipsitz comments that songwriters rarely think of themselves as historians and do not necessarily intend their work to reflect history or shape reality. So what are we to make of Carlos Varela, whose work reflects a self-conscious effort to narrate the history of his particular times and especially that of his generation? And what are we to make of Cuba, a country where music plays such a tremendous role as a form of alternative truth telling, social criticism, and community building, filling the void left by externally blockaded and internally circumscribed traditional media?

As many contributors to this book have emphasized, the emotional power that Varela holds among those who came of age in the 1980s and 1990s must not be underestimated. "Guillermo Tell" is, of course, his best-known and perhaps most stirring generational anthem – "our hymn of independence," as Cuban journalist Marta Maria Ramirez put it in 2004.[3] But many of his other works have also come to be identified as generational classics, for reasons skilfully laid out by the contributors to this book. "Once again Carlos Varela snatched new images from our memory," wrote one commentator, describing a 2007 Havana concert.[4] "There is no other songwriter in Cuba with the gift for drawing people in," declared Frank Padrón in 2006.[5]

As a social historian, I've learned many alternative research strategies: archival tricks of the trade developed by those who want to push past traditional historical subjects and themes. I need no convincing that "History" is not the exclusive preserve of great men whose great deeds are recorded in newspapers and government documents. But it wasn't until I arrived in Cuba in 2004, to research the history of Operation Peter Pan (a child migration scheme of the early 1960s intended to "save" children from Fidel Castro) that I thought about music as part of the historian's toolkit.[6] The case for Varela as historian was made, forcefully, by my new colleague Caridad Cumaná, who was helping me research immigration themes in Cuban film archives. "If you want to understand anything about the recent history of this country," my friend told me, "you have to start with the music of Carlos Varela." In this chapter I review a few of the most prominent historical themes in Varela's work; I also consider why this musician has come to occupy a place of both rebellion and loyalty in contemporary Cuba.

Unlike the Cuban contributors to this book, I don't hear the traumas and dreams of my youth narrated in Varela's music. But in "Jalisco Park" and "Memorias," to name the most prominent examples, I have found evocative and instructive examples of epic poetry (or, as Susan Thomas calls such songs here, urban *crónicas*). Each is a subtle but powerful history lesson that evokes Bruce Springsteen's wise reflection: "we learned more from a three minute record, baby, than we ever did in school." Operation Peter Pan forms the backdrop for "Jalisco Park," which uses images of empty playgrounds, spinning carousels, and Cold War espionage to launch the saga of Cuba in the 1960s: the death of Che, the dream of the ten million ton sugar harvest, the music of Silvio Rodríguez. "Memorias," beautifully analysed in this volume by Robert Nasatir, is an equally ambitious march through the popular culture of the same era, accompanied by the films of Tomás Alea, the music of The Beatles, and the cartoons of Elpidio Valdés. In the same song, Varela characteristically gives credit where credit is due (how the revolutionary government exchanged Bay of Pigs mercenaries for baby food and medical supplies) even while lamenting the Revolution's hypocrisy (those who forbade Beatles music officially while enjoying their albums at home).[7]

Varela's acute historical sensibility is evident even in his many songs that are not specifically devoted to historical topics. Consider this reference, from "El enigma del árbol" (The Enigma of the Tree), which describes Havana during the Special Period:

> No había nadie en la calle, la Habana estaba vacía,
> solo el guardia del barrio con su vieja linterna china.

> No one was in the street, Havana was empty
> Only the neighbourhood guard with his old Chinese lantern.

The ludicrous image of the neighbourhood guard protecting empty, deserted streets is underscored by the lantern. Chinese lanterns were used extensively by the thousands of volunteer teachers who worked in the countryside in 1961 during the literacy campaign in Cuba, teaching people how to read. The lantern was a prominent icon during the literacy campaign, a proud moment indeed in Cuban history. By the 1990s, however, such revolutionary iconography had long faded, and Varela employs it in this song as yet one more dated and no longer functional relic. Varela uses what historians call "material history" (the history of objects) in a similar way in "La política no cabe en la azucarera" (Politics Don't Fit in a Sugar Bowl), which begins with these lines:

> Un amigo se compró un Chevrolet del 59
> no le quiso cambiar algunas piezas y ahora no se mueve.
>
> A friend bought a 59 Chevrolet
> He didn't want to change any parts, and now it doesn't move.

Here, the non-functioning relic – one of Cuba's old American cars, for which the island is famous – stands as a metaphor for what happens when one doesn't change or update things (cars, Revolutions) that were built in 1959.

Varela's historical vantage point is the neighbourhood. As Susan Thomas describes in this book, Varela is the man sitting on the curb, leaning out the window, or gazing at the Malecón, to note a few of his often cited locations in Havana. This constant positioning of himself in the noisy streets of the city – even as he occasionally tries to find refuge or solitude – is the spatial manifestation of his social location. Varela is the historian of those who observe, experience, and feel, but never seem to *make*, dramatic historical change.

"Guillermo Tell" is perhaps the most obvious example of this story of powerlessness: in that song, the boy is forever destined to be target practice for the father. A constant theme of Varela's is the lives of people who live just below the grand narratives of history. The collapse of the Soviet Union and the economic cataclysm it unleashed on Cuba are recounted in the rapidly changing imagery and fast pace of "Ahora que los mapas cambian de color" (Now That the Maps Are Changing Colour), which features burning books, falling walls, empty markets, beheadings, and missing money. In the same vein, "Robinson" employs the image of Robinson Crusoe to symbolize Cuba's place in the post-Soviet world – "alone, on an island, like you and I." The impoverished isolation of Cuba's post-Soviet "Special Period" is also evoked in "Muro" (Wall), in which the protagonist repeatedly dips his bread in an empty plate.

"Jaque mate 1916" (Checkmate 1916) tells the story of the Cuban Revolution as a footnote to a game of chess in 1916 between Lenin and Tristan Tzara: "Sometimes I have a feeling that I was a game piece, and that chessboard was my city." That Cubans are bystanders to their own history, whose main protagonists are elsewhere, is a theme repeated in "Robinson" ("in this game of history, we are only playing dominos") and more recently in "Telón de fondo" (Backdrop) ("we discover only in the end that we're nothing more than a backdrop").

The powerlessness of the person sitting on the curb in the neighbourhood is heightened by the hypocrisy of those with power. "Baby I don't know what's going to happen, if the lie dresses up as the truth," he sings in "Colgando del cielo" (Hanging from the Sky) – a song he performed, incidentally, for a million people at the Concierto por la Paz in Revolution Square in 2009. Cuba's political leaders are sometimes a direct target, for example, in "El leñador sin bosque" (The Woodcutter without a Forest): "in the region of His Majesty, everyone repeats what the King says." More recently, in "Telón de fondo," he sings directly to the Revolution from the perspective of middle age: "I gave you my youth and my heart, and in exchange all you gave me was a world full of stages and silly clowns."

The duplicity of politicians is matched by the deceptions of the press and other official channels. In Varela's Havana, vendors sell newspapers that announce there will not be a cloud in the sky, and then promptly take cover because they know rain is coming ("Bulevar"). "There are robbers that hid inside your room, and they hide themselves in our books, in the newspapers and in the television," he declares in "Todos se roban" (Everyone Steals). The school system also creates powerlessness: "Religion starts on the walls of the schools," he sings in "Robinson," a fairly obvious allusion to the photographs of revolutionary heroes that grace every Cuban classroom (an image evoked, as noted in the Introduction, in the 2011 film *Habanastation*). "Once I wanted to share my opinion," he sings in the distinctly autobiographical "Soy un gnomo" (I'm a Gnome), "but here they told me that all there is to say has already been said." In another early, outspoken song, "Como me hicieron a mí" (As They Did to Me), he sings:

> Dirán que todo es tuyo
> y si intentas cambiarlo
> te patearán más duro
> como me hicieron a mí.
>
> They will tell you everything is yours
> And if you intend to change it
> They will abuse you more
> As they did to me.

At times, Varela's lyrics leap over the considerable barriers of official discourse with one simple phrase: "tu y yo." He always credits his listeners with shared or common knowledge, implying that what "you and I" know is something different from what is being said. In "Bendita lluvia" (Blessed Rain), he ponders the uncertainties of Cuba's future, but in a way that creates a community around uncertainty. "You and I," he sings, "we know that tomorrow there will be no cardinal points." Similarly, in "Nadie" (Nobody), he repeats:

> Ni el Sol, ni el aire
> saben lo que sabe el viento.
> Ni Dios, ni nadie
> saben lo que tú y yo.
>
> Not the Sun, not the air
> Knows what the wind knows.
> Not God, not anyone
> Knows what you and I know.

"El humo del tren" (The Smoke of the Train) also suggests the importance of common knowledge: "Havana isn't Jerusalem. But almost everyone knows who is who."

Like many contemporary Cuban singers, Varela sets the traumas of immigration to music. Immigration is a uniquely complicated issue in

Cuba. Both there and in the United States, government policies maintain immigration as part of the arsenal of Cold War cat-and-mouse politics; at the same time, Cubans feel the same migration pressure – economic need – as people in all Third World nations. This is a daunting mix, the effect of which has been to make migration experiences widespread, emotionally exhausting, and sometimes dangerous.[8]

Everyone is affected by immigration, and everyone sings about it. Varela's contemporary, Frank Delgado, in his signature song "La otra orilla" (The Other Shore; 1997), approaches the topic sardonically while pointing to music's power to create, sustain, and reconcile immigration conflicts. Delgado insists it is possible to "dance with Celia Cruz" (the famous Cuban American exile) while "listening to Silvio and Pablo." Younger singers, such as Adrián Berazaín in "Mis amigos se estan yendo" (My Friends Are Leaving; 2011), sing of the sad realities facing young Cubans preparing for their voyage: "Each time, my country gets older." Varela adopts a tone of melancholy. His anger over political hypocrisy, evident in his music and lyrics alike, contrasts with the sadness of his songs about immigration.

The human face of migration is expressed in Varela's best-known immigration song, "Foto de la familia" (Family Photo). Both the film it inspired (*Video de la familia*) and the song itself take us "behind" (a word used repeatedly in the song) the abstractions of institutions and ideologies (such as governments, borders, and religions) to portray one family coping with the grief of immigration. The observer's voice, which Varela adopts when discussing powerlessness, isolation, and political hypocrisy, works equally well as he describes the incalculable losses of immigration. In "Detrás del cristal" (Behind the Glass), he concludes: "Those who leave cry just like those who stay, those who leave grieve, those who stay, more." In "Estas" (You Are), he walks through the streets of Havana, glimpsing an absent friend in the puddles, shop windows, unpainted park benches, and even empty gas stations (a Special Period image if ever there was one). "Each time I blame you, I forgive you," he concludes, voicing the grief of those who stay. Migration affects everyone, but for the children of William Tell, it has particular force. "I lost a friend in the war in Africa," he sings in "Circulo de tiza" (Chalk Circle), "and another, while escaping, was swallowed by the sea." As he declares in "La Comedia silente" (Silent Comedy), "I'm left almost without a generation."

As Xenia Reloba notes in her chapter, it is not surprising that so many Cuban artists use the imagery of the ocean. Those who leave Cuba by sea – often at great danger – hold a special place for Varela's generation and in Varela's music. It is difficult to imagine a sadder or more powerful evocation of Cuba's *balseros* than the opening lines of "Desde ningún lugar" (From Nowhere), from *Nubes* (2000):

> Cuando el cielo de la noche huele a sal
> cuando los cuervos salen solos a mirar
> Cuando la luz del faro barre la ciudad
> y en las ventanas ya queda nadie más.
> Rezando a Dios, se lanzaban al mar.
> Dejándonos, hacia ningún lugar.
>
> When the night sky smells of salt,
> When the ravens come out just to look,
> When the light from the lighthouse sweeps the city,
> And there's no one left looking through the windows.
> Praying to God, they set out to sea,
> Leaving us, for nowhere.

Like a good historian, Varela embraces complexity rather than prescription. In "La política no cabe en la azucarera," questioning the panacea of immigration, he sings, "Felipito left for the U.S., there it's cold, here it was boring," The same song includes the much sung-along-with line, "listen to me brother, [*in English*] fuck your blockade." For Varela, immigration represents people looking for "a place to breathe" (in "Lucas y Lucia"), or for "a little hope" that doesn't always work out: "In spite of everything, he didn't find the Virgin" (in "No es el fin"). For all his efforts to address Cuba's contradictions and tragedies, he is well aware that change is not straightforward and that neither are solutions. In "Échate a correr" (Start to Run), he offers a warning:

> Nena no sé cómo será el destino
> si ya no queda nada que perder
> pero si ves que está creciendo el río
> será mejor que te eches a correr
>
> Baby I don't know what destiny will be
> If already we have nothing to lose
> But if you see the river is rising
> You better start to run

Varela's clearest commentary on the ambiguities and complexities of change is in his recently recorded "Todo será distinto" (Everything Will Be Different). Addressing himself to someone who "prefers to look at the North" instead of "at the songs of Silvio," he offers this double-edged view of Cuba's future:

> Quizás mañana salga el Sol
> y todo será distinto,
> lo triste será que entonces
> ya no seremos lo mismo.
>
> Maybe tomorrow the sun will come out
> And everything will be different
> The sadness will be that then
> We won't be the same.

Varela keeps his eyes, and ears, trained to the lived experiences of people rather than to ideological abstractions, while recognizing that concepts such as "change" can be uncertain. In "El viejo sueño acabó" (The Old Dream Is Over), he asks, "who cares anymore, who won or who lost, if in the end the dream is over." Perhaps the best one can do is preserve the integrity of the intimate sphere and the precious space for human relations. He explained this philosophy decades ago in "La política no cabe en la azucarera," which, as Xenia Reloba explores in this book, uses the symbol of the family dinner table with two empty chairs to highlight the consequences of political conflict for Cuban families. As if to underscore his point, he dedicated that song to two Cuban singers who are famously on opposite sides of the political spectrum: Silvio Rodríguez and Celia Cruz. For Varela, abstract concepts of politics and ideology mean nothing compared to the realities of people and personal relationships.

Finally, like any good historian, Carlos Varela not only does his research but also credits his sources. He is well known for citing passages from his mentor Silvio Rodríguez in his own songs – for example, in "Jalisco Park" and "La política no cabe en la azucarera." "I knew Silvio's songs better than he did," he jokes in the interview he has provided for this book. Varela has cited others musically as well. "Ahora que los mapas están cambiando de color," a commentary on post-Soviet Cuba, begins with the voice of Vladimir Lenin delivering a rousing speech. "Bola de nieve" (Snowball), a tribute to the celebrated

Cuban musician Ignacio Jacinto Villa, who died in 1971, ends with his voice in performance. Similarly, "La comedia silente" (Silent Comedy), which compares the voicelessness of Varela's generation with the era of silent movies, incorporates the actual voice of Cuban comedian Armando Calderón, who for several decades provided the Spanish-language voice-overs for televised silent films such as those of Laurel and Hardy and Charlie Chaplin.

"History is a songbook for anyone who would listen to it," writes Canadian composer and sound researcher R. Murray Schaffer.[9] In this brief excursion through a few significant historical themes, we have seen that Varela has been listening to, and singing, Cuban history for many years. His lyrics exemplify well Lipsitz's suggestion that our historical understanding is enriched when we consider histories that have "never been written but instead sung, played, danced and shouted."[10] That said, there are other features of Varela's historical sensibility that accompany his lyrics and indeed go beyond them. As Simon Frith, another insightful music scholar, reminds us, popular songs are not primarily "general statements of sociological or psychological truth." Rather, they are more likely to be examples of "personal rhetoric" that derive their meaning in part from the "persuasive relationship set up between singer and listener." And in Cuba, that relationship is unique, as many would point out who have studied the peculiar conditions of creating music in contemporary Cuba.[11]

Here I want to explore how Varela has emerged as a trusted figure in contemporary Cuban culture. As Joaquín Borges-Triana observes here, Varela is loyal. In a 1994 interview he was asked why he wrote so few "romantic" songs. His answer was revealing: "Love is present in my work, but in another way. I love my neighbourhood, my friends and my country."[12] In Cuba, such a statement from a socially aware and active rock star means something different than it would in North America or Europe.[13] The strong connection between artist and audience is what makes Cuba – for all its huge political and economic problems – such a cauldron for creativity. Cuban musicians have their share of advantages (among them, the right to travel and the chance to earn foreign currency), but they do not drive around in limousines. The distance between the lives of successful Cuban musicians and those of other Cubans is not nearly as wide as in other parts of the world. What has Cuba's direct censorship meant for its artists' creativity? In his interview for this book, Varela commented on the Janus-faced nature of censorship: "It is certainly an advantage to live in a country where your music means something to people. From the very beginning, I would put out a disc, it would get very little airplay, but thousands of people would come to my concerts and sing along with every word."

When my Canadian university students learn about Varela, they immediately equate him with Bono, perhaps the most widely recognized "political" musician of their generation. Varela, like Bono, helps create community through music, but he – along with many other Cuban musicians – provides an intriguing counterpoint to the European and North American style of celebrity activism. Musicians like Bono use their celebrity to create armies of donors and shoppers; something very different is going on in Cuba.[14]

The intimacy of Varela's lyrics is more than matched by his ability to generate emotion in concert. As Caridad Cumaná explains in this volume, Varela's early training as an actor made him acutely aware of the theatrical qualities of musical performance and of the various ways, beyond the text alone, that musicians can evoke an emotional response. As early as 1995 he told a Spanish journalist that his concerts were an "authentic catharsis" for his legions of young listeners. Years later, even journalists in skeptical Miami concurred: "I don't know when I've ever seen a crowd so live and involved," wrote Jordan Levin in the *Miami Herald* after one of Varela's 2010 concerts. "Anyone might have been moved by the way that an artist's music can speak so powerfully to and for people's deepest longings."[15]

The catharsis Varela allows his listeners, this connection between singer and audience, generated through both music and performance, has made him a highly revered figure in Cuba. There are many examples of this in the island's everyday life and culture. "In those turbulent years, Carlos Varela dared to say what we all knew, but weren't accustomed to hearing," remembered journalist Irina Echarry in 2009, speaking of the deprivations of the Special Period.[16] Writing about crime in Havana, blogger Yoani Sanchez evoked Varela to describe an attack on some of her friends: "The whole story reminded me of a song from Carlos Varela that says ... 'the city is not the same anymore.'"[17] Recently, attempting to describe the mood of a popular alternative café in Vedado, one writer termed it a place for "cups of espresso and Carlos Varela music"; both helped establish its bohemian atmosphere.[18] And as Cumaná notes, when Varela's music is heard in Cuban films, it is typically to mark a moment of rebellion. Varela and his continued popularity can also be invoked to illustrate just how far Cuba has come since the 1970s, the "grey years" of extreme cultural repression.

Writing about the controversial history of Beatles music in Cuba, journalist Ernesto Juan Castellanos cites the appearance of fans at a typical Varela concert – long-haired, pierced, tattooed – when marvelling at how much has changed in a short time.[19]

Varela the iconoclast circulates through Cuban culture, always the rebel speaking truth to power. This isn't always a compliment. One Cuban father wrote of his anger towards Varela, one of his children's favourite performers: "I blamed Varela for having composed and written works like Guillermo Tell and others that inspired my children, and served as trampolines" – that encouraged them, in other words, to immigrate, which indeed his children did. But on revisiting Varela's work many years later, after attending a concert, this father realized that his children made their own choices about immigrating. He now counts himself as one of Varela's many admirers, and thanks him for singing about "things that get stuck in our throats."[20] Varela's fan mail overflows with similar sentiments. Letters from the global Cuban diaspora (from Miami to Spain, from Singapore to Florence) recount the personal significance of his music. "I left Cuba nineteen years ago," wrote a Miami-based listener in 2009, "and I have never been closer than when I hear 'Foto de la familia.'"[21] The sentimental hold Varela maintains on his generation is perhaps why CubaLlama, a telecom company popular with Cubans in the diaspora, used an image of an early Varela cassette in an ad campaign in 2013. To sell telephone and texting services, the ad encouraged Cubans of Varela's generation to remember the parties of their youth (which they termed "the Facebook of yesterday"), when they spent their weekends meeting new people and listening to music.[22]

Cuban journalist Mario Vizcaíno Serrat observed in 1994 that "Varela is the model for his songs," pointing to what would be Varela's dual role for years to come: pundit *and* protagonist.[23] Varela has often said that he sees his role as "destroying the myths on both sides" – of the Cuban–US divide most particularly. In 1998, when he played his first Florida concert, it was in a private house in Miami so as to avoid the widespread protests that greeted Cuban performers of that era. He was direct on and off stage, vowing he would not let his Miami concert be used "to sanctify one kind of Cuba or another." When someone in the crowd shouted, "Sing without fear!", he responded, "I sing without fear in Cuba, why should I sing with fear here?" Several years later, during the Bush era, when the US government denied him a visa to return for a series of planned concerts, he responded with a statement reflecting his philosophy of music: "My songs don't need a passport."[24] Most recently, he has lent his support to efforts to lift various US-imposed travel and economic embargos, and he has participated directly in lobbying US policy makers through visits to Capitol Hill in Washington.

So when the journalist Bertrand de la Grange asked, after Varela's 2009 and 2010 appearances in the United States, "Can one be an artist in Cuba and publically criticize the government of the Castro brothers?", anyone acquainted with Varela's music and history would have agreed that the question missed the point,[25] for it overlooked the many ways in which musical critique *is* political critique, which can generate a momentum the consequences of which are almost impossible to predict. As others have described with regard to Mexico, Hungary, China, South Africa, and the German Democratic Republic – to take only a few relevant examples – popular music, particularly when it is layered with meaning and exists "half openly," can become a space in which social crises are dramatized, political alternatives are imagined, and new forms of political citizenship are created.[26] For all the problems with censorship, the Cuban music world illustrates well political scientist Carollee Bengelsdorf's comments on state–civil society imbalances in Cuba: "Silence is not the pervading theme in contemporary Cuba; Cubans have never been silent."[27]

This was certainly true in the venerable Chaplin Theatre in Havana on 29 April 1989, when Varela performed, for the first time, "El hijo de Guillermo Tell." That moment has acquired a symbolic meaning for Varela's generation in much the same way that other landmark moments of the Cuban Revolution resonate through the consciousness of an earlier generation: it was a cherished test of defiance and a statement of common purpose. Almost everyone now of a certain age remembers they were there. The year 1989 saw a number of landmark events around the socialist world. *Glasnost* and *perestroika* were in the air in the Soviet Union; in March, the first multi-candidate elections were held there, a victory for Gorbachev's reform campaign. On 15 April in China, protesters began filling Tiananmen Square. A few months ahead lay the September protests in Germany (in which, music historians argue, rock musicians played an important albeit unaccredited role) that led to the fall of the Berlin Wall in November.[28]

That spring in Havana, the artistic world was pushing to see how far *perestroika* would go in Cuba. It is not coincidental that "Guillermo Tell" premiered the same month that Cuban artists organized a rotating exhibition, the *Proyecto del Castillo de la Fuerza*, which included works by well-known artists René Francisco and Eduard Ponjuan that played with the image of Fidel Castro. In one work, Castro was depicted speaking to a crowd from a podium; the faces of the crowd were exact replicas of his own. According to one commentator, the exhibition was "so obvious one was left wondering if the artists were not actually inviting censorship." It was, in fact, quickly shut down by the government. A year later, a group exhibition containing some of the works toured Europe. That exhibition was titled "Fourteen Sons of William Tell."[29]

So the force of Varela's "Guillermo Tell" is important to this day, but so is the force of moment in which it was born. Recently, Havana-based journalist Irina Echarry wrote a bittersweet epitaph for that historical moment:

> The joy was contagious as the cassettes passed from hand to hand. Twenty-two years have passed since that concert, but when I hear the whistles, the screams and the audience's euphoric ovations on the recording, I can't contain the questions: What happened? Where did all the energy go? What happened to the longings for freedom, the rebelliousness, the irreverence? Those of us who screamed and shouted that day at the Chaplin Cinema or at any one of his concerts of the '90s are today dispersed around the world, each in their individual vortex. Those who left as well as those of us still on the island continue to see that nothing has changed in our country. We continue to hold up the fruit threatened by the arrow of William Tell, who doesn't let anything change. And us? We quietly obey.[30]

The thousands of sons and daughters of William Tell who were at the Chaplin Theatre that day might echo the sadness and frustration of Echarry's conclusion. So too might Varela himself, who, in his interview for this book, speculates that more than 90 per cent of the people who attended his early concerts have left Cuba. All of this illustrates the powerful connections between the song, the songwriter, and the audience – connections that generate powerful insights about Cuban history.

NOTES

1 Thanks to Susan Belyea, Scott Rutherford, Stephanie Jowett, and the Toronto Latin American Research Group (especially Anne Rubenstein and Alan Durston) for their helpful comments on this paper.

2 George Lipsitz, *Footsteps in the Dark: The Hidden Histories of Popular Music* (Minneapolis: University of Minnesota Press, 2007), pp. vii, xi.
3 Marta Maria Ramirez, "Carlos Varela: Un hijo de Guillermo Tell," *La Ventana*, 9 November 2004, http://laventana.casa.cult.cu/modules.php?name=New&file=article&sid=2215 (accessed 8 September 2009).
4 Michel Hernández, "Carlos Varela: The Return of the Woodcutter," *Cuba Now.Net*, 16 January 2007, http://www.cubanow.net/articles/carlos-varela-return-woodcutter (accessed 23 August 2010).
5 Frank Padrón, "El cronista del asfalto," *Encuentro en la Red*, 20 March 2006, reprinted in *Los Que Soñamos* 16 (March 2006).
6 Karen Dubinsky, *Babies without Borders: Adoption and Migration across the Americas* (New York: NYU Press and Toronto: University of Toronto Press, 2010).
7 On the controversies of The Beatles in Cuba, see Deborah Pacini Hernandez and Reebee Garofalo, "Between Rock and a Hard Place: Negotiating Rock in Revolutionary Cuba, 1960–1980," in *Rockin' Las Américas: The Global Politics of Rock in Latin/o America*, ed. Deborah Pacini Hernandez, Héctor Fernández L'Hoeste, and Eric Zolov (Pittsburgh: University of Pittsburgh Press, 2004), pp. 43–67; and John M. Kirk and Leonardo Padura Fuentes, *Culture and the Cuban Revolution: Conversations in Havana* (Gainsville: University Press of Florida, 2001), pp. 1–16.
8 Among the many studies of the politics of Cuban immigration, see, for example, Felix Maasud-Piloto, *From Welcomed Exiles to Illegal Immigrants* (New York: Rowman and Littlefield, 1995); and Maria Christina Garcia, *Havana USA: Cuban Exiles and Cuban-Americans in South Florida, 1959–1994* (Berkeley: University of California Press), 1996.
9 Murray Shafer, "Open Ears," in *The Auditory Culture Reader*, ed. Michael Bull and Les Back (Oxford: Berg, 2003), p. 30, as cited in Stephanie Jowett, "Quebec's Not So Quiet Revolution," PhD diss. in progress, Queen's University, Kingston.
10 Lipsitz, *Footsteps*, 264.
11 Simon Frith, *Performing Rites: On the Value of Popular Music* (Cambridge, MA: Harvard University Press, 1996), pp. 163, 166. A few good examples of contemporary Cuban musical studies are Joaquín Borges-Triana, *La luz, bróder, la luz, Canción Cubana Contemporánea* (La Habana: Ediciones La Memoria, 2009), Robin D. Moore, *Music and Revolution: Cultural Change in Socialist Cuba* (Berkeley: University of California Press, 2006); Sujatha Fernandes, *Cuba Represent! Cuban Arts, State Power, and the Making of New Revolutionary Cultures* (Durham, NC: Duke University Press, 2007); Geoffrey Baker, *Buena Vista in the Club: Rap, Reggaetón, and Revolution in Havana*

(Durham, NC: Duke University Press, 2011); and Vincenzo Perna, *Timba: The Sound of the Cuban Crisis* (Aldershot: Ashgate, 2005).
12 Mario Vizcaíno Serrat, "Carlos Varela: el gnomo y el guerrero," *La Gaceta de Cuba* 1 (1994): 20.
13 Reebee Garofalo, ed., *Rockin' the Boat: Mass Music and Mass Movements* (Boston: South End Press, 1992).
14 Lisa Ann Richey and Stefano Ponte, *Brand Aid: Shopping Well to Save the World* (Minneapolis: University of Minnesota Press, 2011), pp. 12, 51–2.
15 Cristina Gil, "La música puede cambiar ideas," *El Periódico*, 24 October 1995; Jordan Levin, "Carlos Varel's Music Speaks to the Audience," *Miami Herald*, 17 May 2010.
16 Irina Echarry, "Three Kings Day in Cuba," *Havana Times*, 5 January 2009, http://www.havanatimes.org/?p=3533 (accessed 2 May 2010).
17 Yoani Sanchez, "Red Chronicles or "the city is not the same anymore ...," *Generacion Y*, 7 January 2008, http://lageneraciony.com (accessed 12 January 2009).
18 Leopoldo Luis, "Café G, Sueño y pesadilla del arte," *El Caimán Barbudo*, May–June 2010, http://www.caimanbarbudo.cu/articulos/2010/06/sueno-y-pesadilla-del-arte (accessed 19 November 2010).
19 Ernesto Juan Castellanos, *John Lennon en la Habana – With a little help from my friends* (La Habana: Editiones Unión, 2005), p. 21.
20 "Tengo fe en que pueda establecerse un puente entre Cuba y EEUU," *Cubadebate*, 4 December 2009, commentario, http://www.cubadebate.cu/noticias/2009/12/04 (accessed 12 February 2010).
21 Carlos Varela, personal correspondence files.
22 Cuballama, Facebook.com, 23 August 2013, https://www.facebook.com/CubaLlama?fref=ts (accessed 27 August 2013). For more on the commodification of the Cuban diaspora, see Catherine Krull and Jean Stubbs, "Commodification, Cityscapes, and Cultural Negotiations of Belonging in Post-1989 Cuban Diasporas," in *The Cuban Diaspora: Post-Soviet Migrations and Exiles*, ed. Nadine Fernández and Ariana Hernández-Reguant (Gainesville: University of Florida Press, forthcoming).
23 Vizcaíno Serrat, "Carlos Varela," 20.
24 Jordan Levin, "Cuban's Songs Bring Message," *Miami Herald*, 6 March 1998, p. 1A; Fidel Díaz, "A Famous Cuban Singer Is Sure of That," *Juventud Cubana* 29 September 2004.
25 Bertrand de la Grange, "Los hijos de Guillermo Tell," *Diario de Cuba*, 26 May 2010.
26 See, for example, Eric Zolov, *Refried Elvis: The Rise of the Mexican Counterculture* (Berkeley: University of California Press, 1999). See also the

following, all in Garofalo, *Rockin' the Boat*; Peter Wicke, "The Times They are A-Changin': Rock Music and Political Change in East Germany"; Anna Szemere, "The Politics of Marginality: A Rock Musical Subculture in Socialist Hungary in the Early 1980s"; Tim Brace and Paul Friedlander, "Rock and Roll on the New Long March: Popular Music, Cultural Identity, and Political Opposition in the People's Republic of China"; and Denis-Constant Martin, "Music Beyond Apartheid?" The phrase "half open" comes from 1980s China and refers to the informal, hand-to-hand circulation of cassettes of foreign popular music, which had been neither explicitly banned nor embraced by authorities.
27 Carollee Bengelsdorf, *The Problem of Democracy in Cuba: Between Vision and Reality* (New York: Oxford University Press, 1994), p. 179.
28 Peter Wicke, "The Times They Are A'Changing."
29 Luis Camnitzer, *New Art of Cuba* (Austin: University of Texas Press, 2003), p. 258. See also Antonio Eligio Fernández, "Ending the Century with Memories ...: Paper Money, Videos, and an *X-Acto* Knife for Cuban Art," in *Cuba in the Special Period: Culture and Ideology in the 1990s*, ed. Ariana Hernandez-Reguant, (New York: Palgrave Macmillan, 2009), 179–96; and Rachel Weiss (ed.), *To and From Utopia in the New Cuban Art* (Minneapolis: University of Minnesota Press, 2011).
30 Irina Echarry, "Cuba's Children of William Tell," *Havana Times.org*, 24 April 2011, https://www.havanatimes.org (accessed 28 April 2011).

Chapter Five

A Singer Who Uses the Guitar as a Camera: The Cinematic Quality of Carlos Varela's Songs

MARÍA CARIDAD CUMANÁ

In his study of contemporary Cuban music, musicologist Vincenzo Perna has noted that historically, songs "included the names of places in Havana, references to urban spaces which avoided realistic descriptions and articulated a mythological cartography of the city."[1] I begin with this quote to suggest that the "mythological cartography" of Carlos Varela's Havana is one of melancholy, love, and desire. And it is also extremely visual.

Carlos Varela's connection with the city is a declaration of love between a poet and the desire that never abandons him. For Varela, the city is a stage, a place where people are like ghosts, travelling to the rhythm of his songs. The theatre is, without a doubt, his favourite medium. It was in the theatre that Varela became a professional, an artist, a musician by calling, and the *trovador* of an entire generation. Through theatre he learned about performance, set design, and stage production, all of which have informed his musical productions throughout his career. An early commentary published in Cuba in 1989 by Iván de la Nuez Carrillo put it this way: at a Carlos Varela concert, "we are not in the presence of a musician but a concept ... whose compositions are closer to Andy Warhol than Paul McCartney."[2]

In 1990, as part of his graduation requirements for the Instituto Superior de Arte (ISA), Varela wrote a thesis titled "Theatricality in Song" in which he outlined the aesthetic precepts of all his subsequent work. From the beginning, he ascribed the greatest importance to the song's text. In his thesis he affirmed that "the *show* idea does not fit the way my songs are constructed; the musical ideas serve the text."[3] In the theatre, Varela learned how to be the actor that "all musicians should be on stage," complete with distinctive clothes, lighting, personality, and character (which he described as "gnome-like-Chaplinisque"). Just as an actor can create subtext and ambiguities when performing in film or theatre, musicians can "sing a text with a distinct sound" in such a way as to "generate codes and signs that multiply the possible readings of a song."[4] The various ways in which his songs have inspired those of us who are contributing to this book are enduring examples of the complex quality of his work.

As a film scholar, I am constantly drawn to Varela's work by its visuality and by its close relationship to Cuban cinema. At the beginning of Varela's career, Nuez Carrillo compared the "visual sharpness" of his compositions to images from music videos.[5] I would extend this metaphor to argue that Varela's songs can be heard as miniature film scripts. In this chapter, I explore some of the cinematic links Varela has established over his career. Those links go both ways: cinematic references appear in many of Varela's songs, and at the same time, Varela's work has enriched a number of important Cuban films. For example, the song "Bola de nieve" (Snowball; 1989) seems to have drawn inspiration from Mayra Vilasís's 1988 documentary *Yo soy la canción que canto* (I Am the Song I Sing). Both this film and the song are dedicated to Ignacio Villa (nicknamed Bola de Nieve), an important figure in the history of Cuban song. Varela's lyrics echo the beginning of Vilasís's documentary: he establishes the scene with the dimmed lights of the Monseñor bar where Bola de Nieve played, and his guitar/camera zooms in on a man sitting at a piano, a glass of rum in hand. He ends with a similarly powerful image of what happens when the bar closes: a voice emerges from the walls, and the piano keys mysteriously seem to play themselves.

The cinema is everywhere in Varela's songs. When he sings, his words sometimes recount actions that are occurring simultaneously, as if to reflect parallel editing or flashbacks. His lyrics are in current time but return us suddenly to the past. "Bulevar" (Boulevard) provides a good example:

> En el bulevar los curiosos
> pegan su nariz en las vidrieras,
> y el viejo que vende la prensa
> se fue porque sabe que va a lloviznar.
> pegan su nariz en las vidrieras,
> y el viejo que vende la prensa
> anuncia que el cielo no se va nublar

> On the boulevard the curious
> Stick their noses to the glass
> And the old man who sells the papers
> Left because he knows that it's going to drizzle
> They stick their noses to the glass
> And the old man who sells papers
> Announces that it's not going to be cloudy

Two actions occur simultaneously in this verse: curious people stick their noses to the windows of the shops (action 1); at the same time, the old man who sells newspapers has left because he knows it will rain (action 2). "Memorias" (1989), a tribute to filmmaker Tomás Gutiérrez Alea, provides other examples of Varela's use of flashbacks: children discover their parents listening to forbidden Beatles records at the same time as mercenaries are being exchanged for baby food at the Bay of Pigs; meanwhile, everyone goes to parties wearing their sugar cane harvesting boots, singing along to Lennon songs.

Varela fills his songs with famous characters: from literature (William Tell, Robinson Crusoe, Snow White, Romeo and Juliet, Don Quixote), art (Tristan Tzara), pop music (The Doors, Jim Morrison, Bob Dylan, The Beatles, Cher, Madonna, Matamoros, Silvio Rodríguez), politics (Saddam Hussein, Vladimir I. Lenin), science (Galileo), animation (Elpidio Valdés, Kermit the Frog, Peter Pan), and even sports (the mascot Misha the Bear). Varela uses them the way a film director uses actors in a film: they are the protagonists through whom the story evolves.

Varela's ties to cinema are also evident in the fact that his music has been used in a number of Cuban films. *Mujer transparente* (Transparent Woman), for example, Mario Crespo's 1991 film, describes an encounter between Zoe, an unconventional and obviously rebellious art student, and the strict, unbending student leader who has been assigned to watch her because she has been missing classes. One day he pays a surprise visit to her house to check up on her. While surveying her apartment, he turns on her record player and hears a fragment of Varela's music. He shudders and quickly turns it off. This alarmed reaction, which itself is a comment on Varela's place in Cuban culture, is more understandable when we analyse the content of the song that is cued on Zoe's record player. The music we hear briefly in *Mujer transparente* is from one of Varela's first recordings. "Jaque mate 1916" (Check Mate 1916) is a song is about the friendship between Vladimir I. Lenin and Tristan Tzara, the founder of the Dadaist movement. With characteristic brevity, even terseness, Varela connects these characters to his contemporary reality: he likens himself to a chess piece in a game that Tzara and Lenin once played. Varela refers to "Jaque mate" specifically in his ISA graduating thesis. It is, for him, an example of how the monotonous voice of a distant narrator – the voice he adopts in this song – can sometimes be an effective means of conveying complex emotions. "When an emotion is contained by the performer," he writes, "the spectator can finish it."[6]

Varela's music is heard in many other films. In 1989, he wrote the music for Víctor Casaus's *Bajo presión* (Under Pressure), a film about a worker who suffers an accident and has to leave his job. Several contributors to this book have emphasized the importance of Varela's captivating elegy on immigration, "Foto de familia," which provides a strong and moving closing for Humberto Padrón's *Video de familia*. In 1999, Cuban filmmaker Pastor Vega asked Varela for a song for his film *Las profecías de Amanda* (Amanda's Prophecies), the story of a Cuban fortune-teller. Although the film did not get good reviews, the song "25 mil mientras sobre la verdad" (25 Thousand Lies about the Truth) became an instant hit for the way in which it presented the issue of the truth and its various shades. More recently, in 2010, young Cuban filmmaker Lester Hamlet used Varela's work as the ending for his film *Casa vieja* (Old House). The song "De vuelta a casa" (Coming Home) is a strong finale for film about a returning Cuban who hasn't seen his family in many years. As Dubinsky also points out in this volume, immigration and its impact on the Cuban people is a prominent theme in Varela's music. That theme becomes even stronger in "De vuelta a casa" as Varela steps out of his customary role as chronicler and focuses on himself. In an elegant illustration of his constant emphasis on the intimate (love) over the abstract (the nation), he declares that "my country is hiding in your heart."

These are a few examples of how Varela's work has been taken up by filmmakers, and no doubt this will continue. There could have been one more such example. After Tomas Gutiérrez Alea heard "Habáname," Varela's classic love song to Havana, he declared that if he had known the song when he was shooting *Fresa y chocolate* (Strawberry and Chocolate), he would have used it in the scene in which Diego shows his Havana to his new friend David.[7]

The cinematic quality of Varela's music is also evident in the structure of his songs. When we approach his recorded works as movements of the camera – as angles, takes, formats, styles of cinematic narration, and so on – we can see much more clearly how the cinema has influenced his work.

Long Shot

Varela's first album, *Jalisco Park* (1989), provides a general shot of Havana, his most precious referent, in three emblematic songs, "Tropicollage," "Guillermo Tell," and "Jalisco Park." The first song refers to a Cuban phenomenon: foreign tourists are allowed to enjoy everything on the island, while Cubans, unfairly, are not. This was especially true during the 1980s, when "Tropicollage" was written and when Cubans (of whatever class) were forbidden to stay in hotels. "Tropicollage" also comments on the often false ideas about Cuba that tourists take with them when they return home: they remember palm trees, cigars, hotels, and cabarets, all of these forming a "tropicollage" for tourist consumption. "Guillermo Tell," for its part, describes the confrontation between young Cubans and the state, whose ideologues prevent them from proving their courage with their own crossbows. This song, as many have noted, encapsulates the highly controversial political, artistic, and social scene of the 1980s. "Jalisco Park" could be viewed as this first album's documentary film, in that Varela is reviewing important moments in recent Cuban history. He ends with a declaration of principles: "I know that with songs I want to make a Revolution."

Medium Shot

In his second album, *En vivo* (Live; 1991), Varela's guitar/camera begins with the shot/song "Todos se roban" (Everybody Steals), about the challenges of daily life in a society in which the prevailing survival principle is theft in all its diverse forms. For many people, crime almost dictates how they live their lives, and this destroys their spirit and their values. As Varela puts it, there is so much theft in Cuba, they even steal "your desire for love." "Cuchilla en la acera" (Knife on the Sidewalk) continues the same theme, detailing a violent robbery on the streets of Havana, passers-by who "turn their heads and keep their mouths shut," and a useless police force. In just one line, Varela summarizes the situation of Havana in the 1990s: social conformity, the lack of an efficient policing, and rising crime and violence. All of these things are present in this verse: "And despite the blood, the cries and God, the police will never arrive." In a perfect intermediate take, we can picture the sprawled, motionless body of the person who has been attacked and left on the sidewalk.

Shot and Reverse Shot

In 1992, Cuba was in the depths of one of the most severe economic crises in its history, which grew more and more acute until it culminated in the so-called Rafters' Crisis of 1994. Varela's *Monedas al aire* (Coins in the Air) was released in 1992. Its songs evoke the cinematic resource used in fiction: the shot and reverse shot, in which two characters or objects appear in the same take, one facing the other, one facing the camera and the other back to the camera. The songs on this album establish a dialogue between general topics, for example, between world politics and specific accounts of Cuban daily realities.

"Enigma del árbol" (Enigma of the Tree) describes well the mood of post-Soviet Havana: "there was no one in the streets, Havana was deserted." A similar mood is evoked in "Robinson," which uses the tale of *Robinson Crusoe* to explain how it felt to live alone on a "solitary little piece of land." The solitude and isolation of Havana described in "Enigma de árbol" and "Robinson" contrasts with the tremendous activity going on simultaneously in the rest of world, as depicted in "Ahora que los mapas cambian de color" (Now That the Maps Are Changing Colour):

> Están quemando los libros, están cortando cabezas,
> están poniendo en peligro las cartas sobre la mesa.
> Está lloviendo en la tierra, están vaciando mercados,
> están jugando a la guerra y están borrando el pasado.
>
> They are burning books, they are cutting off heads
> They are risking the cards they have played
> It's raining on the land, they are emptying the markets
> They are playing at war and erasing the past

Monedas al aire thus establishes a perfect synchronized dialogue between the world and the island, between the outside and the inside. While everything is crumbling apart, the "Robinsons" of Cuba watch the sky to see what happens. As the world convulses, all they can do is observe their profound isolation.

"Muro" (Wall) also visualizes the economic crises of the 1990s in two locations: at the dinner table, and at the Malecón. The main character in this song is the person from Havana, whose back is to the camera while the Malecón faces forward. The Malecón, another recurring character in Varela's work, is a barrier that reminds us of our condition as an island, marginalized, isolated, estranged, the end of the road. It stands between Havana and the imposing ocean, arrogant in its immensity, the uncertain and dangerous path to what Cubans refer to obliquely as "the other shore."

The dialogue with the world returns within the same song, as if by a camera cut, through the media, the only connections Cubans have with the outside world:

> Te compras la prensa y notas que al mundo
> le ha cambiado el rostro para bien o mal
>
> You buy the newspaper
> And you notice the face of the world

In "Como me hicieron a mí" (Like They Did to Me), Varela is facing "the camera," telling the audience (in a reverse shot) about his experiences of living in Cuba. This song, as Dubinsky also notes here, is a remarkably direct indictment of Cuban censorship ("they are going to blindfold you," "no one is listening to you"). Its intensity is made even more powerful by the use of the reverse shot: Varela alone, speaking his truth to the unseen but very much present audience.

Monedas al aire more than confirmed Varela's status as an independent thinking outlaw. His use of cinematic conventions continued with his next album.

Travelling Shots

In film, the movement of the camera is usually made sideways, following the actions of the characters. In his fourth album, *Como los peces* (Like Fish), Varela follows the stories of the protagonists. He walks with them, moves around them, re-creating the ambiences in which they move and develop.

Like many of his influences and contemporaries, such as Chico Buarque and Bob Dylan, Varela specializes in marginalized characters. As Xenia Reloba de la Cruz explains in this book, all of the characters in *Como Los peces* are acute examples of marginality: they are Cubans living through the economic and spiritual deprivations of the Special Period of the early 1990s. It is not difficult to imagine the oppressive world inhabited by the young woman who is the protagonist of "Como un angel" (Like an Angel). She is an "angel in prison," locked in her room with incense, the music of The Doors, and marijuana. With this background, what is described so powerfully and so visually in the next "scene" makes complete, tragic sense:

> Yo la ví saltando del balcón
> y en el aire quiso tocar el Sol.
> ¿Dónde fue? Solo lo sabe Dios.
> Como un ángel se desapareció.

> I saw her jumping from the balcony
> And in the air she wanted to touch the sun
> Where did she go? Only God knows
> Like an angel, she disappeared

Subjective Camera

Subjective camera is a narrative resource filmmakers use when they want the viewer to see through the eyes of one of the characters. And this is exactly the approach Varela takes in his fifth album, *Nubes* (Clouds), released in 2000. These are deeply intimate and often anguished songs, which Varela recorded in Havana after he returned there alone from a tour of Spain, where his entire band had decided to remain.

Nubes is Varela's only acoustic album, and thus his guitar – ever the subjective camera – is especially important, recalling his pain as he observes his surroundings. In *Será sol* (It will be sun), for example, he laments both powerlessness and complacency:

> En vano fue cerrar los ojos
> y no saber dónde mirar.
> En vano fue quedarnos solos
> frente a la colina de los tontos
> viendo pasar el mundo
> en silencio

> In vain we go along with our eyes closed,
> Not knowing where to look.
> In vain we remain on our own,
> Faced with a hill of fools,
> Watching the world go by,
> In silence.

The song that names this album, "Nubes," is a sombre and highly subjective piece that captures the loneliness of a generation on a personal scale. As Nasatir also explores in this book, this song uses references to nature – storms, the moon, and, of course, clouds – to express the loneliness of those who have stayed. Varela mourns the losses caused by immigration, but he also laments those who close paths, destroy roads, censor ideas, block development, and abuse power. "Muros y puertas" (Walls and Doors) is a metaphor for this: some, he sings simply, make walls, others make doors.

Tilt Up/Tilt Down

Tilt down and tilt up are camera angles used in cinema. Tilt-down shots are taken from above, tilt-down shots are taken from below. Varela's album *Siete* (Seven) uses both to capture the citizen in relation to his or her surroundings.

In *Siete*, the narrative codes in Varela's songs become more universal, although the referent of Havana is never lost. When Varela looks at the universe, it is from above, as an omniscient narrator. In "Siete," his guitar/camera moves from the top: he observes "seven lives, seven seas, seven marvels and seven cities," and so on, until he sees himself on the streets of Havana during his childhood. He then recounts, from a child's perspective, how the halcyon days of his youth in the 1970s (when "the street was a playground") were soon replaced by the conflicts of the 1980s (which "divide[d] us into those who stayed and those who left"). Varela evokes his youth – something he does often – to reinforce the camera angle. The camera/song tilts up at the emerging international political events of the 1980s, which are about to change forever the world of Havana's street children.

Close-Up

Varela's most recent recording, "*No es el fin*" (It's Not the End), released in 2009, can be seen as a close-up of some of his most central themes. In songs like "Telón de fondo" (Backdrop), "Todo será distinto" (Everything Will Be Different), "La comedia silente "(Silent Comedy), and "El viejo sueño acabó" (The Old Dream Has Ended), he recounts his obsessions: the end of illusions, promises unfulfilled, the death of utopia, the absence of faith, the persistence of the past, and the uncertainty of the future. These songs are close-ups of a fifty-year period in the life of a country.

Several of the songs on this album are written in first person. He voices his own experiences, standing in front of the camera in close-up. In "Castillos de arena" (Sandcastles) he seems to be sitting on the Malecón, offering a monologue as the waves break against the rocks. Of all the songs in this profoundly pessimistic collection, perhaps "Nadie" (No One) best illustrates the near-absolute loss of hope that pervades contemporary Cuba, a place where "not God, not anyone, can save what is lost."

Yet in characteristic Varela fashion, there is always possibility. In the title song "No es el fin," there is a small space for hope, as suggested by the title, which is repeated as a mantra throughout. Similarly, "Historia de un descapotable" (Story of a Convertible), which takes place at a drive-in cinema, suggests that love is a way to salvation. This song is an intimate close-up of two lovers who, by surrendering to their passions, are able to rise above their troubles. It is also a beautiful tribute to romantic cinema, which can make the audience forget that what they see on the screen is only an illusion. It is telling that for Varela, love, salvation, and hope can sometimes be found in the world of cinema.

Conclusion

In his 1990 ISA thesis, Varela declared his philosophy of songwriting: "My intention is for each song to lead into the next, that is, to create an unbroken thread of action. My songs are as precise as a theatrical text. I have the advantage of music that binds and accompanies each soliloquy. This is my idea of a song."[8] In Varela's work we find coherence, rhythm, meaning, and a wide variety of readings and interpretations. One approach to interpreting his songs is by remembering that he has always shown a tremendous appreciation for the visual language of cinema.

NOTES

1 Vincenzo Perna, *Timba: The Sound of the Cuban Crisis* (Aldershot: Ashgate, 2005), p. 172.

2 Ivàn de la Nuez Carrillo, "La canción como laberinto hacia una totalidad otra," *La Gaceta de Cuba*, July 1989, p. 5.
3 Carlos Varela, "La teatralidad en la canción," Tesis de graduación, La Habana, Instituto Superior de Arte, 1990, p. 1.
4 Varela, "La teatralidad," p. 3.
5 Nuez Carrillo, "La canción como laberinto."
6 Varela, "La teatralidad," p. 3.
7 Juan "Pin" Vilar, *Carlos Varela* (Madrid, Fundación Autor, 2004), p. 43.
8 Varela, "La teatralidad."

Chapter Six

Singing the Cityscape: Varela as Urban Chronicler

SUSAN THOMAS

Described as "palimpsestic" by José Quiroga,[1] Havana's architectural, historical, and social layers have long been inscribed and reinscribed with changing narratives of national and local belonging. While much of the scholarship of Havana's allegorical power as both a "memory city" and an ephemeral "non-space" has focused on literary and visual depictions,[2] some of the city's most powerful representations have been *heard* rather than read or seen. In the imaginations of Cubans and non-Cubans alike, music is central to the construction of Havana, and the city's musical (re)incarnations illustrate how its physical geography continues to serve as the site for contested narratives of Cuban identity. As I've written elsewhere, the city of Havana has been visited and revisited musically through musical and textual references that bind together past and present experiences of urban space.[3] No musician stands out in this regard as sharply as Carlos Varela, the city's consummate chronicler.

Perhaps more than any other Cuban singer/songwriter, Carlos Varela is intensely associated with the city of Havana. In a recording career that spans eight albums and three decades, Varela has revealed a "very special relationship" with the Cuban capital, in which he experiences "Havana not only as a city, but Havana as something very deep and very personal ... and Havana as a woman as well."[4] Indeed, in his music and lyrics Varela constantly references the streets of Havana, especially the leafy, symmetric blocks of the Vedado district, where he grew up and continues to live. Called the "Poet of Havana" by *Beat Magazine*[5] and a "unique urban rapporteur"[6] by leading Cuban music critic Joaquín Borges-Triana, Varela has been widely hailed as a chronicler of Havana's promise, its contradictions, and its decay. Thus his poetic depiction of Havana is central to this chapter, just as his skill at situating his songs in a broader historical and literary context is one of the hallmarks of his work. Yet as Varela himself has noted, "I'm not only a writer of songs or a singer of texts, I am also a musician, and many times the music says more than the words."[7] A primary goal of this chapter, then, is to contribute to our understanding of how, compositionally and in his performance practice, Varela has developed musical codes to represent the city and the emotions it evokes, particularly nostalgia.

The Sung City

Varela's multifaceted use of Havana as muse participates in a larger trend in Cuban songwriting that developed in the late 1980s in which the city became a protagonist with whom songwriters engaged in ways both individual and intimate. Unlike the earlier generation of Nueva Trova musicians, who tended to avoid specific references to place, Varela and his contemporaries – such as Gerardo Alfonso and Frank Delgado – created a repertory that celebrated, critiqued, and, above all, *experienced* the city. Described at street level, local urban experience is lyrically claimed as an assertion of Cuban identity, an identity that increasingly has had to reinvent and reassert itself as the geopolitical boundaries of "Cubanness" have become increasingly amorphous. Such songs are attempts to renegotiate Cuban (or at least *habanero*) identity within the spaces and places that created it, and they often converse with the past, whether that past is personal or imagined.

Taking overt (and often controversial) inspiration from the sounds of Argentine, North American, and British rock music, Varela's early musical style was self-consciously urban and cosmopolitan. Yet while his sound palette stressed international cosmopolitanism, his lyrics stressed the local, with graphic depictions of Havana serving as the backdrop for acute social and political commentary ("Tropicollage") as well as for love songs and nostalgic laments ("Callejón sin luz" [Dark Alley]). Avoiding the kind of cartographic specificity found in the songs of Gerardo Alfonso, Varela only occasionally named specific streets or places (as in the children's amusement park described in "Jalisco Park" or the Chinese Cemetery referenced in both "Ahora que los mapas están cambiando de color" (Now That the Maps are Changing Colour) and "Callejón sin luz"). At the same time, however, these songs are undeniably "Havana-centric," and Varela's slow-moving gaze and acute attention to detail allow his descriptions to be simultaneously general *and* personal, allowing the listener to fill in the specifics. Thus, the neighbourhood curb in "Memorias" and the gas station and rain puddles in "Estás" (You Are) can be appropriated into the imaginations of individual listeners.

Narrating the City

Varela has described his early songs as having been written from a photographic viewpoint,[8] a characteristic that Caridad Cumaná discusses in this book. Yet as José Quiroga has discussed, a historic relationship exists in Cuba between image and narrative. "It seems," he writes, "as if no picture has been taken there without being subjected to reflections of a 'writerly' sort."[9] These reflections look back to other texts as well as to the identities of those who wrote them. Quiroga writes that "for the foreign observer, as well as for many *habaneros*, walking around Centro Habana as late as 2002 invited the stroller, or *flâneur*, to apprehend different temporalities of the same structure."[10] Quiroga is speaking here of architectural palimpsests, of the ability to read simultaneously Havana's transtemporal layers, as Varela does in "Memorias." Yet in referencing the figure of the nineteenth-century strolling voyeur, Quiroga's statement reveals the tendency of contemporary viewers of the city to position *themselves* palimpsestically, that is, to identify with and appropriate earlier narrative positionalities, such as the *flâneur*.

Elsewhere, I have compared the *trovador* who emerged in Havana prior to the collapse of the Soviet Union with the bohemian *flâneur* of nineteenth-century Paris.[11] Educated, male, and with time for leisure, the *flâneur* was an urban figure, an "eternal vagabond"[12] who spent his time in the street observing the fabric of city life. Indeed, for the *flâneur* the city *was* life; his obsession with Paris reflected that French life focused on the capital.[13] Similarly, the prominence of Cuba's capital city in songs written from the late 1980s onward is indicative of Havana's increasing gravitational pull on nearly all aspects of Cuban economic, cultural, and political life. The affinity of the *flâneur* – a figure whose existence was propelled by the social and economic upheavals of early capitalism – with songwriters who documented both the apex and the crumbling of a socialist experiment might not seem initially apparent were it not for the intervention of the spaces in which they wrote/composed. The Havana cityscape, itself strongly influenced by that of nineteenth-century Paris, shaped the explorations and the observations of the *trovador*, much as the arcades and boulevards of Paris formed the world view of the *flâneur*. The Parisian *flâneur* and the Cuban *trovador* thus emerge as figures whose relationship with their respective cities is both " a present and immediate reality, a practico-material and architectural fact," and "a social reality made up of relations that are to be conceived of, constructed or reconstructed by thought"[14] (or in song). Such meta-(re)constructions draw on what Jameson has called the "nostalgia for the present,"[15] and both nineteenth-century Parisian and late-twentieth-century Cuban explorations of the urban landscape occupy an ephemeral temporal space in which the past and the present coexist.

With the figure of the *flâneur* in mind, "Bulevar" (Boulevard; 1991) evokes the consumerist spectacle of Benjamin's arcades. Only someone familiar with the Cuban economic situation in the early 1990s would hear the irony (and the nostalgia) in the song's depiction of shoppers alternatively fascinated by and rushing past windows and display cases. Just as Benjamin had been fascinated by the use of glass and mirrors within the arcades, and the new material's ability to shape, manipulate, and reflect the gaze of the viewer, Varela focuses on the viewer's relationship with glass, in this case as a barrier against which viewers can only "stick their noses." Varela's songs repeatedly reference glass and mirrors, which frame, reflect, and refract Havana in a variety of ways. "Detrás del cristal" (Behind the Glass), for example, uses the metaphor of refraction to broach alternative ephemeral histories of Havana as well as a failed relationship that never came to be. The protagonist in "Estás" (You Are), from the album *Siete* (Seven; 2003), seeks truth and lost love in reflections (in mirrors, puddles, glasses); similarly, "Sombras en la pared" (Shadows on the Wall) uses the image of light shining on or through glass as a metaphor for longing.

The *flâneur*, described by Benjamin as a "chronicler and philosopher,"[16] has a Latin American counterpart in the *cronista moderna* (modern chronicler), who emerged around the same time period. Described by Julio Ramos as "an ideal medium for reflection about change,"[17] the literary *crónica* (chronicle) narrated Cuban encounters with the promise and contradictions of modernism. A blend of documentary journalism and descriptive and colouristic prose that could "overwrite" the emerging medium of photojournalism,[18] the modern *crónica* that emerged in Cuba in the late nineteenth century was promoted by writers based both on the island and abroad, such as José Martí, Julián del Casal, and Ramón Meza. The *crónica*'s close identification with José Martí inevitably links its literary and descriptive conventions to the rhetoric of Cuban nationalism and Cuban identity, and these associations are prominent in Varela's own urban *crónicas* (most famously in "Jalisco Park") from a century later. As self-referential as they were descriptive, *cronistas* universalized their everyday encounters by positioning themselves as actors personally affected by modern change. This activist role differentiated the *cronista* from the *flâneur*, who was a mere spectator. The *crónica*'s historical associations with modernism – in particular, with the contradictions arising from the inequalities generated by Latin American modernization[19] – make its conventions particularly useful for Varela: Havana's messy, contradictory, and often frustrated relationship with modernity is a central theme in his work.

By personalizing his encounters with the city, Varela transforms the anonymity and vastness of urban space into something intimate. "In the act of strolling," Ramos writes, "the *cronista* transform the city into a *salon*, into an intimate space [and] into an object of aesthetic and even erotic pleasure."[20] The intimacy with which Varela treats the city is notable, and while his lyrics tend to deal with public rather than private space, he uses a "domestic" sound palette in his songs about the city, most of which are accompanied by piano or acoustic guitar and are produced to give the effect of a performance in an intimate setting. An example is "Detrás del cristal," the final track from *Siete*, which begins with a transparently bare introduction in which the beautiful imperfections of live acoustic guitar performance are exquisitely foregrounded. The ear is drawn to the rasp of a callus pulling across a string, the minute buzz of fingernail against vibrating wire, the near-silent deadening of a tone under the weight of a fingertip. The arrangement is minimalist and skeletal, suggesting the bones of the city on which Varela is reflecting. Yet it is also a deeply textured and detailed look at the architecture of a city (or of a relationship), one that pauses to reflect on scraped edges, on dust, on unattainable beauty. The song maps Havana's landscape onto a lover, projecting the city's tragic decadence onto a beautiful yet troubled love affair.

Like the nostalgic travelogues written by the *flâneur* and the *cronista*, Varela's songs present urban life as "before all else a *system of signs* in which even the most trivial phenomenon is replete with meaning," signs that when linked together can "disclose a universe of significance."[21] When I interviewed him in 2004, Varela noted that the intimate and local character of his songs is a metaphor through which more universal messages can be understood:

With the years you learn, with a more universal vision, to discover that loneliness, nostalgia, fury, hope, and disillusionment are the same in every city, whether it be New York or Havana or Moscow. Inevitably, this [understanding] comes with the years, with maturity, and also with the possibility that you can also see your country from the outside, this gives you a vision a lot more open and more extensive of the reality in which you live, that's why when you listen to the albums you realize that there are themes that stay connected to Cuban reality.[22]

The City as Allegory

Richard Burton, channelling the spirit of the Parisian *flâneur*, writes that "tout pour moi devient allégorie" (for me, everything becomes allegory).[23] This statement applies equally well to Varela's treatment of Havana. Throughout his oeuvre, he utilizes detailed references to local places as markers of personal relationships, philosophical stance, and political and social critique. His use of place as a metaphor for the human experience is evident in "Ahora que los mapas están cambiando de color" (Now That the Maps Are Changing Colour) from his 1992 album *Monedas en el aire*. In that song, composed following the collapse of the Soviet Union, he uses outdated international maps and the physical boundaries of Havana's cityscape to construct a political allegory. The music itself, which crosses geo-aesthetic boundaries, is perhaps the most extreme example of Varela's appropriation of an international pop-rock sound, with clear textural and timbral allusions to Argentine, British, and American rock.

Here, as Cumaná has also observed, Varela travels from the general to the local, from the global upheavals caused by the fall of the Iron Curtain to the metaphoric opening of the gates of Havana's Chinese Cemetery. His merging of the graphic representation of political geography with an image that recalls the politics of local human geography is striking. The Chinese Cemetery, closed after the exodus of Havana's Chinese population in the years following the Revolution, is one of the most poignant geographic markers of the island's current diasporic reality.[24]

With his references to the gates of the Chinese Cemetery in "Ahora que los mapas cambian de color," and to the ruined boats in "Jalisco Park," Varela links material metaphors of the local to the ephemeral community of Cubans who visit such spaces only aurally. Varela's relationship to Cuban émigrés who left friends and family behind on the island is simultaneously artistic, professional, and personal. Songs such as "Foto de familia" (Family Photo), "Detrás del cristal," and "Jalisco Park" call up the exquisite hollowness of separation endured by "los que se fueron y los que están" (those who left and those who are here).[25]

Varela's ode to his generation, "Memorias," famously calls up the icons of Cuban childhood in the 1970s, referring to the children's cartoon character Elpidio Valdés, Soviet-made television sets, and the rationed allocation of toys. In the opening stanza of this song, Varela's use of urban space is general, focusing on the transtemporality of the neighbourhood curb to illustrate the slow pace of true sociopolitical change:

> Estoy sentado en el contén del barrio
> como hace un siglo atrás
> a veces me pasan en la radio,
> a veces nada más.
>
> I'm sitting on the neighborhood curb
> just like a century ago
> sometimes they play me on the radio
> sometimes not any more.

On *Siete*, Varela revisits the same curb in "El humo del tren" (The Smoke of the Train), a fast-paced, *timba*-influenced song that features the Cuban dance band Los Van Van. The use of popular Cuban dance music is a departure from Varela's more international rock ballad style, and his reference to the earlier song's lyrics in the opening – "Hey man, sentado en el contén" (Hey man, sitting on the curb) – consciously calls up the stylistic difference as well as the decade and a half that separates the two songs. If "Memorias" affirms post-revolutionary identity in the shared pleasures and traumas of a childhood caught between isolation and globalization, "El humo del tren" is a recognition that while so many more friends have left for other shores, the curb has not budged. Varela thus implicitly critiques those, including himself, who continue to observe from its perch.

Siete itself is a study in contrasts, juxtaposing the thick textures and dance aesthetic of Los Van Van with spare arrangements for voice and acoustic guitar and the sonorities and rhythmic regularity of rock. References to Havana are woven throughout this album, binding together its diversity of sonic textures as well as tying it thematically to the six albums that preceded it. *Siete* also represents an overt recognition that

Varela's popular success has as much to do with his international reach as it does with his local sensibilities; the album was aggressively marketed abroad.

The Ruined City and the Sound of Nostalgia

Travelogues of Havana have long focused on the city's decay. Even in the 1840s, a time of rapid economic growth and urban expansion, the Condesa de Merlin could write of Havana, "I walk among nothing more than a pile of lifeless rocks and an undying memory."[26] That long-ago assessment presages much of the twentieth-century commentary on Havana, which regards the city as prone to ruin and links urban decay to memory and nostalgia.

A number of recent scholars have focused on the image of crumbling Havana. That image is a central theme in Anke Birkenmaier and Esther Whitfield's collected volume *Havana beyond the Ruins*. Geoffrey Baker picks up the same topic in his study of Cuban hip hop, *Buena Vista in the Club*, in which he describes a desirous touristic gaze bent on consuming nostalgia through scenes of Havana's rubble. He contrasts this with a more critical and realist (and implicitly local) viewpoint as expressed by writers like Pedro Juan Gutiérrez and rappers Los Aldeanos and Hermanos de la Causa, whose texts represent the messy and contradictory underbelly of the city with all its grit, and do so – in Gutiérrez's *Trilogía sucia de La Habana* – with a total lack of moral platitudes.[27] Equating the nostalgic treatment of ruins in songs like "Jalisco Park" with a touristic gaze, however, fails to recognize the long tradition of Cuban musicians, artists, and writers experiencing a romantic yet ultimately transformative *saudade* for their city and expressing it in terms of its physical deterioration. According to Quiroga, Varela and other artists from the second Nueva Trova generation experience a kind of "messianic time" in which the present is deemed integral to the realization of the future.[28] In this respect, Varela's focus on Havana's material decadence is not an obsession with the past, but rather a redemptive impulse, a desire to see the city and all it represents as "an ongoing national project."[29]

Notwithstanding his references to a more distant past in songs like "Memorias," "Habáname," and "Foto de Familia," Varela's nostalgia is not a nostalgia for "the city that time forgot." Rather, his songs return again and again to the experience of lost innocence, lost love, and a painfully beautiful and ultimately transformative coming of age. This sense of redemption is found in mid-twentieth-century literary explorations of Havana by Alejo Carpentier and José Lezama Lima but is largely absent among more recent writers. Most notable here is Gutiérrez, who unromantically drags readers on a relentless slog through Havana's gritty, smelly, and often violent underbelly. Yet even Gutiérrez recognizes nostalgia as an inescapable force. The solution, asserts his protagonist Pedro Juan with his characteristic deadpan pragmatism, "is to learn to live with it."[30] Yet even Pedro Juan can't resist the impulse to see nostalgia as potentially redemptive provided that it serves as a catalyst for finding "the arms of a new lover, a new city, a new era, which, no matter whether it's better or worse, will be different. And that's all we ask each day; not to squander our lives in loneliness, to find someone, to lose ourselves a little, to escape routine, to enjoy our piece of the party."[31] In spite of the line that contemporary critics have drawn, then, between representations of the city that rely on "realist grit" and those that showcase "nostalgic romanticism,"[32] I would argue that in some ways the perspectives of Gutiérrez and Varela are not so far apart, only their methods. Gutiérrez shocks with painful ugliness, Varela with painful beauty. The excruciatingly static tempo of "El viejo sueño se acabó" (The Old Dream Has Ended) on *No es el fín* (2009), for example, forces the listener to experience the real-time, unrelenting anguish of a break-up, while the use of the close-miked piano and warbled falsetto "tuu-uu-uu-uu" bring the listener into a claustrophobic domestic space from which (s)he might like to escape.

"El viejo sueño se acabó" ends with the sound of a music box playing Steven Sondheim's "Send in the Clowns," with the mechanism winding down and cutting off mid-phrase. It is not unusual for Varela to end an album with nostalgia. *Siete*, for example, ends with "Detrás del cristal," *Nubes* with the nearly a cappella "Una palabra," and *Como los peces* with "Habáname." What is unusual is Varela's frank embrace of personal sorrow and loss, which he expresses without the distancing effect of metaphor. Perhaps this song is as painful as it is precisely because it is *not* told through the metaphor of Havana's public spaces, but rather through an unseen yet inescapable domestic space.

The Sound of Nostalgia

Varela's output, with its reliance on memory as a poetic trope, its fascination with palimpsests and transtemporality, its focus on ruins, and its concern with loss and loneliness, is unquestionably nostalgic. Beyond the lyrics, however, what aural signifiers link Varela's music with nostalgia and urban experience? What does Varela's nostalgia *sound* like? While he references Havana in a number of non-nostalgic songs (usually protest songs), most of his Havana songs can be described as nostalgic. The lyrics connect with memory and the historical past; there are also textual connections between songs that foster a sort of intertextual, interstitial nostalgia. All of this is present in the repeating images of mirrors/glass/reflections (discussed earlier) and in poetic allusions to fish, clouds, angels, photo albums, curbs and rocks, and so on, that tie one song – with all of its accompanying semiotic freight – to another. Sound plays a similar role in Varela's music: his Havana songs are linked by a number of general characteristics and sometimes by direct sonic citation. Also, they tend to be in a minor key or to fluctuate between major and minor. Their most common accompaniments are acoustic guitar and piano, and many of them feature a particular finger-picking guitar style characterized by rapid "filigree" turns that evoke the city's baroque ornamentation. The instruments are close-miked to heighten intimacy and suggest a small (domestic) space and are often backed by a synthesizer that sometimes suggests a string section and other times is overtly electronic. Occasionally, Varela evokes urban ephemera, including laughter ("Nubes"), sampled sounds from the urban environment ("Callejón sin luz"), or a live, local, and temporally specific audience (in his now iconic Teatro Carlos Marx performance on *En vivo*).

In discussing the sound of nostalgia in Varela's music, it makes sense to begin with the two most iconic examples – "Jalisco Park," which is specific to Havana, and "Guillermo Tell," which is not. Both songs are coming-of-age stories that struggle with lost illusions. "Jalisco Park" is told from the perspective of memory, while "Guillermo Tell" functions as a parable/manifesto for Cuban youth frustrated by their lack of opportunities. The two songs share a collective past of lost innocence, a frustration with present-day stagnation, and a desire for change. Musically, they also share some characteristics, and as two of Varela's most significant early compositions, they shape the musical treatment of nostalgia in his future work. A distinguishing musical feature of "Jalisco Park" is the finger-picked guitar, which features a repeated descending third motive in the upper voice that is later picked up by the vocal line and is undergirded by a repeated descending figure in the bassline. The falling interval is repeated at different pitches, and its fragmentary nature and constant repetition evoke memory – they are the aural equivalent of someone running a thought over and over through his head. A similar falling third motive with descending bassline is worked into the guitar accompaniment to "Guillermo Tell." In these two songs, this guitar pattern functions as an aural signifier for memory, childhood, disillusionment, and coming of age.[33] The opening changes of "Guillermo Tell" return on the 2003 album *Siete*, where in "25 mil mentiras sobre la verdad" (25 Thousand Lies about the Truth) they make their appearance as a synthesized music box. Here, the reference to the earlier song evokes memory as well as a sense of disillusionment and betrayal. The music box, which suggests domesticity and childhood, is replaced by an organ once the voice enters, a shift that calls up simultaneously religious symbolism and the repetitive irony of an organ grinder.

Varela's best-known ode to Havana, "Habáname," shares with the previously described "Detrás del cristal" a poetic conflation of the aesthetic and the erotic as well as a similar sonic vocabulary. Like "Detrás del cristal," "Habáname" features a spare, almost architectural fingerpicked accompaniment; this is embellished with melodic turns and is close-miked to capture audible "squeaks" as the fingers slide on the guitar. "Habáname" also features a descending ostinato in the lower voice of the guitar, illustrating that this particular harmonic arrangement remains strongly associated with memory and nostalgia in Varela's later music. While the close miking of voice and guitar provides a sense of domestic intimacy, the instruments are backed by atmospheric synthesized strings. Vocally, Varela shifts back and forth between a breathy falsetto and occasional focused, more nasal/angular "o" vowels in words like "todo," "quitó," "Matamoros," "Tesoro," and "derrumbando," which prevents the listener from being completely lulled into complacency. This also pulls the song away from being a mere nostalgic ode, and personalizes it by placing the *cronista* and his perspective at the centre of the performance.

Conclusion

Varela's most recent album, *No es el fin* (2009), initially seems to have little in common with his previous output, an effect due largely to a significant change in the sound of the band, which now includes Tony Rodríguez on piano and Julio Cesar Gonzáles Ochoa on bass, with *coros* sung by Diana Fuentes. Piano is more prominent than before. The sound production differs from his previous recordings as well: the microphones are set farther back, producing a more spacious sound, and the paired use of piano and guitar on many songs, augmented by Diana

Fuentes's vocals, amplifies this effect by further defining the space. Besides all this, the sense of the local that pervades Varela's earlier albums is much less overtly present. Speaking to personal issues of separation, heartbreak, and redemption, the album's themes initially seem more general and less "Varela-like" than listeners might have expected. This is reflected in fans' comments posted on numerous fan sites, where a common refrain has been that they didn't particularly like the album on first hearing but came to appreciate it more and more with later listenings. I suggest that it is in later listenings that we can pick out familiar nostalgic musical tropes such as the timbre of Varela's guitar and his characteristic finger-picked embellishments (heard as Varela describes the now separated lovers playing as children along the Almendares River). Even Varela's distinctive vocal shifts, from gravelly to falsetto to a nasal "Dylan-esque" declamatory style, are camouflaged by the new sound palette, especially with the addition of Fuentes's back-up vocals. As a consequence, listeners have to retrain their ears to refamiliarize themselves with his voice. Yet while the street does not dominate *No es el fin* as much as it did previous albums, the Havana context is still recognizable, not only in the guitar turns of "No es el fín" mentioned previously but also in the spare architectural sound and angular melody of the piano introduction to "El viejo sueño acabó" and in that song's equally spare, chorus-free vocals. Aurally, that song *sounds* like a Havana song, even if it is not, and its extended dirge-like lament "túu-uu-uu-uu y yo" recalls the upbeat and exhilarating "solo túu-uu-uu-uu" in "Solo tú (puedes traer el sol)" (Only You Can Bring the Sun), creating a textual and sonic link to the earlier work.

The redemptive nostalgia evoked by the sound of the city is so integral to Varela's compositions that it has contextualized his later work. Thus, as Joaquín Borges-Triana has written, even though *No es el fin* lacks the quotidian realism of earlier albums, its songwriting "stands out for its systematic tribute to the Cuban capital, in what might be defined as 'an attitude that arises from its *habanero* context.'"[34] It is that context, and its ultimate expression as a series of musical signs woven throughout Varela's eight albums, that gives Varela's work its signifying power. Whether singing of a young girl's suicide by leaping from a balcony ("Como un angel"), or the suddenly increasing crime and corruption resulting from Cuba's headlong entry into the tourist economy ("Tropicollage"), or stolen private moments taken within the collective intimacy of the city ("Sombras en el pared"), Varela uses the local and the deeply personal to speak to larger truths – societal, political, and human. Here I have suggested that by paying close attention to both the lyrics and the sound of Varela's Havana, we can appreciate more fully the recent history of this complex and evocative city.

NOTES

1 José Quiroga, *Cuban Palimpsests* (Minneapolis: University of Minnesota Press), 2005.
2 See Marc Augé, *Non-Places: An Introduction to Supermodernity* (London: Verso, 1995); Velia Ceilia Bobes, *Los laberintos de la imaginación: Repertorio simbólico, identidades y actores del cambio social en Cuba* (Mexico City: El Colegio de México, 2000). See also the recent volume edited by Anke Birkenmaier and Irene Whitfield, *Havana beyond the Ruins: Cultural Mappings after 1989* (Durham, NC: Duke University Press, 2011).
3 Susan Thomas, "Musical Cartographies of the Transnational City: Mapping Havana in Song," *Latin American Music Review* 31, no. 2 (Fall–Winter 2010): 124–43.
4 Carlos Varela in an interview with Alexis on *Trapicheo Online*, 23 June 2011, http://los2musicales.blogspot.com/2011/06/alexis-carlos-varela-entrevista-y.html (accessed 25 November 2011).
5 http://www.artemapale.com/CarlosVarela.html (accessed 2 February 2014).
6 http://www.lajiribilla.cu/2011/n539_09/539_05.html (accessed 2 February 2014).
7 Mabel Machado, "Conectado con la memoria y los corazones de los cubanos," *La Jiribilla* 9, 12–18 March 2011, http://www.lajiribilla.cu/2011/n514_03/514_25.html (accessed 15 November 2011),
8 Interview with the author, 1 November 2004.
9 Quiroga, *Cuban Palimpsests*, 83.
10 Quiroga, *Cuban Palimpsests*, 32.
11 Thomas, "Musical Cartographies."
12 Walter Benjamin, "From the Arcades Project," in *The Blackwell City Reader*, ed. Gary Bridge and Sophie Watson (Malden, MA: Blackwell Publishing, 2002), 399.
13 Elizabeth Wilson, "From *The Sphinx in the City*," in *The Blackwell City Reader*, ed. Gary Bridge and Sophie Watson (Malden, MA: Blackwell Publishing, 2002), 419.
14 Henri Lefebvre and Elizabeth Lebas, eds., *Writings on Cities* (Oxford: Blackwell Publishers, 1997), 103.

15 Fredric Jameson, "Nostalgia for the Present," *South Atlantic Quarterly* 18, no. 2 (1989): 517–37.
16 Benjamin, "El París del segundo imperio en Baudelaire," in *Iluminaciones II (Poesía y capitalismo)* (Madrid: Taurus, 1972), 51.
17 Julio Ramos, "Un medio adecuando para la reflexión sobre el cambio," in *Desencuentros de la modernidad en América Latina: Literatura y política en el siglo XIX* (Mexico City: Editorial Cuarto Propio, 2003), 150.
18 Kelley Kreitz, "On the Beat in the Modern City: The *Crónica Modernista* and Nineteenth-Century News," paper presented at the 2009 Congress of the Latin American Studies Association, Rio de Janeiro, Brazil, 11–14 June 2009, p. 5, lasa.international.pitt.edu/members/congress.../files/Kreitz Kelley.pdf (accessed 25 Nov. 2011).
19 See Ramos, *Desencuentros de la modernidad*, 12.
20 "En el paseo, el cronista transforma la ciudad en *salon*, en espacio íntimo [y] en objeto de placer estético e incluso erótico." Ramos, *Desencuentros de la modernidad*, 129.
21 Richard D.E. Burton, *The Flaneur and His City: Patterns of Daily Life in Paris, 1815–1851* (Durham, UK: University of Durham, 1994), 2.
22 Carlos Varela, interview with the author, Havana, 1 November 2004.
23 Burton, *The Flaneur and His City*, 2.
24 Havana's Chinese inhabitants, including the neighbourhood that recalls their absence, is similarly the focus of Gerardo Alfonso's song "Barrio Chino" (*El ilustrado caballero de Paris*; 2001), which, like "Sábanas blancas," refers to specific streets.
25 Lyrics from "Detrás del crystal."
26 Santa Cruz y Montalvo, María de las Mercedes, *Viaje a La Habana* (La Habana: Arte y Literatura, 1974).
27 Geoffrey Baker, *Buena Vista in the Club: Rap, Reggaetón, and Revolution in Havana* (Durham, NC: Duke University Press, 2011), 223–43.
28 Quiroga, *Cuban Palimpsests*, 154.
29 Quiroga, *Cuban Palimpsests*, 113.
30 Pedro Juan Gutiérrez, *Dirty Havana Trilogy* (New York: HarperCollins, 2002), 54.
31 Gutiérrez, *Dirty Havana Trilogy*, 54.
32 See Baker, *Buena Vista in the Club*, 223–43.
33 Further evidence of this occurs in "Memorias," which also makes use of a descending bass pattern. The use of such cellular repetition thus can be seen as a mnemonic trope in Varela's early repertoire.
34 Joaquín Borges-Triana, "Carlos Varela-No es el fín," www.carlosvarela.com/client/news/show.php?news_id=67 (accessed 30 November 2011).

Chapter Seven

Carlos Varela, Protest Song, and Cuban Music History

ROBIN MOORE

Carlos Varela has established himself as one of the most important and influential composers of Cuban music in the last twenty years. This book attests to his unique abilities and to the resonance of his music for many listeners. One aspect of Varela's music making that may not be as apparent is the extent to which it builds on or harkens back to Cuban repertoire of past generations even while establishing new ties with international sounds and musical trends. Especially in terms of the politically and socially engaged aspects of his lyrics, Varela can be viewed as continuing a well-established Cuban tradition. And his strong interest in international rock- and guitar-based music builds on the work of countless other local performers since the late 1950s.

As I have discussed elsewhere, Cuba's tumultuous political history has long lent itself to musical and other artistic expressions that engage with contemporary social concerns.[1] Certainly the comic theatre derived much of its popularity from an engagement with political topics, beginning in the early nineteenth century and continuing through the 1930s. Together with the *danza* and *danzón* (creolized forms of local dance music), early comic stage productions featuring music performed by racialized character types (the *negro bozal*, the *negro catedrático*, the *mulata*, etc.) came to be associated with local realities during the struggle for independence from Spain (1868–98) and thus had political significance even beyond their overt content. Even the well-documented Kings' Day street celebrations dating back to the early years of colonization can be considered protest music of a sort, in that they were public presentations of African-derived culture on an island that embraced slavery and yet failed to valorize African heritage of any sort.

In the final decades of the nineteenth century, guitars became a central feature of Cuban music with the rise of the *trovador* tradition. The eastern end of the island, especially the city of Santiago, proved central to the emergence of this type of performance, which was first heard in modestly affluent urban black communities. Performers like José "Pepe" Sánchez (1856–1918) helped develop the Latin American *bolero* with its fusion of European and Caribbean influences; they also promoted other local song forms, including the *canción*, the *clave*, and the *criolla*. Early *trovadores* usually sang duets to the accompaniment of two guitars, one providing a bassline and chordal accompaniment, the other filling in between vocal phrases with improvised melodies. Often they incorporated *clave* sticks into the ensemble as well. Pieces tended to be harmonically sophisticated, reflecting the influence of light opera and parlour song. Much of the early repertoire featured patriotic or nationalist lyrics.[2] This is not surprising, given that this style of music became popular during periods of frequently intense fighting that culminated first in independence from Spain (1898) and then in US occupation (1898–1902) and subsequent struggles for full autonomy.

Songs of political commentary continued to be written with some frequency in later decades. A certain resentment existed in Cuba (and elsewhere in the region) to the strong cultural and political influence exerted by Europe and the United States. Thus, most composers of that period chose to couch their commentary in music featuring local instruments, rhythms, and song styles. Famous examples of political song from the early to mid-twentieth century include Miguel Matamoros's "Bomba lacrimosa" (Tear Gas Grenade, 1928) and the Eliseo Grenet's "Lamento cubano" (Cuban Lament, 1932). Both were responses to the excesses of security forces associated with the Gerardo Machado administration. That conflict escalated until a civil war broke out, which led to Machado's ouster in 1933. Grenet's composition, in its early versions, is slow, sad, and lyrical.[3] Musically, it references the *habanera* and the *danzón*, two popular, nationalistic genres of the day, with its frequent use of the five-note *cinquillo* rhythm (an African-derived pattern common to much Caribbean music) in the instrumental accompaniment and its sectional switches between major and minor keys.

> O Cuba hermosa, primorosa
> ¿por qué sufres hoy tanto quebranto?
> O patria mía, ¿quién diría
> que tu cielo azul nublara el llanto?

Oh beautiful, elegant Cuba
Why do you suffer such affliction?
Oh, my country, who would guess
That your blue sky concealed weeping?

"Bomba lagrimosa," by contrast, demonstrates a different trend in Cuban music: the mixing of social commentary with humour or bawdy double entendre.[4] Jorge Mañach commented famously on this characteristic of Cuban society in his essay "Indagación sobe el choteo."[5] Music of this nature is found as often in the era of Carlos Varela as in decades past (most notably in *timba*, discussed below). The Matamoros composition is a jaunty dance tune in a major key. Its musical setting seems to clash with the rather serious lyrics at the outset, but this tension resolves itself in the chorus as Matamoros jokingly suggests both that Machado's forces will not prevail in their clashes with the people and that they are sexually impotent. Choral responses are indicated below by italics.

Hoy lo que pasa en La Habana
Sólo lo sabe mi moza:
Juegan los guardias con ganas
Con la bomba lacrimosa
Tírate una bomba lacrimosa
Que tengo ganas de llorar
Hoy se han puesto las cosas
Que no se pueden comprar
Guardia Tu bomba no tira
Guardia Tu bomba no suena

Today what happens in Havana
Only my girl knows:
The police enjoy playing
With tear gas grenades
Throw a tear gas grenade
Cause I feel like crying
Things have gotten so expensive
You can't buy them
Policeman Your grenade won't fire
Policeman your grenade won't go off

The 1940s and 1950s saw a lull in political songwriting, while the production of fun-loving, apolitical dance music exploded. This period represented a Cuban musical heyday in terms of the island's international influence, the sheer number of artists performing, and the vibrancy of Havana nightlife. *Son, mambo, cha cha chá,* big band *boleros,* jazz orchestras, trios, and countless other styles became popular at home and around the world. Lavish cabaret shows, funded largely through revenues derived from gambling, became synonymous with Havana.[6] This period was also one of rapid economic expansion and affluence for a surprisingly large urban middle class. Politically, however, the island continued to face many challenges, the most serious of which was a military coup instigated by Fulgencio Batista in the early 1950s that effectively ended democratic governance and led to an escalating civil war against him.

The 1960s and 1970s, the decades of Carlos Varela's childhood, witnessed a radical break with the previous era of commercial music making. Following the triumph of Cuban revolutionaries and the departure of Batista in 1959, the island's new leaders found themselves forced to intervene in the cultural sector much more quickly than they had anticipated. The outlawing of gambling, especially, eliminated a key source of revenue for Cuba's music industry and meant that state revenues had to be used to support performances of all kinds. Political tensions between the United States and Cuba in the early 1960s led to a decline in tourism and the departure of many well-known artists. In the aftermath of the Cuban Missile Crisis, the failed Bay of Pigs invasion, and an economic embargo imposed by the United States, not to mention Cuba's abrogation of international copyright law, commercial music making as it had existed earlier became largely impossible.

Various performers of traditional music aligned themselves with the revolutionary government from the very first years – Los Compadres, Carlos Puebla, Eduardo Saborit, Pello el Afrokan. However, their traditional-sounding repertoire was soon overshadowed by a new form of music known as Nueva Trova. This is the repertoire most closely associated with the Cuban Revolution today, and most directly influential on Varela. Nueva Trova began as a youth movement; it developed on the streets and in parks, private homes, and other informal settings as an expression of the first generation of Cubans to be raised under socialism. Such music is usually considered a form of protest, although some songs avoid overt political references. Most Nueva Trova musicians had little formal training; they often began their careers in the military or in amateur groups, or they learned to play in community settings. Early stars of the movement included Pablo Milanés, Silvio Rodríguez, and Noel Nicola.

Artists of the late 1960s and early 1970s consciously attempted to break with commercial culture as it had existed previously. Much like Bob Dylan in the United States, Victor Jara in Chile, and Caetano Veloso and Gilberto Gil in Brazil, they experimented with new sounds and new musical formulas. Dressing informally and influenced by the counterculture movement, Cuban artists wrote songs that questioned many aspects of contemporary life. Following the egalitarian ideals of socialism, most of them worked to erase divisions between performer and audience, mingling with crowds and continuing to play in informal settings even after becoming famous. In both an aesthetic and a lyrical sense, musicians of this period expanded the boundaries of Cuban music as it was understood at the time.

Rock'n'roll became increasingly popular among Cuban youths of the 1960s and 1970s; indeed, some have suggested that by the mid-1970s, rock music overshadowed all other styles on the island. This is not always evident when we read existing literature on Cuban music history, for it is not something that the nationalistic cultural establishment is terribly proud of. Government officials and state-supported cultural organizations took a dim view of rock for some time and chose not to financially support or formally recognize many local rock musicians. They considered rock to be "music of the enemy," a style compromised by its associations with consumer capitalism and related values. Nevertheless, some recent authors such as Humberto Manduley have documented the extensive rock scene that existed in Havana and elsewhere as early as the 1950s.[7] Many Nueva Trova artists began their performance careers as members of rock bands and continued to perform and listen to rock'n'roll despite its marginal status. They used the official acceptance of the Nueva Trova movement in the mid-1970s to develop an artistic forum for themselves, incorporating influences from rock and folk-rock into their compositions. Other groups, such as Los Kent, Los Dada, Nueva Generación, Sonido X, Arte Vivo, and Metal Oscuro, continued to play "pure" rock informally in the capital; these groups were direct antecedents to music performed by Varela and others a decade later. Even well-known dance band musicians like Juan Formell and Los Van Van began their careers playing rock-inspired work.

Support for rock began to increase in the mid-1980s, and performers found more opportunities to take to the stage in formal, state-sponsored contexts. Various factors contributed to this, including the widespread appeal of rock music internationally, its popularization throughout Latin America, a degree of rapprochement between Cuban and US officials under the Carter administration, and ongoing social and cultural reforms in Cuba that began to liberalize the musical environment and led to its diversification. Carlos Varela was one of several influential artists who took advantage of new performance opportunities, catering to the strong desire for rock music among younger Cubans, who until that time had often been denied access to it. As Robert Nasatir has explored in this book, Varela's career received a strong boost from Silvio Rodríguez, by then an established figure with strong revolutionary credentials, who invited him to share the stage during national and international events in the late 1980s. This led to increased recognition for Varela, and by 1990 he had emerged as one of the most influential artists of the period.

Xenia Reloba de la Cruz has written here about the unique qualities of Cuban cultural production during Cuba's Special Period of the early to mid-1990s.[8] The collapse of the Soviet Union and the loss of Cuba's special economic relationship with the Eastern Bloc resulted in widespread economic hardship and led Cubans to question whether the socialist revolution was succeeding. Cubans, for the first time in decades, witnessed the arrival of relatives and foreign tourists from capitalist countries who enjoyed a standard of living far superior to their own. This contradicted official state discourse about the decadence and slow decline of capitalism. The tensions of the Special Period imbued the music of those years with a certain edginess, sarcasm, and irreverence that implicitly or explicitly challenged socialist doctrine. Also, many musicians began to discuss formerly taboo subjects through their lyrics, thus creating a space for commentary outside the state-controlled media.

Carlos Varela's music exemplifies all of this. His were among the first state-sponsored events to embrace showmanship and theatrics and thus to reject the notion of the performer as conceived by most Nueva Trova figures of an earlier generation. His wholesale adoption of foreign rock and pop styles also generated controversy, as he was perhaps the first nationally recognized artist to do so. And in a lyrical sense, Varela's music constantly referred to the social ills and ideological dissonance of 1990s Cuba. His music became a "chronicle of the people," documenting increasing street violence ("Cuchilla en la acera"), the excesses and ironies of the new tourist economy ("Tropicollage"), generational tensions in political ideology ("Guillermo Tell"), state censorship and control ("Como me hicieron a mí), and the pain of separation caused by exiled family members ("Foto de familia"), as well as loneliness, depression, and countless other quasi-forbidden subjects. In the first half of the 1990s, he became a musical sensation among Havana's youth, which led to close supervision of his concerts by the police.

Varela lost some of his public profile in the later 1990s, partly because he had had to reorganize his band. His musical director and principal arranger, Elio Villafranca, had left for the United States, and this caused logistical problems in terms of live performances, the development of new material, and so on. But since 2004 he has resurfaced with a series of new CDs and high-profile international tours, including of the United States. He has also collaborated on film scores and other projects. Varela is now as much an international artist as a Cuban one.

Since the early years of Varela's popularity, two other important genres of protest song have developed in Cuba. The first, *timba*, is a highly percussive dance music that fuses the traditional rhythms of *son* and *salsa* with elements of funk, rap, and jazz as well as Afro-Cuban drumming and song. *Timba* emerged together with the rise in foreign tourism in the early 1990s; it came to be associated with venues frequented by foreigners and with hedonism and excess (reflected in the lyrics of many songs) that flew in the face of socialist dogma. *Timba's* catchy choruses, sexually suggestive dance moves, and embrace of material pleasure presented unique challenges to Cuba's cultural establishment. Songs such as "El temba" (roughly, "Sugar Daddy") became emblematic of changing social and cultural realities as the island re-engaged with its capitalist neighbours.

The Cuban *rap consciente* movement gained momentum slightly later, in the mid-1990s, and peaked in popularity about 2003. As with *timba*, most *rap* performers were black or of mixed race. Even more than *timba*, rap lyrics reflected themes that were directly pertinent to the Afro-Cuban community. Even though they had appropriated a foreign style in the same way as rock performers, Cuban rappers quickly secured state support for their activities. In part, this reflected the attitude of a new and more liberal Culture Minister, Abel Prieto; it also reflected a more tolerant attitude towards foreign culture in recent years, and the fact that *rap consciente* performers more consistently identified with socialist ideals. The few CD releases of *rap consciente* that are available demonstrate serious engagement with issues such as racism, discrimination, and prostitution; they also promote Afro-Cuban religion and related expressions, denounce sexism, and address other social concerns.⁹

Despite a recent decline in political song on a national level, and greater interest in the promotion of music with broad commercial appeal – as Geoffrey Baker has recently observed in his study on *reggaeton* – it is safe to assume that the history of Cuban political song is far from finished and that countless new topics and new forms of expression remain to be developed.¹⁰ As a musician with an established record of social engagement, and one with increasing international connections and financial autonomy, Carlos Varela will undoubtedly continue to play a key role in Cuba's political songinto the future.

NOTES

1 Robin Moore, *Music and Revolution: Cultural Change in Socialist Cuba* (Berkeley: University of California Press, 2006).
2 Margarita Mateo Palmer, *Del bardo que te canta* (La Habana: Letras Cubanas, 1988); Carmela de León, *Sindo Garay: Memorias de un trovador* (La Habana: Letras Cubanas, 1990).
3 Eliseo Grenet, n.d. "Lamento cubano," Esther Borja con la Orquesta Numidia y Luis Carbonell, CBMF radio station recording #E636.
4 Miguel Matamoros, "Bomba lacrimosa," 78 RPM LP, Victor 46691-B, 1928. See also Ezequiel Rodríguez Domínguez, *Trío Matamoros: treinta y cinco años de música popular* (La Habana: Arte y Literatura, 1978).
5 Jorge Mañach, *Indagación del choteo* (La Habana: La Verónica, 1940).
6 See Bobby Collazo, *La última noche que pasé contigo. 40 años de la farándula cubana* (San Juan, Puerto Rico: Editorial Cubanacán, 1987); Cristóbal Díaz Ayala, *Del areyto al rap cubano*, 4th ed. (San Juan, Puerto Rico: Fundación Musicalia, 2003).
7 Humberto Manduley, *El Rock en Cuba* (Bogotá: Atril Ediciones Musicales, 2001).
8 See also Ariana Hernández Reguant, ed., *Cuba in the Special Period: Culture and Ideology in the 1990s* (New York: Palgrave Macmillan, 2009).
9 Ariel Fernández and Pablo Herrera, prod. *The Cuban Hip Hop All-Stars*, vol. 1 (Madrid: Papaya Records, 2001).
10 Geoffrey Baker, *Buena Vista in the Club: Rap, Reggaetón, and Revolution in Havana* (Durham, NC: Duke University Press, 2011).

Epilogue

Carlos Varela: A Cuban Who Knows the Past but Can Also See the Future

PAUL WEBSTER HARE

Carlos Varela has been a wind that blows through Cuban fields of rice. But in the opposite direction.

Varela sings the story of the Revolution: the death of Che in 1967, the ten million ton sugar harvest of 1970. His Cuba went to war in Africa, where he lost friends. His songs centre on his experiences over time, and he has seen all the phases of the Revolution. He knew of Christmas trees and Christmas toys, but, as he sings, he never had them. His television was Russian, he listened secretly to the Beatles. Like so many Cubans, his friends Lucas and Lucia left for a country where the "cielo" stops and it becomes the "sky." He hasn't been the only Cuban to satirize aspects of the Revolution and speak his mind. But Varela's music tells the unvarnished story of his life, and the lives of eleven million Cubans. His music is the conduit for truth, rejecting the silence of conformity. As he sings in "Todo será distinto" (Everything Will Be Different), "We pass our time looking only at the past / without realizing what we have silenced."

To non-Cubans, Carlos comes as a surprise. I lived in Cuba from 2001 to 2004 as the British Ambassador. When I first encountered Varela, I could not believe his audacity. How can this be? A man who lives in Cuba but who behaves with no preordained conformity. Aren't Cubans afraid, brainwashed even? Don't they avoid expressing their inner pain and soul in public? Cubans who have stayed, not fled to the North and become Miamized, must be of a different mindset. So Varela poses challenges for the foreign observer as well as the Cuban fan. That is his gift and that is his fascination. Varela keeps Cuban individuality alive. He has shown through his talent that he will be listened to, that he cannot be jailed, merely frozen. As he sings, he's neither a child nor an old man, he represents neither peace nor war. In the Cuban–US stand-off, this refusal of simplistic, opposing positions means a great deal.

One pledge Carlos Varela made and kept is that he would never leave. So the 15 per cent of the Cuban nation living "fuera" know what he means as well. He has seen so many come and go: some whose political fame has been fleeting, some whose artistic reputation was short-lived. Every Cuban, whether in Cienfuegos, Fort Lauderdale, New Jersey, or Madrid, knows what he is saying. Born in 1963, Carlos is the ideal age for a Cuba in transition, because he is a Cuban with a past but also a future. He will continue observing the Cuban revolution as a curious, compassionate, and independent observer.

Carlos was born a child of the Revolution who lived as a teenager through years when Cubans seemed to have made their system work. Cuba gave him the education, in the beautiful setting of the ISA, the old country club golf course of Havana. The largesse of the 1980s gave Cubans a lot, more than they could have imagined, thanks to Fidel Castro's deal with the Soviet Union, which bankrolled the system. Carlos did not grow up in deprivation, but things were happening that he disapproved of. Cuba had gone overseas to war. It was a troubling time for youth yearning for freedom of expression. Varela studied at a state school that groomed talent in the dangerously rebellious world of the arts. And the school nurtured in Carlos the knowledge that there was a world beyond Cuba – just listen to The Beatles. Cuba could teach the world something, but Cuba had to learn and listen as well.

What of the man who created the Cuba into which Carlos was born? Insurgent, orator, a politician who made his own party and called it communist, Fidel Castro has always been an intellectual, and he likes to be seen as one. He is a rare combination – a populist intellectual. He likes ideas, statistics, and books, but also sport, and we know that he and Carlos share a liking for at least one song – "Imagine" by John Lennon. Fidel Castro is complicated, and the Cuba he has built is complicated: a mosaic of mass mobilization, a culture that placed the collective ahead of personal material motivations and attempted to impose uniformity in education and political activity. Uniformity brought education and health care, national pride, baseball, and the arts, all for free. And if you did not like the system, the choice was simple: leave, or keep your mouth shut.

But Fidel Castro has always known that it is not possible to create a false unanimity (his brother Raul's phrase). Art soon seeps out of the container. It refuses to be compartmentalized. Varela and the street comedians, Varela and those who throw themselves to the mercy of the sea and wind on rafts, Varela and today's bloggers: they are representatives of a centuries-old tradition. Ideas abhor boundaries and walls. So the Cuban leadership had a problem. How do you allow the young and talented to comment on serious issues of politics? Conformity could not extinguish the search for invention, originality, melodies, and poetry. For like politics, music must go beyond what is in the sugar bowl. You educate your country, teaching high ideals of socialism and service overseas. But then you are invited to agree with those who – like William Tell – fire arrows at your head. How many phrases from thousands of hours of political speeches are remembered by Cubans? How might this compare to the memories Cubans hold of lines from Carlos's beloved songs?

How do we explain that, in a culture that praises those who wield power, Carlos Varela found success? How do we explain this particularly when the heavily circumscribed media choose which of his music is acceptable to broadcast? How many Cuban media gatekeepers were themselves listening to Varela's music, just as he sings of Cuban parents in the 1960s listening to banned Beatles music in private parties at home? *La doble moral?* Beyond this, is there a political or sociological phenomenon in Varela's music that will impact the transition in Cuba? Did his music sow seeds that predicted – as he does in his songs – that some day "the fog will lift" and tomorrow "there will be sun." Or are the words that Varela writes, as Lennon said of "Imagine," "just bloody songs!"? Did the Cuban government ever "approve" of Carlos, or did it acquiesce to a popularity that developed in a country that values creativity, even it if prefers to use art for political purposes? For Varela is indeed a contrarian, but one whose songs cannot be silenced. Pragmatism is also a hallmark of politicians, even Fidel Castro.

Cuban arts and music have lived on the razor's edge. Varela's career has been unique; his artistic standing and popular reputation are exceptional. Younger and more appealing than the driven revolutionary Silvio Rodríguez, Carlos has mapped a course that he alone has determined. Perhaps more than any other popular Cuban artist, Carlos has asked the questions, not imposed the answers.

Varela sees politics as an intrusion on the individual, as demanding that the individual submit to mass movements and slogans. Like fish, people are driven to leave the country. They don't speak. Like fish, they just look into each other's eyes. For Varela, the smallest "little dreams" are what the individual wants. People want to feel that their actions and words mean something and that an individual can do and say what he or she feels. Varela does not lecture or disapprove, he observes and comments. He observes the neighbourhoods of Havana, and he also chronicles the Cuban nation, its wider community. He asks Cubans on and off the island: Are we all still Cubans? Do we prefer to look to the North rather than to the songs of Silvio? Do Cubans read the books on Marxism or do they wear a cross around their necks? Perhaps Varela sees some value in prayer. His songs contain plenty of references to it. His faith and his soul are strong. Does this account for his optimism, his irony, his humour? His concerts are joyous, laconic, and fearless. My religion is not of the altar, he sings, but after all, we are all a mix of Christ and Lucifer.

My first Carlos Varela concert was at the Karl Marx theatre in Havana in 2003. Why would a British diplomat take his family to hear someone whose songs were still largely unknown in Europe? Cubans I knew talked to me about the importance of Varela's concert, not just as a musical experience but as a weathervane of popular feelings about the government. At a Varela concert one would see what Cubans really thought, they told me. Sure enough, the streets were teeming with people and police. Security vans were parked down side streets and were prominent at the massive Karl Marx theatre, the biggest indoor venue in Cuba.

Our seats were high up, so we had a panoramic view. The audience was the twenty- and thirty-somethings of modern Cuba. The tickets had sold out within minutes. The show was spectacular, with dramatic lighting and great sound quality. It was clear that this crowd had not come to hear new music. They knew every word Varela played, and they knew what to wait for in the songs. Varela has given his fans a career's worth of such inspiring performances. But beyond this, he has displayed, in his music and his life, a wish to fulfil a higher calling. The emotion evident in his music and his voice suggest he believes he has a duty to do more than make a living at music.

Perhaps Varela's largest audience in Cuba was at the massive Peace Concert in Havana in 2009, spearheaded by the popular Colombian singer Juanes. I was not in Havana for this event, but I suspect Carlos was uncomfortable in what was a formal, large-scale setting, with a million people expecting a significant political event. Juanes had asked everyone – performers and the audience – to wear white to symbolize peace. Varela – ever the rebel – wore his customary black. He saw the value of art promoting peace, but he performed on his own terms. Cubans don't always conform.

Many in this anthology have described what Varela means to Cubans, but what does his music say to the overseas listener? Does he have a message for outsiders? There is a lot to learn about Cuba from his songs, including that Elpidio Valdés was the Superman whom Cuban children grew up with. But beyond such specifics of "Cubanidad," Varela sings of universalities: of beauty, of the individual, and of the mysteries and mixtures of real life, which is never so one-dimensional as politicians like to imagine. Varela's insights into Cuban daily life are also universals, despite their Cuban particularities. He sings of the tears of the mothers whose sons have swum away. He explains that Cubans are a mixture of those who have bad days but good nights, who read Marxism but wear a cross. He opens doors rather that builds walls. He does not pretend to be a builder of a fully alternative house; rather, he points out the nonsensical elements he sees in Cuba and in Cuba's opponents.

Varela has helped raise the reputation of Cuban popular music, which is often understood in stereotypical terms, because so much that has been approved or is marketed for tourists is dross – repetitive and unthinking. The official representatives of the artificial Cuba make a living but taint a reputation. Varela believes in talent. He has worked with some of the best musicians, and his musical repertoire is crammed with invention, experimentation, and variety. He has also remained loyal to his fans in the best way possible. He travels the length and breadth of Cuba to give largely free concerts.

So where does he stand in the evolution of modern, post-revolutionary Cuba? Do we know what he thinks, whom he supports? Does he want capitalism? Does he want a Western-style democracy? Why do we want to label him? Does he have a conclusion? Varela often laments the obvious: that it's not clear in Cuba who are the winner or losers. But then we have the song perhaps deliberately placed last on his most recent album: "El viejo sueño acabo." The old dream is over. Has he concluded that a collective project imposed too much on the individual? Yet I doubt whether he sees a balance sheet of life in modern Cuba. Like many Cubans, he has faced complex challenges; also like many, he has applied ingenious solutions to survive. Perhaps his most important legacy for Cubans is that he has ensured that "change" in Cuba means something more profound than cellphones and access to the Internet. Change is for the individuals of Cuba to reassert themselves, those who gave their hearts and their hopes to what was happening but have been, for so long, the backdrop to the Cuban drama rather than the actors on the stage.

Our second contact after the Karl Marx concert was when I invited Carlos to play at our embassy party. "Just come along with your guitar for few songs," I said to him. He did not know me, and perhaps he assumed we would make polite conversation in very British Spanish. He may have thought I just wanted to fill out a routine party. So why would he bother to come to make our party better? But the reply I received from him was warm and generous. Of course he would play, and he brought his full band. They all came, refusing all payment, and rehearsed for at least four hours.

We became friends. Carlos got to know my family, the embassy staff, our cats. This is just one example of how Carlos has used his music to reach out to many outside Cuba. He has taken his guitar to the US Congress. I suspect that Carlos sees most politicians as self-serving, as creating an agenda for their own ends. But they too can be talked to, sung to. Perhaps someone will be listening. He regularly meets with American schoolchildren visiting Cuba. On a recent concert tour in the United States, he played at a famous music club in Boston. Early in the morning, despite a brutal travel schedule and a heavy cold, he had gone to a local middle school in Marblehead to sing for them. The weather was cool and drizzly, and he could have pleaded artistic license. He could have gone just to show up, but he went and he played, and invited the kids to sing with him. He built a bond – their "tio cubano." And so in the evening concert, in front of a packed audience, he took a risk that few artists would: he showed on stage that a Cuban musician could perform with a group of American middle school kids. He had built a real life bridge, an unforgettable memory for these children, all of whom knew his songs as part of their Spanish class. In that moment he showed how music can connect. As he told the audience with obvious contentment: "Tonight we have done more than all the politicians have managed over a long time."

Carlos regularly builds such bridges. He has been the engineer without steel, the carpenter without wood, the politician without a party. The bridges he builds are still standing, and one day Cubans will walk across them. And they will be grateful that over all these years, people like Varela were imagining the future of Cuba. As a grateful Cuban member of our embassy staff wrote to me after his concert in our garden: "I am so happy Carlos Varela played at the embassy. He has been the voice of our generation."

Beginning a New Cuban Dream: An Interview with Carlos Varela[1]

MARIA CARIDAD CUMANÁ
AND KAREN DUBINSKY

This interview took place over several meetings, beginning at Varela's house in Havana in May 2010 and continuing, episodically, after that. At our first session, Varela had just returned from a multi-city US tour; his guitars lay unpacked in the living room. Fuelled by coffee and blockade-breaking imported Splenda, we settled into a long conversation about songwriting, censorship, the death of old dreams, and the beginning of new ones.

Q: You are a Cuban singer, with a loyal national audience, and your songs speak of Cuban realities. Your songs are full of *Cubanismos*. Who else but a Cuban would sing about "la soledad de una gasolinera" (the loneliness of a gas station) or "diecisiete instancias de una primavera" (the title of a Soviet soap opera popular on Cuban TV in the 1970s). But you have an international audience as well. So we wonder, for whom do you write and sing, and how has this changed since you began?

CV: I started like all young composers in Cuba: I was fourteen when I went to the Chaplin Theatre to a concert of Silvio (Rodríguez) and Pablo (Milanés). Of course I couldn't understand all the poetic dimensions of their songs. But I felt profound electricity, a strong connection. And, immediately, like many composers of my generation, I tried to follow the work of Silvio and Pablo; I tried to write like them. A mistake, typical of adolescents. The first songs I tried to write, at the end of the 1970s, with my brother Victor, were like a game, trying to be like Silvio and Pablo. I knew Silvio's songs better than he did.

In the 1980s I was a part of the movement of *Nueva Trova* singers. This movement organized big concerts in factories and schools. It also organized meetings between poets and *trovadores*, we held debates about the songs. It was a beautiful time, especially when you were convinced, when you were certain about things. In 1984, I met Silvio in the *Casa de Joven Creadores*. I sang something, I don't remember what. And Silvio asked, who is that? I lived two blocks from him, on Calle 23. He invited me to the Pizzeria at 23 and 12, an interesting place that formed a part of my childhood and my adolescence. And there we spoke all night. He said, "I'm happy I have had such an influence on you." But he also said, "Try, in every way, to make your songs tell your own story. Tell stories of your friends, your neighbourhood. Use your own vision."

At the time I was a theatre student. But I had studied two years at *CUJAE* (Polytechnical University – Cuidad Universitario José Antonio Echeverría), from 1980 to 1982. My father, who was from Galicia, said, *por sus*,[2] that his son had to be an engineer like him. When he died in 1982, I started to study theatre, and that opened me completely. I did theatre in high school. I used to be a good actor. But I started to study theatre at ISA (Instituto Superior del Arte) in order to gain more insight, and more tools, into how to tell my story, my own vision of reality. I wanted to learn how to tell a story that really moves you.

So the game – copying Silvio and Pablo - became more serious. I was at ISA with actors, musicians, theatre students, writers. We developed a type of friendly competition: "Why didn't you read that, why didn't you see that film?" And then you start to fill all your songs with this; my songs became a kind of vessel for all these influences, from literature, film, painting. In this sense, ISA was very important. Because it had in its hand all my generation, doing super-important things. I remember that the first *peña* I went to was at the Hubert Blank Theatre in Vedado, others were at the Hotel Nacional.[3]

No one knew me, but my songs became distinguished for their sense of urban poetry. Silvio and Pablo came to Havana from the country; I grew up in Havana. My "Cubanidad" is far from the guy in the *guayabera* with a cigar. My songs are deeply embedded in the reality that I live. In my songs you don't see nature, you see asphalt and gasoline. I actually lived above a gas station. I had the constant noise of Calle 23. So I started writing songs like "Apenas Abro los Ojos":

> Todo el silencio se va
> y con el desayuno me trago
> el ruido y el humo que viene
> de la cuidad.

> All of the silence goes away,
> with breakfast
> I swallow the noise and the smoke,
> coming from the city.

And everyone said "What?" "How?" "He's crazy, no?" I started talking about all the billboards and the signage in the city, I started using urban elements. At that time I saw a film at the Havana Film Festival that blew my mind: *Ciertas Palabras con Chico Buarque*. I adored it. People always talk about the influence of Bob Dylan, Silvio, Pablo, Joan Serrat, Joaquín Sabina on my work, but no one has mentioned the real influence of Chico Buarque, especially around urban themes. Songs like "Construction." Wow. This awoke all my creative energy.[4]

I wrote a song, which I didn't sing much, called "La Calle." This is where I really began thinking about urban themes. It has a peculiar harmony. This type of work attracted the attention of lots of my colleagues, people from my generation, Santiago Feliju, Gerardo Alfonso, Alberto Tosca. This made me realize I was creating something new, I was swimming in other seas:

> La calle esta lleno del edificios
> muy bonito
> que tienen antenas
> que son buenas
> para que vengan las pájaros
>
> The street is full
> Of beautiful buildings
> That have antennas
> Which are great
> For when birds come

See, it's all theatrical irony:

> La calle esta lleno del edificios
> muy bonito
> para los pececitos
> La calle esta llena de colillas de cigarros
> La calle esta llena de extremistas
> Y mi apartamento

Todo centro
Se van los detalles de la calle
Se van inundando en un instante
La calle esta llena de tragantes
Menos mal

The street is full
Of buildings which are beautiful
For little fish
The street is full of cigarette butts
The street is full of extremists
And my apartment
In the middle of everything
The details of the street go away
Everything washes away in an instant
The street is full of drains
Thankfully

It's very theatrical. I started to realize the influence of theatre, not just in my self-presentation, but also in my thoughts, my peculiar dress, it's a unique style. I care about the lights, I care about how each musician dresses, I care about the staging of the concert, how is the opening, the order of each song, the tone, the importance of the staging within each song. It is all "how do I tell my story."

Q: You have so many unrecorded songs; how do you choose what to record?

CV: Oh, it's a mystery. Because there are always people very close by who say to you, why not that one? I want my discs to have a dramatic coherence, from song to song. It's not about a group of songs, it's about the coherence between them. I don't want to include a song just because my friends or I think it's good. I want coherence; I want unity, like a work of art.

I come from the generation of vinyl. All the drama that you try to create in a performance, you also put on the disc; the opening, the development, the finale. We still do this, but now that people listen to your music on MP3s or the Internet, it's a great democratic chaos! People decide to play the third song, or the fifth, or the ninth. The other day, I was reading something interesting about Pink Floyd; they don't permit their music on the Internet, not for any reason, because people don't listen to music in the manner that they recorded it.

To return to your initial question: without realizing it, my songwriting began to get tangled up in everything, everything that happens to you, personal things too like love, lovelessness, illusion, disillusionment, what I see, what I hear, what I talk about ... The years pass, and one has a series of experiences that are definitely a good part of all of these songs. Grief, longing, and irreverence are in my songs because they are in my life, my history, and the history of my country.

Q: Your work is full of historical themes and images; with a few phrases you can evoke some of the most complicated experiences of Cuban history. Some of your classic songs, such as "Jalisco Park," or "Memorias," read like poetic history texts. Why is history so important to you?

CV: I don't think I recount the entire history of Cuba through my songs, but I think I do tell a good part of the history of my generation. Take "Jalisco Park," for example. This attracted my attention because I spent my childhood in Jalisco Park, it's my neighbourhood. And then, later, I saw the park completely abandoned. I was always walking around 23rd Street, to school and back. I used to pass by Jalisco Park, full of metal, full of leaves, all the playground equipment was tipping over. And I said, some day I have to write about the loneliness of this park. But I didn't want to make a simple song that says "poor little park all alone." Rather, I tried to use the park to talk about other elements, to talk about, for example, how my friends were taken away from Cuba by their parents. You know all the history Jalisco Park tells, it's about *Patria Potestad* and Peter Pan, it's about the influence of Che, and the influence of Silvio. In "Jalisco Park" I began to use an element that I had never used before in a song, which is to take a whole sentence from Silvio's work. From then on, I began to wink ... In almost all of my discs, I wink at Silvio. It's a poetic wink, I use a phrase of his, or I use a bit of his music, until one day Silvio said, "leave me alone." (laughs)

With the song "Jalisco Park," something really interesting happened. It created a lot of debate, then. At the beginning of the 1990s, they fixed the park. After that both Juan Formell – who for me was also a great storyteller of Cuban realities through popular music – and Silvio, both said to me in different ways, "I knew that songs can touch the heart, and transform the person. But I didn't know that songs could transform space, a park ... That park should have a plaque." And to me, fixing the park seemed a beautiful homage, but it was complicated. Because from this moment, many people ... You know in Cuba that many people feel they have the right to touch you, it's great because you always keep your feet on the ground. People are always commenting about your work, about a song they have listened to. After they fixed Jalisco Park, people immediately started to ask me, why don't I write a song about certain other places that people want to change. And I'd say, I'm not a magician. I'm only a poet, but I am trying.

Q: Can you speak more about your experiences and inspirations for songwriting in the early years?

CV: In 1986, Silvio came to ISA and said to me, "You are going to come with me next week to Spain," and I said, "Wow, no university teaches this experience." To come out and sing for thousands and thousands of people, who weren't from my country, this experience made me grow up, inevitably. From then on, quickly, between 1986 to 1988 I began to write a series of songs, which came out in *Jalisco Park*, my first disc, in 1989. I played these songs a lot, in concerts, in 1988, at the theatre at Calle 23 and 12. But how it is possible that they were never played on TV or on the radio, even though the theatres were overflowing with people, so many people that the police and the security systems of the city were worried.[5] This helped to create myths about my work. These were turbulent years in Cuba; many people began to invent, to see ghosts in many of these songs. Many artists felt they had no other option but to leave their country. Because you don't feel like you left Cuba, but that Cuba left you. I think that 90 per cent of the people who went to my concerts in those years have left Cuba. I meet many of them now, when I travel.

But what I was holding on to was that I was writing more and more songs. I was possessed, I couldn't stop writing songs. It was my therapy. I learned to have patience – there are songs that end in one month, or one year. There are songs that never end. There are songs that emerge in hotels, in airplanes, that emerge in happiness, or in loneliness. And so I was kind of a sponge, always reconverting, recycling everything that I heard and felt and saw.

I continue to defend the job of songwriting. To join, magically, poetry and music, it's really a blessing. And you begin to feel a very serious responsibility. On stage, you can feel the breathing of each one of the spectators, you can feel the vibration of each of the phrases. When you feel that people need to listen to these songs, at least for that night, to take one home with them, to make love with it, or be angry with it, understand it, it's truly a blessing and a responsibility.

Q: There's a quote from a recent newspaper article about you that seems to sum up your own place in Cuban history: "In those turbulent years, Carlos Varela dared to say what we all knew, but weren't accustomed to hearing."[6] People seem to trust you, in a place where political leadership is complicated. You are a poet, not a politician, but do you think people look to you for inspiration?

CV: It's interesting, because in many ways Cuba is completely different from other countries. You know in Cuba we don't use the system of promoting discs with videos. There are some who do this but it doesn't go anywhere. In Cuba, at least for my generation, we grew up with such a thirst for information from literature, film, and music. All of this stirred a generation of youth absolutely more awake, in the best sense of the word. Art is the common denominator of my generation.

In my concerts many people are waiting for the classics. They are accustomed to concerts where I come to sing the classics; I know that if I sing the classics, they will sing with me. So I sing some of the more or less popular ones, but I try to insert some completely new ones. What happens is a kind of catharsis between the audience and me. Sometimes people have a perspective on my work that is a bit frightening. I always say don't make a statue of me. Don't make a statue of anyone. Actually I wrote a song that is called "the statue maker."

In my concerts we don't have time to sing about silly things. And so you can feel a type of connection that is almost religious. When I play "Foto de familia," for example, I can hear the tears. Every night, and in every space, not just in Cuba.

The silences are almost as important as the sounds. It's a subtle act of communication, theatrical, religious, inspiring for everyone, the audience and me too. It's not me that inspires them, I am inspired also. Every song has a different feeling every time. It has been beautiful to see that, with the years, the people who come to listen, they aren't only from my generation, but much younger. This gives you the feeling that this country is still alive.

Q: What's it like performing for the Cuban diaspora? Your songs seem to provide a bridge between Cubans everywhere. There is a good observation the writer Wendy Guerra made about your work; she spoke about the "huge numbers of people who kill their problems and their homesickness" with your songs.[7]

CV: I think Cubans outside Cuba find (or at least maybe they do) a little piece of their neighbourhood, their family, a piece of their history. When I see that I say, "Wow, I had no idea that this reached like that." I mean, it's only a song.

We have received thousands and thousands of letters, from people who use the songs as a talisman, for example, a young man who crossed the ninety miles on a raft, who wrote me a letter and told me, "I only brought water, bread, a compass, and your discs. And I got there." I thought, "Wow." I mean, this gives my work another meaning. Sure, everyone creates the talisman they want. What I could say to you now is that I didn't conceive the songs to have all this meaning, all this significance for many people.

I just returned from the United States, after twelve years without being able to sing there. And the concert, especially in Miami, was practically the same concert it would be in Havana. It was the same experience of communication, of catharsis, many people crying, many people laughing, yelling ... I mean, among Cubans, wherever they are, there is so much accumulated fury, there is so much disillusionment, and there is so much love, that maybe many of these songs wake up all these feelings.

When you say that for many people my songs can be an inspiration, what I know is there is a great expectation about what my songs mean. I always say my role has been to break the myths on both sides. But there are many admirers and many detractors. Many in Miami. Welcome to the real world, right?

When I started writing songs in the era of the 1980s and the beginning of the 1990s, my first songs had a strongly photographic sense of reality. With the years, I began to come and go, to leave Cuba, and that gave me a deeper vision of reality. And that inevitably is noted in one's poetic vision. For example, a song, like one I wrote in 1988, "Tropicollage," it's very Chico Buarque, it's a collage of photos: the Hotel Havana Libre, money changing. There was an urban sensibility in the poetry, but it's very photographic. With the years, I discovered and prefer songs like "Graffiti de Amor." It can be sung in Kingston, Ontario, and Havana and New York. I mean, the song continues to connect, even though it's born from a specific reality. As Tagore says, "If you know the people who live in your village, you know the world." I have dedicated myself to knowing my village, but now I am interested in writing with a deeper poetic sense.

Recently in Miami, a journalist said to me, "What happened to you? Because at the beginning you were singing 'Guillermo Tell' and 'Memorias.' But now" – and he said it in this tone, you know? – "at the Revolution Square, at the Juanes concert, you sang

'Colgando del cielo.'" And I said, "My love, if you think that song doesn't have value for you, I'm sorry. But to me, it seems marvellous to do a song like 'Colgando del cielo,' in Revolution Square." I mean:

> He visto al bien con los ojos del mal
> Como un ciego
> feliz en la oscuridad
> Nena no se lo que va a pasar
> Si la mentira se disfraza como la verdad
>
> I have seen good things with bad eyes
> Like a blind person,
> happy in the darkness
> Baby I don't know what will happen
> If lies dress up as the truth

And I sang it together with "25 mil mentiras sobre la verdad." "The truth about the truth is that / there never is just one. / Not mine, not his, not yours." At Revolution Square!

Q: Your work has been discovered by Hollywood, how did that happen?

CV: When I recorded *Como los Peces* in Spain, in 1994, the musicians made so much money they stayed. All of them. Without telling me. I entered such a deep depression. They were my brothers, and we had plans. I thought, fuck, I'm a victim too. But I'm not a state, I'm not a government. I was super depressed, because I'd created this band, we had worked together for many years, and they stayed. For me it was such a blow.

When I returned, Silvio called me, and he said, "You always told me that your favorite disc of mine was *Mujeres,* an acoustic guitar disc. It's your moment to record that kind of disc." I thought, "You're crazy, who the fuck is interested in that?" But I went to Pablo Milanés's studio, and I recorded *Nubes*. I thought no one would be interested in that disc. That disc included 'Una palabra.'"

I was still very depressed, and Silvio said, "You have to understand that discs, and songs, are like children. Let them grow up, give them their time." But with *Nubes,* immediately people in the music industry said, "How can you do this? After you have done songs like 'Muros y puertos,' and 'Como los peces,' you make a little disc with one little guitar?"

Anyway, time passed, and I got another band and I recorded *Siete*. And then, all of a sudden, Alejandro González used "Una palabra" in the short film *Powder Keg*, and then Tony Scott used "Una palabra" in *Man on Fire* and it all blew up. It's my most recorded song; there is a Polish version, Hungarian, Russian, Portuguese ... All the music companies began to call to ask for *Nubes*.

Q: But how did they know about it? How does a Cuban *trova* singer get to Hollywood?

CV: Oh, that's easy. Because Alejandro González was in Cuba in 2001, when his film *Amores perros* was nominated for an Oscar. I had recorded *Nubes* in 2000, and I gave it to him when he was here. And later he called me, and he said, "I love all your songs, my brother, you are the Bob Dylan of Latin America. Some day, we are going to work together." And I said, "Good luck with the Oscar." And I'm watching the Oscars, and of course, *Amores perros* didn't win. And that night he called me and he said, "I'm calling you because I won." I said, "I don't understand." He said, "Brother, I didn't win the little statue." But that night Jack Nicholson took Alejandro to his house after the Oscar ceremony, and they had a meeting with different filmmakers. Tony Scott and Guy Ritchie were there. And this is where the BMW project came from: everyone was going to make a short film. And Alejandro González decided to make *Powder Keg*, a film about a war photographer, and he used "Una palabra" at the end. When they were shooting it, he called me again and said, "Everyone is asking me who fuck is that with the little voice at the end." Then shortly after that Tony Scott wanted it for *Man on Fire*. Apparently he said, "Go to the end of the earth to find the guy that wrote that song." And so this created a great promotion – look what happened with *Nubes*, everyone wanted it, it became the best-selling disc. So mine hasn't been a speedy career, but it has been interesting.

Q: What do you think about the Cuban music scene today, especially the significance of hip hop? Everyone in Cuba – at least the young ones – seems to be listening to Los Aldeanos these days. We read a while ago in *La Ventana* that someone called you "like Los Aldeanos with a guitar." What's your response to that?[8]

CV: Wow. I like Los Aldeanos. I have listened to a lot of their music, everything that is circulating, I mean by MP3, and the videos. And it seems to me absolutely unjust what has been happening to them.[9] Hip hop music of course feeds urban energy, and they have a talent for storytelling. Cuba has a big hip hop movement. Many of them, not Los Aldeanos, imitate what they sell in the US hip hop industry. You know they are more worried about how they dress, or they use codes that belong to the US. But Los Aldeanos, it seems to me they are interesting. In the last few months they have been working with new instruments, including some of my musicians, my pianist, my drummer, they are incorporating instruments, not just machines or techno music.

There is a big hip hop movement developing in Cuba, including *reggaeton*. It's a great step, kids from marginal neighbourhoods who go out to the street and make poetic rhymes. Not all have something to say – truly, there are some who write silly things. But Los Aldeanos, they are really interesting. Because especially Aldo, more than El B, he has an explosive chemistry when he's writing his vision of reality. It's really bad that they haven't been allowed to leave Cuba. Because I think … First of all, that's a fundamental right we all have, as citizens of Cuba and as musicians. They have been invited to rap festivals in other countries, I hope they can go. I think their music, and their vision of Cuba, will deepen if they are allowed to see it from outside. Here they face so much aggression, so much censorship, so much misunderstanding. It makes them lose their focus. And to concentrate only on this dispute, between them and the censors, it's an absolutely stupid dispute. I hope they don't lose. I admire them, and I would like to meet them some day.

I'd like to see them reconvert all the spirit and the energy they have, including the experience of marginalization, not only inside but also outside Cuba. We are marginalized by other aspects of the reality we live in, not just censorship. They are constantly being hit, so they are going to concentrate on this blow, on this whip.

It seems to me that people are always looking for a label, to try to locate or pin down your work. I don't think the label "Los Aldeanos with a guitar" is a good analogy to describe my work. But I have faith that these *muchachos* won't provoke so much anger against themselves. Possibly they have enough talent to broaden themselves, to become more poetically open, like Calle 13 from Puerto Rico, for example. The best thing would be to just leave them alone to develop their career. They deserve it.

If someone says I am Los Aldeanos with a guitar, tomorrow they will say I am Yoani Sanchez with a guitar. Everyone wants to label. But it seems to me that neither Los Aldeanos, nor the blogs of Yoani, nor my songs, are any more critical than the reality in which we are living. Reality is always more critical than any song.

Q: You said in an interview a while ago that you live in the only place in the world where time isn't money.[10] There are many disadvantages to living and creating in Cuba. What are some of the advantages?

CV: Oh yes, there are many. I know songwriters like Joaquín Sabina, or Joan Serrat, who have said, on various occasions, that if they lived in Cuba they would write twenty songs a day. The filmmaker Pedro Almodóvar has said that if he lived in Cuba he'd make a film every month.

I can never say that. Living here, it's like a sort of historical sentence. It's like we are condemned. I mean, when people say, "Oh how beautiful is Havana, leave it as it is, with its deterioration." Everything is falling, but when you see it from outside, well, you aren't speaking about the people who live here. You aren't speaking of the propped-up buildings, which are propping up their own disillusionment. Sure, as postcards, they are beautiful. We've heard for a long time, "Oh, how beautiful is Havana, full of bicycles, it's much healthier, you can breathe." (everyone laughs) "Look at their bodies, everyone looks so healthy." I mean, it's a vision, true, it's beautiful, but, profoundly, it's also a sentence; I don't have other options.

But in terms of music, literature, and film, *wow* ... This country is eternally boiling, I mean, wherever you look. If you have very open eyes, and the sensibility to connect with what's happening, there is incredibly creative energy and motivation. I think there are creative impulses all over the world, but in Cuba there is so much passion and so many contradictions in everything that happens, every day, it's fuel for the creator. You know there is an expression here – you kick a stone and out pops an artist. It's true.

Maybe some day I'll go write in Canada, but the winter ... Truly, I am fucked. I don't know if it's the dead who call me, but there are many parts of my family who are under the ground here, and I feel them, they talk to me. There are also the friends that one has, you know, your environment. What is the homeland? The *patria* could be a flavour, a smell. For me, all these elements become converted into songs.

There are plenty of disadvantages to being a musician here. There are many talented people here who can't make a living, people who don't know how to organize themselves as cultural producers. For example, there isn't a culture of sound. Cubans speak loudly, they put music on loud, they put the television on loud. And so when you play on stage, you play loud. And then you realize ... calm down!

There isn't a culture of disc production either. There are a lot of frauds in this country, and in the ministries ... There are people who are absolutely inexperienced. And so, to put the work of young, talented people in these hands, it is ridiculous. I think that, well, I hope that it might be that things will wake up, that a real recording business will be created. What more or less every musician has done, inside or outside Cuba, they all have their own little business, for recording and promotion, you know, because if you put yourselves in the hands of the Cuban music industry or ministry ...

So sure, here are many disadvantages, but the advantages, for me, are greater from the creative point of view. Because of course also it's not just about what we *have been* living, what's really interesting is what we are *going to* live.

It is certainly an advantage to live in a country where your music means something to people. And there is no formula for musical success, because you sold so many discs. Here it's all the same, it doesn't matter if the disc exists, the people still sing your songs. From the very beginning, I would put out a disc, it would get very little airplay, but thousands of people would come to my concerts and sing along with every word. Historically, the people have copied or pirated music for good reasons.

For me the advantages outweigh the disadvantages because for a long time I haven't lived with the disadvantages. I'm not interested in being on Cuban TV or being in the Cuban press. It doesn't matter to me if they play me on the radio or not. I survive by ignoring them. I don't listen to Cuban radio. When they play me now, occasionally a friend will call to tell me. I say, "Wow, how great, things have changed." Before, in the 1980s, they only played me during dawn or late at night. You know they don't call that censorship – they call it "selection criteria." Often it is just safer for them to play Julio Iglesias.

Q: Tell us more about the economic conditions of musical production in Cuba today. What are the options for musicians starting out today?

CV: Probably 90 per cent of the musicians you know in Cuba, and the painters as well, live on the border. They have their feet in at least two countries. But we chose to live here, with the advantages of creating here. Here in Cuba I have time, nothing more. I don't earn anything from my Cuban concerts. Sure, they pay, but I have to pay the technicians and the musicians, because I am always concerned that my concerts have a high level of organization and logistics.

I have arrived at an agreement with the Cuban music industry to make copies in *moneda nacional* (Cuban pesos). I don't want my discs sold in Cuba for CUCs.[11] However, this becomes another problem, because Cubans are very clever, some of them buy lots of discs in *moneda nacional* and then take them around to hotels to sell to tourists in CUCs. This is a great big chaotic mess that that no one has been able to solve.

It's like the story of the Palacio del Salsa, which was the most important salsa place in Cuba for a while. It was very profitable, made a lot of money, the musicians started to make so much money they didn't want to leave Cuba. Every day they had this popular music show, it was superpowerful. But then this created a conflict – Why did the musicians earn so much money, when the workers in the sugar mills did not? And the musicians said to the authorities, "Well, the problem of the sugar workers is your problem to fix. Me, I'm earning money from tourists, and besides, we are all earning money from tourism."

In Cuba we have this paternalistic mentality that we are all equal. So in art, the artist who does nothing makes the same salary as one who fills stadiums. These are things that people have to change. It's a false equality; we are not all equal, *por favor*. I think it would be great if this state supported some important cultural projects like the national symphony.

I come from a profoundly disillusioned generation of artists, people who have given their lives for their careers. But how do they present their work to the public, how do they make a living? Some have been left behind; it's not their fault. No one says it's easy, to live from your artistic work – you can spend your whole life trying. It's difficult but not impossible.

Q: You were born in 1963, Ground Zero of the Cold War. You grew up in a rigidly divided ideological climate. We've noticed that you often combine opposing images or concepts: walls and doors, crucifixes and Marxist books, good things and bad eyes – there are lots them in your songs. We wonder if all these binaries reflect the climate in which you grew up?

CV: That is a super-interesting question. When I'm writing, I don't think about my work in this way. But now that you have pointed this out, I say "Wow," and I'm thinking of more examples. I'm thinking of a line from "Cris y Lucy," "we are only puppets of Christ and Lucifer." It's not something that I intended. I like to show two faces in my music. This is something that Joaquín Sabina likes to do too, even more than me. People in Madrid have said that I've been influenced by Sabina's style, and this is true. But you know my work, and if you are saying I use binaries a lot, this is really interesting.

Q: We've also noticed that when you speak of history, often you take the voice of a child. It's the voice of innocence, with questions but no answers. But it seems as though on your latest disc, *No es el fin*, perhaps you have decided this voice of childhood innocence is over. Where did the child go?

CV: The child is still there. But the child grew up. You've reminded me of another song I have, which I never recorded, that says, "If an older person doesn't understand your dream / it's because they forgot that one time they were young."

With my new disc, I have another vision, almost twenty years after "Guillermo Tell," in "Telon de fondo." It tells something of the same story as Guillermo Tell did, but he's older now.

> Yo te di mi ilusión,
> mi niñez, mi país y mi corazón.
>
> y en cambio solo
> tu me diste un mundo
> lleno de escenarios y
> payasos tontos
>
> I gave you my dream
> My childhood, my country and my heart
>
> And in return all
> You gave me was a world
> Full of stages
> And silly clowns

But still, I think this disc, *No es el fin,* has a sweetness. I like, poetically, that it is sweet. I also like that this is my first disc where the music also has a poetic element and where the musicians have a prominent role. None of my songs would be possible without the music. None of these verses would exist without the music behind them, because there is a connection.

Q: Are you inspired by the same things as at the beginning of your career? What is the inspiration for your new disc?

CV: Like my other songs, "No es el fin" is inspired by real things. There are many songs that are absolutely real, but there are other songs created from real things. "Como un Angel," for example. Of course the girl didn't intend to touch the sun from her balcony. But poetically, I thought, how can I tell her story? The girl was actually fourteen years old, she smoked marijuana, she listened to The Doors, she was a fan of mine. And somebody told me her story – she lived here in the neighbourhood. One day, one day she threw herself from the balcony, my God. So I re-created the story in "Como un Angel." Well, the song "No es el fin" is also something like that. They met each other in childhood. The years pass, and they began to lose the chemistry, and he throws himself into the sea. Again, the same theme, he throws himself into the sea and he's gone. Although this song was written to console someone, it can be read on another level, it has other dimensions. Similar to "Monedas del aire," which was written especially for my mother. I was at Santiago de Compostella in Spain when I found out my mother was near death. She was sick for many years, she had cancer. So I went to the cathedral at Santiago and put my hand on the Witches' Column, and asked for her, and I thought, "Maybe, maybe, a miracle will descend, even here."

Now, years later, this phrase has another dimension. Not just the phrase but the fact that at concerts, during this song, "Monedas al aire," people started to light matches and throw coins in the air. I mean, it's a very interesting catharsis, something very strange, in a country like ours.

There are people who think the songs on the new disc are pessimistic. "El viejo sueño acabó," for example.

> Qué más da
> quién ganó, quién perdió
> si es que al final
> el sueño acabó
>
> Who cares anymore
> Who won, who lost
> If in the end
> The dream has ended

But I insist, *el viejo sueño acabó*. But another dream starts. That's why, *no es el fin*. Let's close this chapter. But another dream begins.

NOTES

1 A version of this interview appears in the *Latin American Music Review* 34, no. 2, Fall–Winter 2013
2 *"por sus,"* a Cuban colloquialism, a version of "por sus cojones," indicating *machismo*.
3 These early concerts are detailed by Joaquín Borges-Triana in chapter 1 of this anthology and in his *La luz, bróder, la luz, Canción Cubana Contemporánea* (La Habana: Ediciones La Memoria, 2009), pp. 29–57.
4 Buarque, "the master of political critique and double entendre," would have much to teach a young Varela about censorship, theatre, and urban poetic sensibilities. Christopher Dunn, *Brutality Garden: Tropicália and the Emergence of a Brazilian Counterculture* (Chapell Hill: University of North Carolina Press, 2001), p. 162. See also Charles A. Perrone, "Dissonance and Dissent: The Musical Dramatics of Chico Buarque," *Latin American Theatre Review*, Spring 1989, pp. 81–94; and Perrone, *Masters of Contemporary Brazilian Song, 1965–1985* (Austin: University of Texas Press, 1989). Brazil's *Tropicália* sound was introduced to Cuba via Alfredo Guevara, the longtime director of the Instituto Cubano de Arte e Industria Cinematográficos (ICAIC), who became an enthusiast of Tropicália's combination of rock, traditional music, and social activism. Historians suggest that this not only provided youth of Varela's generation with musical inspiration, but also offered an earlier generation of political songwriters such as Rodríguez and Milanes a degree of protection from state harassment. Deborah Pacini Hernandez and Reebee Garofalo, "Between Rock and a Hard Place: Negotiating Rock in Revolutionary Cuba, 1960–1980" in *Rockin' Las Américas: The Global Politics of Rock in Latin/o America*, ed. Deborah Pacini Hernandez, Héctor Fernández L'Hoeste, and Eric Zolov (Pittsburgh: University of Pittsburgh Press, 2004), pp. 43–67.
5 Varela has a long and complicated relationship with censorship, in both Cuba and the United States. Besides being occasionally blacked out by Cuban radio and television, his music was forbidden at some of the *escuelas al campo*, the country schools that Cuban pre-university students attended in the 1980s and 1990s. Mario Vizcaíno Serrat, "Carlos Varela: el gnomo y el guerrero," *La Gaceta de Cuba* 1, 1994, p. 20. On censorship in Cuban artistic production in general in this era, see the important essay by the artist

Tonel: Antonio Eligio Fernández, "Ending the Century with *Memories* ...: Paper Money, Videos, and an *X-Acto* Knife for Cuban Art," in *Cuba in the Special Period: Culture and Ideology in the 1990s*, ed. Ariana Hernandez-Reguant (New York: Palgrave Macmillan, 2009), 179–96.
6 Irina Echarry, "Three Kings Day in Cuba," *Havana Times*, 5 January 2009, http://www.havanatimes.org/?p=3533 (accessed 2 May 2010).
7 Wendy Guerra, "Llamada local: Carlos Varela," *Habaname*, 22 September 2008, http://www.elmundo.es/blogs/elmundo/habaname (accessed 23 October 2009).
8 Eyder La O Toledano, "Entrevistas: Un gnomo contra los leones," *La Ventana*, 3 October 2007, http://laventana.casa.cult.cu/modules.php?name=News&file=article&sid=3867 (accessed 2 January 2009).
9 Los Aldeanos had been denied exit visas to perform outside Cuba. The Cuban government eventually did grant them visas, and they performed in Miami in November 2011.
10 Mario Vizcaino Serrat, "Entrevistas: Le toca a Carlos Varela la manzana en la cabeza?," *LaVentana*, 30 July 2005, http://laventana.casa.cult.cu/modules.php?name=News&file=article&sid=2667 (accessed 23 October 2009).
11 Cuba's two-currency system, in which the CUC (convertible peso) basically replaced the US dollar as the currency of foreigners.

Appendix

Lyrics of Varela's Recorded Songs

Discography:

No es el fin 2009
Carlos Varela: All His Greatest Hits 2009
Los Hijos de Guillermo Tell Vol 1 2005
Siete 2003
Nubes 2000
Como los Peces 1995
Monedes al Aire 1992
Carlos Varela en Vivo 1991
   Jalisco Park 1989

25 MIL MENTIRAS SOBRE LA VERDAD (*SIETE*)

Nostradamus nunca tuvo la verdad
ni los Beatles, ni Galileo.
Hare Krishna nunca dijo la verdad
ni Jesús, ni Julieta, ni Romeo.

Los poetas nunca escriben la verdad
ni la Biblia, ni los diarios.
Los profetas no adivinan la verdad,
ni los pobres, ni los millonarios.

La verdad de la verdad
es que nunca es una
ni la mía, ni la de él, ni la tuya.
La verdad de la verdad
es que no es lo mismo
parecer
que caer en el abismo
de la verdad.

Los maestros
nunca enseñan la verdad
ni los reyes ni los Mesías.
Los ejércitos
no tienen la verdad
ni las leyes ni la astrología.

La verdad de la verdad
es que nunca es una
ni la mía, ni la de él, ni la tuya.
La verdad de la verdad
es que no es lo mismo
parecer
que caer en el abismo
de la verdad,
de la verdad.

25 THOUSAND LIES ABOUT THE TRUTH (*SIETE*)

Nostradamus never found the truth
Nor the Beatles, or Galileo.
Hare Krishna never spoke the truth
Nor did Jesus or Juliet or Romeo.

Poets never write the truth
Nor the Bible, nor the newspapers.
Prophets can't guess the truth,
Neither can the poor, nor the rich.

The truth about the truth
Is that there never is just one.
Not mine, not his, not yours.
The truth about the truth
Is that it's not the same
To feign
As to fall into the abyss
Of the truth.

Teachers
Never teach the truth
Nor do kings, nor the messiahs.
Armies
Don't have the truth
Nor laws, nor astrology.

The truth about the truth is that
There never is just one.
Not mine, not his, not yours.
The truth about the truth
Is that it's not the same
To feign
As to fall into the abyss
Of the truth,
Of the truth.

AHORA QUE LOS MAPAS CAMBIAN DE COLOR (*MONEDAS AL AIRE*)

Están tocando la puerta, están rezándole al cielo
están sacando la cuenta y está faltando el dinero.
Están tumbando los muros, están cruzando fronteras.
El día está más oscuro y están usando mi antena.

Ahora que los mapas están cambiando de color.

Están quemando los libros, están cortando cabezas,
están poniendo en peligro las cartas sobre la mesa.
Está lloviendo en la tierra, están vaciando mercados,
están jugando a la guerra y están borrando el pasado.

Ahora que los mapas están cambiando de color.

Cementerio Chino
creo que esta vez veo tu destino
y abrirán tus viejas puertas de una vez.

Abraza a tu fe
abraza a tu fe.
Ahora que los mapas están cambiando de color.

APENAS ABRO LOS OJOS (*NUBES*)

Apenas abro los ojos
todo el silencio se va
y con el desayuno
me trago el ruido y el humo
que viene de la ciudad.

Apenas salgo a la calle
alguien se empieza a quejar,
se pone a hablar de mi anhelo
dice que es muy largo ya
y en la esquina hay un letrero

NOW THAT THE MAPS ARE CHANGING COLOUR (*MONEDAS AL AIRE*)

They are knocking on the door, they are praying to the heavens.
They are working out the bill, and money is missing.
The walls are falling, and they are crossing borders.
The day is darker, and they are using my antenna.

Now that the maps are changing colour.

They are burning books, they are cutting off heads.
They are risking the cards that they've played.
Its raining on the land, they are emptying the markets,
They are playing at war and erasing the past.

Now that the maps are changing colour.

Chinese Cemetery
This time I think I see your destiny
And they are going to open your old doors once and for all.

Embrace your faith,
Embrace your faith,
Now that the maps are changing colour.

AS I OPEN MY EYES (*NUBES*)

As I open my eyes
All the silence goes away
Along with my breakfast
I swallow the city's
noise and smoke.

As I go out to the street
Someone begins to complain,
They start to talk about my dreams,
They say they are already too big
And on the corner there is a sign

que dice: Libertad
dice mi verdad.

Así me voy descubriendo
cruzo la calle corriendo
me pierdo entre tanta gente
queriendo fantasear
y lo cotidiano
me hace soñar.
Apenas abro los ojos.

ÁRBOLES RAROS (*JALISCO PARK*)

Dejó la nieve de Estocolmo
y salió a buscar otra estación
quiso un paisaje sin otoño
y aquí llegó con la ilusión.

Ella miraba en la avenida
esos árboles raros de boliches verdes.
Sus hojas son como estos días
que a pesar de la lluvia
tampoco florecen.

Pasó seis años y otro poco
viviendo igual, pero soñando
y hasta cantó con esos locos
que el tiempo ya nos va cansando.

Pero ella vio en la avenida
a esos árboles raros de boliches verdes
sus hojas son como estos días
que con el viento sucio
algunas se mueren.

Dejó la nieve e Estocolmo
y salió a buscar otra estación

That says: Freedom
That says my truth.

So I try to find myself.
Cross the street running
And get lost among all the people
Wanting to fantasize
And daily life
Makes me dream.
As I open my eyes.

STRANGE TREES (*JALISCO PARK*)

She left the snow of Stockholm
And went searching for another season
She wanted a country without autumn
And she arrived here with that illusion.

On the avenue, she saw
Strange trees with green *boliches**
Their leaves are so much like these times
Despite the rain
They never blossom.

Six years and a bit later
Still living like this, but always dreaming
She even sang with these lunatics
Of how the times tire us.

But on the avenue she saw
Those strange trees that looked like green *boliches**
Their leaves so like these times
In the dirty wind
Some die.

She left the snow of Stockholm
And went in search of another season

quiso un paisaje sin otoño
y aquí llegó con la ilusión.

Dejó la nieve de Estocolmo
y en mi ciudad paró su tren
quería un paisaje sin otoño
y se encontró
que aquí las hojas
se caen también.

BENDITA LLUVIA (*NO ES EL FIN*)

Soñé
que solo con tu mirada
es tan frágil el pasado
que perder no vale nada.
Tú sabes que
la gente de las ventanas
hablan solo a la vez
y al final no escuchan nada.

Como las nubes de porcelana,
como la sombra de tus pies.
Deja que el Sol te dé en la cara
y que no puedas ver.

Tú y yo
sabemos que mañana
no habrán puntos cardinales
solo manchas en el alma.
Tanto tiempo haciendo zapping
con tu maldita desilusión.
Quién te dijo que era fácil
el precio de la razón.

Como las nubes de porcelana,
como la sombra de tus pies.

She wanted a country without autumn
And she arrived here with that illusion.

She left the snow of Stockholm
And her train stopped in my city
She wanted a country without an autumn
But she found that
Here the leaves
Also fall.

Boliches are small seed-like fruit.

BLESSED RAIN (*NO ES EL FIN*)

I dreamt
That in your eyes
The past was so fragile
And losing was worth nothing.
You know that
The people in the windows
All speak at the same time
And in the end, they don't hear anything.

Like porcelain clouds,
Like the shadow of your feet.
Let the sun shine on your face
So that you can't see.

You and I
We know that tomorrow
There will be no cardinal points
Only stains on the soul.
So much time zapping
With your damned disillusion.
Who told you that the truth
Would be easy to buy.

Like porcelain clouds,
Like the shadow of your feet.

Deja que el Sol te de en la cara
y que no puedas ver.

Lluvia de agua bendita!
Lluvia que te da y te quita.
Bendita lluvia
de los deseos!
Lluvia que ojalá
se lleve de una vez lo feo.

BOLA DE NIEVE (*JALISCO PARK*)

En la penumbra del Monseñor
todas las noches tocaba
sentado al piano bebiendo ron
muy tarde hasta la mañana.

Bola de Nieve
negro piano man
con la voz rajada
ya de tanto trasnochar.

En la penumbra del Monseñor
la gente escuchaba al Bola
cantando con su traje de Lord
como su piano de cola.

Bola de Nieve
negro piano man
con la voz rajada
ya de tanto trasnochar.

Un día el Bola no regresó
y no se supo más nada
solo que tuvo un extraño amor
oculto en la madrugada.

Let the sun shine on your face
So that you can't see.

Rain of blessed waters!
Rain that gives and takes.
Blessed rain
Of hope!
Rain I pray
That takes all the ugliness away.

SNOWBALL (JALISCO PARK)*

In the semidarkness of the Monsignor
He played, every night.
Sitting at the piano, drinking rum
From late until morning.

Snowball
Black piano man
With a voice raspy
From so many late nights.

In the semidarkness of the Monsignor
The people listened to Snowball
Singing with his Lord's costume
Like his grand piano.

Snowball
Black piano man
With a voice raspy
From so many late nights.

One day Snowball didn't return
And no one heard anything more of him
Only that he had a strange love
Hidden in the dawn.

Snowball
Black piano man
With a voice raspy
From so many late nights.

Y cuando cierra el Monseñor
dicen que pasa algo extraño
por las paredes se oye una voz
y tocan solas las teclas de piano.

BLUES DEL BOXEADOR (*JALISCO PARK*)

Regresa a su casa con la madrugada
pasado de tragos sin pagarse nada
se bebió la noche y antes de acostarse
se encontró un amigo y empezó a acordarse.

Que fue boxeador hace ya unos años
que rompió sus manos en una pelea
te habla de la vida lo que se le ocurre
conoció la fama, pero ahora se aburre.

Ya no sale su foto en los diarios
ya no hay más medallas, ya no hay más contrarios
y el último golpe será cuando un día
solo lo recuerden los viejos del barrio.

Ahora tiene un perro para la nostalgia
y las cicatrices que fueron quedando.
Regresa a su casa cuando duermen todos
la calle da vueltas y él va silbando
solo.

And when the Monsignor closed
They said something strange happened
Through the walls one could hear a voice
And piano keys played on their own.

*Ignacio Jacinto Villa, "Snowball" 1911-1971, Cuban singer-pianist.

THE BOXER'S BLUES (*JALISCO PARK*)

He returns home as the sun is rising
Full of drinks that he didn't pay for
He drank the night away and before going to bed
He found a friend and began to reminisce.

He was a boxer some years ago
Who broke his hands in a fight
He tells you of his life, and of what happened to him
and of the times when he was famous, but now he's just tired
of it.

Now his picture isn't in the newspapers
Now there aren't any more medals
Now there aren't any more opponents
And the last blow will be when one day
Only the old men in the neighbourhood remember him.

Now he has a dog for his nostalgia
And scars that won't fade
He returns home when everyone is sleeping
The street spins around and he walks on whistling
all alone.

BULEVAR (JALISCO PARK)

En el bulevar la gente corre,
tienen algo que encontrar
y las tiendas son peceras
reflejando la ciudad.

En el bulevar los curiosos
pegan su nariz en las vidrieras,
y el viejo que vende la prensa
se fue porque sabe que va a lloviznar.
pegan su nariz en las vidrieras,
y el viejo que vende la prensa
anuncia que el cielo no se va nublar.

En el bulevar la gente corre,
tiene algo que encontrar
y las tiendas son peceras
reflejando la ciudad.

En el bulevar los juguetes
provocan la risa de algún pequeñín,
pero otros muchachos prefieren
mirarle los senos a un maniquí.

En el bulevar la gente corre,
tienen algo que encontrar
y las tiendas son peceras
reflejando la ciudad.

Cuando el bulevar cierra todo,
hay que ver los ojos del barrendero,
es como contar las estrellas
y no saber por dónde empezar primero.

En el bulevar la gente corre,
tiene algo que encontrar
y las tiendas son peceras
reflejando la ciudad.

THE BOULEVARD (JALISCO PARK)

On the boulevard people run
They are looking for something
And the stores are fishbowls
Reflecting the city.

On the boulevard the curious
Stick their noses to the glass,
And the old man who sells the papers
Left because he knows that it's going to drizzle.
They stick their noses to the glass,
And the old man who sells papers
Announces that it's not going to be cloudy.

On the boulevard people run,
They are looking for something
And the stores are fishbowls
Reflecting the city.

On the boulevard the toys
Make the little ones laugh
But other boys prefer
To look at the mannequin's breasts.

On the boulevard people run
They are looking for something
And the stores are fishbowls
Reflecting the city.

When the boulevard is all closed,
You have to see the eyes of the street cleaner.
It's like trying to count the stars
But not knowing where to begin.

On the boulevard people run
They are looking for something
And the stores are fishbowls
Reflecting the city.

En el bulevar los curiosos
pegan su nariz en las vidrieras,
y el viejo que vende la prensa
se fue porque sabe que va a lloviznar.

CALLEJÓN SIN LUZ (*SIETE*)

Justo detrás del Cementerio Chino
en el viejo callejón sin luz
detrás de la bandera
en el balcón de los vecinos
te me desnudabas tu.

Yo no era más que un duende sin abrigo
tu buda tu rabino y tu gurú
y justo en el oscuro cementerio
descubrí la vida encima de una cruz
hicimos el amor ,sudamos el misterio
en el viejo callejón sin luz.

La vida es como un remolino
de polvo y hojas se hace la ilusión
los sueños envejecen como el vino
y el olor de una canción.

Justo en el borde del camino
en vez de aquella silla estabas tu
debajo de tu falda yo era el asesino
de aquel callejón sin luz.

Hoy te busqué en el Cementerio Chino
por el viejo callejón sin luz
y aún sigue la bandera en el balcón
de los vecinos
solo que ya no estás tu.

Mi amor fue un remolino
que daba vueltas cuando el viento eras tu

On the boulevard the curious
Put their nose to the glass,
And the old man who sells newspapers
Left because he knows it's going to drizzle.

DARK ALLEY (*SIETE*)

Just behind the Chinese Cemetery
In the old dark alley
Behind the flag
On the neighbours' balcony
You undressed for me.

I wasn't more than a sprite without a coat
Your Buddha, your rabbi, and your guru
And just there in the dark cemetery
I discovered life on top of a cross
We made love, we sweat the mystery
In the old dark alley.

Life is like a whirlwind
An illusion made of dust and leaves
Dreams age like wine
And the smell of a song.

Just on the edge of the road
Instead of that chair, was you
Under your skirt I was the assassin
Of that dark alley.

Today I looked for you in the Chinese Cemetery
In the dark alley
And although the flag on the neighbours' balcony
Is still there
You are not.

My love was a whirlwind
That spun round with the wind

y ahora mi vida y mi destino
no son más que un callejón sin luz.

CAMBIA (*NO ES EL FIN*)

Te hace mal
la desilusión, la noche, el día.
Te hace mal no reír
y te hace mal que otros se rían.
Te hace mal
los diarios, la televisión,
las viejas profecías.
Te hace mal
la ciudad que no fue
como el sueño que una vez tenías.

Y es que nunca nos dimos cuenta
que vivir no es solo ir y venir de vuelta,
dime para que sirvieron tantos sueños
escondidos tras las puertas.

Cambia
cambia de color, de gurú, de chamán
cambia el Norte, cambia el Sur
y hasta cambia el mar
y verás que va cambiando todo lo demás.

CASTILLOS DE ARENA (*NO ES EL FIN*)

Hoy no
no sientas pena,
no te dejes engañar.
Rompe todas tus cadenas
y echa tu alma a volar.

Ya no sé quien soy
cuando te siento lejos.

And now my life and my destiny
Are no more than an dark alley.

CHANGE (*NO ES EL FIN*)

It bothers you
The disillusionment, the night, the day.
It bothers you not to laugh
And it bothers you that others laugh
It bothers you
The newspapers, the TV,
The old prophesies
It bothers you
The city that never was
Like the dream that you once had.

And we never realized
That to live isn't only to come and to go
Tell me what's the use of so many dreams hidden
Behind closed doors.

Change
A change of colour, of guru, of shaman
Change in the north, change in the south
Even the sea changes
You'll see that everything else changes.

SANDCASTLES (*NO ES EL FIN*)

Not today.
You don't feel sadness
You won't let yourself be fooled
Break all your chains
And let your soul fly

I don't know who I am
When I feel you are distant

Tus ojos son espejos
para mi corazón.
Hay un lugar cerca del mar
que me recuerda a ti,
una ilusión del más allá
como castillos de arena
que suelen durar
lo mismo que un sueño
a orillas del mar.

Hoy no
no tengas pena,
no hagas como los demás
que se esconden en la arena
para no ver más allá.

Ya no sé quien soy
cuando te siento lejos.
Tus ojos son espejos
para mi corazón.
Hay un lugar cerca del mar
que me recuerda a ti,
una ilusión del más allá
como castillos de arena
que suelen durar
lo mismo que un sueño
a orillas del mar.

Lama
si en vez de tantas penas
se iluminara el alma de los demás.
Mañana
yo encenderé una vela por cada huella
perdida en el mar.

Your eyes are mirrors
For my heart
There is a place near the sea
That reminds me of you
A dream of the great beyond
Like sand castles
That usually survive
Like a dream
At the sea shore

Not today.
Don't be sad
Don't be like all the rest
Who hide themselves in the sand
So they can't see beyond.

I don't know who I am
When I feel you are distant
Your eyes are mirrors
For my heart
There is a place near the sea
That reminds me of you
A dream of the great beyond
Like sand castles
That usually survive
Like a dream
At the sea shore

Lama,
What if instead of all this sadness
Everyone's souls could shine
Tomorrow
I will light a candle
For every footprint lost in the sea

CIRCULO DE TIZA (*MONEDAS AL AIRE*)

Pintaba el asfalto con trozos de cal
En mi sucio barrio de La Habana oscura.
"Cuba declara la guerra en contra de ..."
Mi religión no es de cruz, ni de altar,
Pero voy a rezar porque un día
Se acabe la niebla.
Yo perdí un amigo en la guerra de Africa
Y a otro que escapando se lo tragó el mar.
"Cuba declara la guerra en contra de ..."
Mi religión no es de cruz, ni de altar,
Pero voy a rezar porque un día
Se acabe la niebla.
No creo en los diarios con la foto de Sadam
Ni en ideologías, ni en lo que vendrá.
El mundo declara la guerra en contra de ...
Mi religión no es de cruz, ni de altar,
Pero voy a rezar porque un día
Se acabe la niebla.
Pintando el asfalto con trozos de cal
Están los muchachos de La Habana oscura.
Yo no sé en contra de quién
Ni en contra de
Pero voy a rezar porque un día
Se acabe la niebla.

COLGANDO DEL CIELO (*SIETE*)

El predicador se aburre
los dados solo salen una vez
los trucos del mago se descubren
las brujas ya no creen en el poder.

Unos son el Yin y otros son el Yang
y aunque no te olvides de tus barrotes
nos vendría bien ponernos a bailar
la antigua danza del peyote.

CHALK CIRCLE (*MONEDAS AL AIRE*)

The pavement is painted with bits of limestone
In my dirty neighbourhood, in dark Havana
"Cuba declares war against ..."
My religion is not the cross nor the altar,
But I'm going to pray so that one day
The fog will lift.
I lost a friend in the war in Africa
And another, while escaping, was swallowed by the sea.
"Cuba declares war against ..."
My religion is not he cross nor the altar,
But I'm going to pray so that one day
The fog will lift.
I don't believe in the newspapers with the photo of Saddam
Nor in ideologies, nor in what's coming.
The world declares war against ...
My religion is not the cross, nor the altar,
But I am going to pray so that one day
The fog will lift.
The boys of dark Havana
Are painting the pavement with bits of limestone
I do not know who or what
They are against
But I am going to pray so that one day
The fog will lift.

HANGING FROM THE SKY (*SIETE*)

The preacher got bored
The dice only win once
They discovered the magic tricks
The witches don't believe in power.

Some are Yin and some are Yang
And although you don't forget the bars
We could use a dance
The old dance of peyote.

Pero Dios,pero Dios
sigue siendo tu anzuelo
colgando del cielo.
Pero Dios, pero Dios
sigue siendo tu anzuelo
colgando del cielo.

Ni el oráculo sabe
lo que pueda pasar
ni las líneas en el mapa
de tus manos
y a falta de fe
la gente suele inventar
talismanes embrujados.

La lluvia apagó
la hoguera del chamán
La bola de cristal
ya no dice nada
y los chicos de hoy
no saben a donde van
soñando con llegar al nirvana.

Pero Dios, pero Dios
sigue siendo tu anzuelo
colgando del cielo.
Pero Dios, pero Dios
sigue siendo tu anzuelo
colgando del cielo.
Pero Dios, pero Dios
sigue siendo tu anzuelo
colgando del cielo.

Yo he visto al bien
con los ojos del mal
como un ciego feliz
en la oscuridad.
Nena, no sé lo que va a pasar
si la mentira se disfraza
cómo la verdad.
Si la mentira se disfraza
cómo la verdad.

But God, but God
Is still your hook
Hanging from the sky
But God, but God
Is still your hook
Hanging from the sky

The oracle doesn't know
What can happen
Nor the lines on the map
Of your hands
And without faith,
People have to invent
Bewitching talismans.

The rain puts out
The shaman's bonfire
The crystal ball
Says nothing
And the boys of today,
I don't know where they're going
They dream of reaching Nirvana.

But God, but God
Is still your hook
Hanging from the sky
But God, but God
Is still your hook
Hanging from the sky
But God, but God
Is still your hook
Hanging from the sky

I have seen good things
With bad eyes
Like a blind man happy
In the darkness.
Baby I don't know what's going to happen
If lies dress up
As the truth.
If lies dress up
As the truth.

Pero Dios,
si la mentira se disfraza
cómo la verdad.

COMO ME HICIERON A MÍ (*MONEDAS AL AIRE*)

Te contarán la historia
y cuando pase el tiempo,
te vendarán los ojos
como me hicieron a mí.

Te enseñarán el hacha
y cuando pase el tiempo
te esconderán el árbol
como me hicieron a mí.

De nada sirve que sepas la verdad,
si cuando gritas sabes que
ya no te escuchan.

Te pedirán que jures
te pedirán que marches
te pedirán lo mismo
como me hicieron a mí.

Dirán que todo es tuyo
y si intentas cambiarlo
te patearán más duro
como me hicieron a mí.

De nada sirve que sepas la verdad,
si cuando gritas sabes que
ya no te escuchan.

Te contarán la historia
y cuando pase el tiempo,
te vendarán los ojos
como me hicieron a mí.

But God,
If lies dress up
As the truth.

AS THEY DID TO ME (*MONEDAS AL AIRE*)

They are going to tell you the story
And when time passes,
They are going to blindfold you
As they did to me.

They are going to teach you to use an axe
And when time passes
They are going to hide the tree from you
Like they did to me.

It's useless to know the truth,
If when you shout, you know that
No one is listening to you.

They will ask to you swear
They will ask you to march
They will ask you the same
As they did to me.

They will tell you everything is yours
And if you try to change it
They will kick you harder
As they did to me.

It's useless to know the truth,
If when you shout, you know that
No on one is listening to you.

They are going to tell you the story
And when time passes,
They are going to blindfold you
As they did to me.

COMO UN ÁNGEL (*COMO LOS PECES*)

Como un ángel en una prisión
la dejaban encerrada en su habitación.
Un incienso y un disco de los Doors
y un cigarro marihuana calmaban su dolor.

Nadie le dio algo de amor. Nadie.
Nadie abrigó su corazón. Nadie.

Y su padre no hacía más que pelear.
Y su madre se pasaba todo el día
sin dejar de llorar.
Una virgen colgada en la pared
y el tatuaje de una cruz en la espalda,
donde no se ve.

Nadie le dio algo de amor. Nadie.
Nadie abrigó su corazón,
por eso quiso buscar como escapar,
por eso se fue buscando otro lugar.

Así fue que un día se escapó
donde nadie, nadie la encontró
Y de nada sirvió que avisaran a la policía
la buscaron varios días, pero nunca
nunca aparecía.

Nadie le dio algo de amor. Nadie.
Nadie abrigó su corazón. Nadie.

Yo la ví saltando del balcón
y en el aire quiso tocar el Sol.
¿Dónde fue? Solo lo sabe Dios.
Como un ángel se desapareció.

Nadie le dio algo de amor. Nadie.
Nadie abrigó su corazón,
por eso quiso buscar como escapar,
por eso se fue buscando otro lugar.
Como un ángel.

LIKE AN ANGEL (*COMO LOS PECES*)

Like an angel in a prison
They left her locked up in her room.
Incense, a Doors record
And marijuana calmed her pain.

No one told her anything about love. No one.
No one warmed her heart. No one.

And her father didn't do anything but fight.
And her mother can't pass a day
Without crying.
A virgin hung on the wall
And a tattoo of a cross on her back,
Where it can't be seen.

No one told her anything about love. No one.
No one warmed her heart,
That's why she wanted to look for an escape,
That's why she went looking for another place.

And so it was that one day she escaped
Where no one, no one could find her
And it was no use telling the police
They looked for her for a few days, but
She never appeared.

No one told her anything about love. No one.
No one warmed her heart. No one.

I saw her jumping from the balcony
And in the air she wanted to touch the sun.
Where did she go? Only God knows.
Like an angel, she disappeared.

No one told her anything about love. No one.
No one warmed her heart,
That's why she wanted to look for an escape,
That's why she went looking for another place.
Like an angel.

COMO UN PEZ (*SIETE*)

Ahora entiendo
cuando un día
le tiré piedras al Sol
y entre el humo gris
de la neblina
tú me hacías el amor.

Sin amor nada es posible
sin amor nada vendrá
sin amor no somos libres
como un pez sin el mar
sin amor, sin amar.

Ahora entiendo
si te vas tan lejos
ahora entiendo
cuando ya no estás.
Los recuerdos
solo son espejos
que te miran
más y más.

Y es que sin amor
nada es posible
sin amor nada vendrá
sin amor no somos libres
como un pez sin el mar
sin amor, sin amar.

Si me pierdo
estaré en la orilla
arrojando piedras
contra el mar
para ver si al menos
algún día
nos volvemos a encontrar
más allá.

LIKE A FISH (*SIETE*)

Now I understand
How one day
I threw stones at the sun
And between the grey smoke
Of the fog
You made love to me.

Without love nothing is possible
Without love nothing will come
Without love we aren't free
Like a fish out of water
Out of love, out of loving.

Now I understand
When you go far away
Now I understand
When you aren't here.
The memories
Are only mirrors
That see you
More and more.

Without love nothing is possible
Without love
Nothing will come
Without love we aren't free
Like a fish out of water
Out of loving, out of love.

If I disappear
I will be at the shore
Throwing rocks
At the sea
To see if at least
Some day
We'll return to find
The great beyond.

COMO LOS PECES (*COMO LOS PECES*)

Las iglesias hablan de la salvación
y la gente reza y pide cosas en silencio
como los peces
y en la cara de Jesús hay una lágrima rodando
lágrimas negras.

Y los padres ya no quieren hablar de la situación
sobreviven prisioneros y acostumbran a callar
como los peces
y en la cara de sus hijos hay una lágrima rodando
lágrimas negras.

"Aunque tú me has echado en el abandono,
aunque ya han muerto todas mis ilusiones,
lloro sin que sepas que este llanto mío
tiene lágrimas negras"
lágrimas.

Las noticias hablan de resignación
y la gente traga y se miran a los ojos
como los peces
y en la cara de la virgen hay una lágrima rodando
lágrimas negras.

Los muchachos hablan de desilusión
y en silencio van al mar y se largan
como los peces
y en la cara de una madre hay una lágrima rodando
lágrimas negras.

"Aunque tú me has echado en el abandono,
aunque ya han muerto todas mis ilusiones,
lloro sin que sepas que este llanto mío
tiene lágrimas negras"*
lágrimas.

Las iglesias hablan de salvación
y la gente reza y pide cosas en silencio

LIKE FISH (*COMO LOS PECES*)

The churches speak of salvation
And the people pray and ask for things in silence
Like fish
And a tear rolls down the face of Jesus,
Black tears.

And the parents don't want to talk about the situation
Prisoners survive and learn to keep quiet
Like fish
And a tear rolls down their children's faces,
Black tears.

"Even though you have abandoned me
Although all my illusions have died
I cry without you knowing
That I am crying black tears."*
Tears.

The media speak of resignation
And the people swallow and look at each other
Like fish
And there's a tear rolling down the virgin's face
Black tears.

Teenagers speak of disillusionment
And in silence they go to the sea and swim off
Like fish
And a tear rolls down a mother's face
Black tears.

"Even though you have abandoned me
Although all my illusions have died
I cry without you knowing
that I am crying black tears."
Tears.

The churches speak of salvation
And the people pray and ask for things in silence

como los peces
y en la cara de Jesús hay una lágrima rodando
lágrimas negras.

*De Miguel Matamoros, en "Lagrimas negras"

CUATRO LUNAS (*NUBES*)

Ella siempre se esconde
entre los campanarios de la cruz.
Nadie supo su nombre,
nunca enseñó sus ojos a la luz.

Pero sé, pero sé
que algo pasa cuando faltan las palabras.
Y ella fue, y ella fue
cuatro lunas más adentro de mi alma.

Ella siempre se esconde
detrás de los secretos del jardín
nadie supo hacia donde
se fue de pronto y nunca más la vi.

Pero sé, pero sé
que algo pasa cuando faltan las palabras.
Y ella fue, y ella fue
cuatro lunas más adentro de mi alma.

Ella siempre se esconde
entre los campanarios de la cruz.
Nadie supo su nombre,
nunca enseñó sus ojos a la luz.

Like the fish
And there's a tear rolling down Jesus' face.
Black tears.

From "Lagrimas Negras" by Miguel Matamoros (1874–1971), Cuban trovador

FOUR MOONS (*NUBES*)

She always hides
In the bell tower of the cross,
No one knew her name,
She never showed her eyes to the light.

But know, but know,
That something happens when you can't find the words,
And she went, and she went,
Four moons deeper inside my soul.

She always hides
Behind the secrets of the garden
No one knew where she was heading,
Suddenly she left and was never seen again.

But know, but know
That something happens when you can't find the words.
And she went, and she went
Four moons deeper inside my soul.

She always hides,
In the bell tower of the cross,
No one knew her name,
She never showed her eyes to the light.

CUCHILLA EN LA ACERA (*EN VIVO*)

Le pusieron la cuchilla en el cuello
y después le quitaron la ropa,
los transeúntes que lo vieron
viraron la cara y se callaron la boca.

Y aunque no le encontraron dinero,
lo dejaron tirado en la vía,
y a pesar de la sangre, los gritos y Dios
nunca llegó la policía.

Qué está pasando mi amor
que ya la ciudad no es la misma.

Qué está pasando mi amor
que ya la ciudad no es la misma
de ayer.

Te pondrán la cuchilla en el cuello
y después te van a quitar la ropa,
los transeúntes que te vean
te virarán la cara y van a callar la boca.

Y aunque ya no te encuentren dinero,
te dejarán tirado en la vía,
y a pesar de la sangre, los gritos y Dios
no llegará la policía.

Qué está pasando mi amor
que ya la ciudad no es la misma.

Qué está pasando mi amor
que ya la ciudad no es la misma
de ayer.

KNIFE ON THE SIDEWALK (*EN VIVO*)

They put a knife to his neck
And after they took all his clothes
The passersby who saw him turned their heads
And kept their mouth shut.

And although they didn't find money,
They left him sprawled on the street
And despite the blood, the cries and God
The police never arrived.

What's happening, my love,
Is that the city isn't the same.

What's happening, my love,
Is that now the city isn't the same
as yesterday.

They'll put a knife to your throat
And then they are going to take your clothes,
The passersby who see you
Will turn their heads away and keep their mouths shut.

And although they won't find your money,
They will leave you sprawled on the street,
And despite the blood, the cries and God
The police won't arrive.

What's happening, my love,
Is that now the city isn't the same.

What's happening, my love,
Is that the city isn't the same
as yesterday.

DE VUELTA A CASA (*NO ES EL FIN*)

Tengo un reloj, tengo sed,
no tengo Dios, pero tengo fe.
Ya conocí New York, ya conocí París
sin embargo siento que no soy feliz.
Me voy mi amor, otra vez me voy,
me voy sin saber que pasa.
Tú sabes bien que soy como soy,
pero sigo regresando a casa.

Si ves mi amor que otra vez me fui,
me fui sin entender que pasa.
En tu corazón se esconde mi país
y el jardín que me conduce a casa,
de vuelta a casa.

Tengo una ilusión y un collar sin diamantes,
pero tengo una canción que es mi mejor amante.
Ya conocí La Habana, ya conocí Madrid
sin embargo hermana, siento que no soy feliz.
Por eso
hoy mi amor,
otra vez me voy,
me voy sin saber que pasa.
Tú sabes bien que soy como soy,
pero sigo regresando a casa.

Si ves mi amor que otra vez me fui,
me fui sin entender que pasa.
En tu corazón se esconde mi país
y el jardín que me conduce a casa,
de vuelta a casa,
de vuelta a casa.

COMING HOME (*NO ES EL FIN*)

I have a watch, I'm thirsty
I don't have God, but I have faith.
I already know New York, I already know Paris
However I'm still not happy.
I'm leaving, my love, again I'm leaving,
I'm leaving without knowing what's going on.
You know well that I am what I am,
But I will always come home.

If you see, my love, that again I'm leaving,
I leave without understanding what's happening.
My country is hiding in your heart
And the garden that leads to my home
Back to my home.

I have a dream and a necklace without diamonds,
But I have a song that is my best lover.
I already know Havana, I already know Madrid
However, my sister, I'm still not happy.
That's why
Today, my love,
I'm leaving again,
I'm leaving without knowing what's happening.
You know well that I am what I am,
But I'll keep coming home.

If you see, my love, that again I'm leaving,
I leave without understanding what's happening.
My country is hiding in your heart
And the garden that leads to my home
Back to my home,
Back to my home.

DELICADEZA (*SIETE*)

El viento puede envejecer
el sol nacer
la tierra detener.
Se puede oír un alfiler caer
y a Dios toser,
cuando una mujer besa a otra mujer,
tanta belleza,
delicadeza,
se nos confunde con naturaleza
de mujer a mujer.
Un angel puede aparecer,
puede llover
y hasta podría habanecer.
El cielo se puede romper
Y el mar arder,
pero cuando una mujer besa a otra mujer,
tanta belleza,
delicadeza,
se nos confunde con naturaleza
de mujer a mujer.

DESDE AQUEL DÍA EN QUE LO DIVIDIERON TODO (*MONEDAS AL AIRE*)

Tenía que robarle al padre de la billetera
algún dinero para sus pastillas.
Un día vio llorando a su madre en el cuarto
y algunos muebles tirados contra la pared
y descubrió que entonces algo se había acabado
desde aquel día en que su padre se fue.

Desde aquel día en que dividieron todo
las ilusiones, las fotos y la cama,
desde aquel día en que sólo vio a su padre
los fines de semana.

DELICACY (*SIETE*)

The wind could age
The sun be born
The earth move slower.
One could hear a pin drop
And God coughing,
When a woman kisses another woman
So much beauty,
Delicacy,
It confuses us with naturalness
From woman to woman.
An angel could appear
It could rain
And even Havana could see a new dawn.
The heavens could break
And the seas burn,
But when a woman kisses another woman,
So much beauty,
Delicacy,
It confuses us with naturalness
From woman to woman.

SINCE THAT DAY THEY DIVIDED EVERYTHING (*MONEDAS AL AIRE*)

He had to rob his father's wallet
To get some money for his pills.
One day he saw his mother crying in the bedroom
And some furniture thrown against the wall
And he discovered then that something had stopped
Since that day when his father left.

Since that day when they divided everything
The hope, the photos, the bed,
From that day on he only saw his father
On weekends.

Tenía que sacar buenas notas en la escuela
para poder salir con su pandilla.
Tenía que pedirle a la madre que le diera
algún dinero para sus pastillas.

Un día tuvo miedo y no supo qué hacer
cuando se vio desnudo con una mujer,
y descubrió que entonces algo le había faltado
desde aquel día en que su padre se fue.

Desde aquel día en que dividieron todo,
las ilusiones, las fotos y la cama,
desde aquel día en que sólo vio a su padre
los fines de semana.

Tenía que sacar buenas notas en la escuela
para poder salir con su pandilla.
Tenía que robarle a la madre en la cartera
algún dinero para sus pastillas.

Un día lo agarraron robando en una casa
y terminó con los brazos contra la pared
y descubrió que entonces algo se había acabado
desde aquel día en que su padre se fue.

No digo que eso sea la razón de su desgracia,
ni que por eso el muchacho está en cana,
pero lo cierto es que el solo vio a su padre
los fines de semana.

Desde aquel día en que dividieron todo
las ilusiones, las fotos y la cama,
desde aquel día en que sólo vio a su padre
los fines de semana.

He had to get good grades in school
To be able to go out with his gang
He had to ask his mother to give him
Some money for his pills.

One day he was afraid and he didn't know what to do
When he saw himself naked with a woman,
And he discovered then that something had been missing
Since that day his father left.

Since that day when they divided everything,
The hope, the photos, the bed,
From that day on he only saw his father
On weekends.

He had to get good grades in school
To be able to go out with his gang
He had to steal from his mother's purse
To get money for his pills.

One day they caught him robbing a house
And he ended up with his hands against the wall
And he discovered then that something had stopped
Since that day his father left.

I'm not saying that this is the reason for his disgrace,
Or that it's why the boy is in prison,
But what is certain is that he only saw his father
On weekends.

Since that day when they divided everything,
The hope, the photos, the bed,
From that day on he only saw his father
On weekends.

DESDE NINGÚN LUGAR (*NUBES*)

Cuando el cielo de la noche huele a sal
cuando los cuervos salen solos a mirar
Cuando la luz del faro barre la ciudad
y en las ventanas ya queda nadie más.

Rezando a Dios, se lanzaban al mar.
Dejándonos, hacia ningún lugar.

Cuando en la calle todo sigue igual
y en los tejados alguien sueña con volar
Cuando la gente se disfraza de animal
cuando no queda más remedio que callar.

Rezando a Dios, se pierden por el mar
Dejándonos, hacia ningún lugar.

Cuando mañana nadie quiera recordar
cuando los años borren toda la verdad,
Aunque los hijos les enseñen a olvidar
y en los diarios no se escriba nada más.

Lejos de Dios, sus almas seguirán
Buscándonos, desde ningún lugar ...
Lejos de Dios, sus almas seguirán
Buscándonos, desde ningún lugar ...

DETRÁS DEL CRISTAL (*SIETE*)

Tu te pareces a la Habana
a la que fue y ya no será.
El forastero viene y se va
se va llevando un poco más.

Cuando te duermes en mi cama
siento que todo me da igual,
pero las luces de la mañana
tocan mi puerta una vez más.

FROM NOWHERE (*NUBES*)

When the night sky smells of salt
When the ravens come out just to look
When the light from the lighthouse sweeps the city
And there's no one left looking through the windows.

Praying to God, they set out to sea.
Leaving us, for nowhere.

When everything goes on as usual in the streets
And on the rooftops someone dreams of flying
When the people disguise themselves as animals
When there's nothing left to do but scream.

Praying to God, they set out to sea
Leaving us, for no place.

When no one wants to remember tomorrow
When the years erase all truth,
Even though the children are taught to forget
And they don't write anything in the newspapers anymore.

Far from God, their souls will follow
Looking for us, from nowhere ...
Far from God, their souls will follow
Looking for us, from nowhere ...

BEHIND GLASS (*SIETE*)

You are like Havana
Like what was, but is no more.
The stranger comes and goes
Always taking a little more.

When you sleep in my bed
I feel that everything will be all right.
But the morning light
Knocks on my door one more time.

Una ciudad rodeada de mar
es un amor detrás de un cristal
los que se fueron lloran
igual que los que están .

Cuando me asomo a la ventana
y miro la misma ciudad,
a veces suele entrar el mar
para llevarse un poco más.

Una ciudad rodeada de sal
es un amor detrás de un cristal,
los que se fueron lloran
igual que los que están.
Los que se van la añoran,
los que se quedan
más.

DUDAS (*SIETE*)

Dudas de mi
yo sé que dudas de mi.
Buscas en mi
yo sé que estás buscando en mi.
Huyes de mi
yo se que huyes de mi
porque me fuí
tan solo porque me fui.

Vuelve a tu pasado de hojas secas
y haz una hoguera con tu vanidad,
con tanta soledad por ahí
con tantas ganas de vivir
y tu no dejas de dudar de mi.

A city surrounded by the sea
Is a love behind glass.
Those who left cry,
Just like those who stay.

When I lean out the window
And look at the same city,
The sea usually flows in
To wash away little more.

A city surrounded by salt
Is a love behind glass.
Those who leave cry,
Just like those who stay
Those who leave grieve,
Those who stay –
more.

DOUBTS (*SIETE*)

You doubt me
I know you doubt me
You question me
I know you are questioning me
Avoiding me
I know that you avoid me
Because I left
Only because I left.

Return to your past of dry leaves
And make a bonfire with your vanity,
With so much loneliness here
And such an urge to live
You can't stop doubting me.

Hablas de mi
yo sé que andas hablando de mi
porque no fui
aquello que soñabas de mi.
Dudas
yo sé que dudas de mi
y jura que ayer jurabas por mi.

Vuelve a tu pasado de hojas secas
y haz una hoguera con tu vanidad,
con tanta soledad por ahí
con tantas ganas de vivir
y tu no dejas de dudar de mi.

Vuelve a tu pasado de hojas secas
y haz una hoguera con tu vanidad,
con tanta soledad por ahí
con tantas ganas de vivir
y tu no dejas de dudar de mi.

Dudas de mi
yo sé que tienes dudas de mi
porque me fui,
tan solo porque me fui.
Dudas
yo sé que dudas de mi
y jura que ayer jurabas por mi.

ÉCHATE A CORRER (*SIETE*)

En mis sueños veo un pájaro en el aire
mirando hacia el mar
y hay un pez que mira al cielo
creo que sueña con volar.

Los muchachos de la calle dicen que
que les va mejor
y la noche solo sabe

Speak of me
I know that you go around speaking of me
Because I wasn't
What you dreamed of
Doubts
I know that you doubt me
And swear that yesterday you stood by me.

Return to your past of dry leaves
And make a bonfire with your vanity,
With so much loneliness here
And such an urge to live
You can't stop doubting me.

Return to your past of dry leaves
And make a bonfire with your vanity,
With so much loneliness here
And such an urge to live
You can't stop doubting me.

You doubt me
I know you doubt me
You question me
I know you are questioning me
Avoiding me
I know that you avoid me
Because I left
Only because I left.

START RUNNING (*SIETE*)

In my dreams I see a bird in the air
Looking towards the sea
And there's a fish that looks at the sky
I think it dreams of flying.

The kids in the street say
That things will get better
And the night only knows

que la Luna quiere ser
como el Sol.

Nena no sé cómo será el destino
si ya no queda nada que perder
pero si ves que está creciendo el río
será mejor que te eches a correr
será mejor que te eches a correr
será mejor.

En el reino de los cielos
todos quieren parecerse a Dios
y en el mundo de los ciegos
solo el tuerto es el más veloz.

Pero hay gente que en la calle
dicen que
que les va mejor
y la lluvia solo sabe
que la hierba no es igual
a la flor.

Nena no sé cómo será el destino
si ya no queda nada que perder
pero si ves que está creciendo el río
será mejor que te eches a correr

Nena no sé cómo será el destino
si ya no queda nada que perder
pero si ves que está creciendo el río
será mejor que te eches a correr
será mejor que te eches a correr
será mejor
será mejor.

Cómo será el destino
no hay nada que temer
pero si crece el río
será mejor que te eches a correr
será mejor que te eches a correr

That the moon wants to be
Like the sun.

Baby, I don't know what destiny will be,
If already we have nothing to lose
But if you see the river rising,
It's better if you start to run,
It's better if you start to run,
It's better.

In the kingdom of heaven
Everyone wants to be like God,
And in the world of the blind
Only the one-eyed is quickest.

But there people in the street
Who say
That things will get better,
And the rain only knows
That the grass isn't the same
as the flowers.

Baby, I don't know what destiny will be,
If already we have nothing to lose
But if you see the river rising,
It's better if you start to run.

Baby, I don't know what destiny will be,
If already we have nothing to lose
But if you see the river rising
It's better if you start to run.
It's better if you start to run.
It's better,
It's better.

What will destiny be?
There's nothing to fear.
But if the river rises,
Its will be better if you start to run.
It's better if you start to run.

será mejor
será major

EL HUMO DEL TREN (*SIETE*)

Ey man
Sentado en el contén
No eres mas que un prisonero
No eras mas que un rehén

La Habana no es Jerusalén
Pero casi todo el mundo
Sabe quién es quién

Yo tengo una visión
Tengo un sentimiento
La televisión no es mas
Que el Muro de los Lamentos

Así que, mama
A ti que mas te da
Si en la calle todos dicen
Que hay un mas alla
Unos dicen que Ala
Y otros que Yemaya
Y es solo una manera
De buscar la verdad

EL LEÑADOR SIN BOSQUE (*COMO LOS PECES*)

Soy leñador
nací detrás del molino.
Yo tuve un jardín
que fue creciendo conmigo.
Años después un humo negro en el cielo,

It's better.
It's better.

THE SMOKE OF THE TRAIN (*SIETE*)

Hey, man,
Sitting on a curb,
You are no more than a prisoner.
You were no more than a hostage.

Havana isn't Jerusalem,
But almost everyone
Knows who is who.

I have a vision,
I have a feeling,
Television isn't more
Than the Wailing Wall.

So, mama,
What do you care
If in the street everyone says
There is a great beyond?
Some say Allah
And others Yemaya
And it's just a way
To seek the truth.

**THE WOODCUTTER WITHOUT A FOREST
(*COMO LOS PECES*)**

I'm a woodcutter,
Born behind the mill.
I had a garden
That grew with me
Years after a black smoke in the sky,

la Inquisición
quemó mi bosque con fuego, mi bosque.

En la comarca de su majestad,
todos repiten lo que dice el Rey,
el les da el agua, les da el vino y el pan,
pero más tarde les cobra la ley.

Por eso vivo alejado
del trono y el dragón,
prefiero ser olvidado
antes que hacer de bufón.

Soy leñador
un leñador sin bosque.

Yo he visto al verdugo matar al juglar
y a los herejes queriéndo escapar.
Escúchame madre, yo te pido que
antes que sea tarde comience a llover.

Inquisidores que me van a hacer
si ya no quiero inclinarme a tus pies.

Soy leñador desde mi niñez
y aunque no tengo bosque
sueño con árboles,
y aunque no tengo bosque
sueño con árboles.

EL NIÑO, LOS SUEÑOS Y EL RELOJ DE ARENA (*COMO LOS PECES*)

Sentado sobre una piedra de la calle Soledad
sentado como si fuera "El Pensador de Rodin".
Esta es la historia de un niño que se detuvo a soñar
y sueña con ver un día que no acaba de llegar.

The Inquisition
Set fire to my forest, my forest.

In the region of His Majesty,
Everyone repeats what the King says.
He gives them water, he gives them wine and bread
But later he uses the law to charge them.

That's why I live far away
From the throne and the dragon
I'd rather be forgotten
Than be the jester.

I'm a woodcutter,
A woodcutter without a forest.

I have seen the executioner kill the minstrel,
And those heretics who wanted to escape.
Listen to me mother, I ask you
Before long it will start to rain.

Inquisitors, what are you going to do to me,
If I don't want to bow at your feet?

I've been a woodcutter since childhood,
And although I don't have a forest,
I dream of trees.
Although I don't have a forest,
I dream of trees.

THE CHILD, THE DREAMS, AND THE HOURGLASS (*COMO LOS PECES*)

Sitting on a rock on Soledad Street
Sitting as though he was Rodin's Thinker,
This is the story of a child who paused to dream
He dreams of seeing a day that still hasn't come.

Pero sabe que hay otros que sueñan igual,
porque tal vez un día ese maldito sueño,
se puede volver real.

Los viejos pasan y ríen viendo al muchacho soñar,
no es que ya nadie confíe, pero es difícil confiar.
El joven mira hacia el cielo y mientras en la ciudad,
la gente vive con miedo, con miedo para esperar.

Pero sabe que hay otros que sueñan igual,
porque tal vez un día ese maldito sueño,
se puede volver real.

Yo tengo un reloj de arena para medir mi dolor,
cada segundo es la pena que va cayendo en mi corazón.
Y aunque no me hago ilusiones, algo tendrá que cambiar,
aunque yo sueñe canciones y otros prefieran callar.

Pero sabe que hay otros que sueñan igual,
porque tal vez un día ese maldito sueño,
se puede volver real.

Sentado sobre una piedra de la calle Soledad
sentado como si fuera "El Pensador de Rodin".
Esta es la historia de un niño que envejeció de soñar
y sigue esperando un día que no acaba de llegar,
de llegar.

EL VIEJO SUEÑO ACABÓ (*NO ES EL FIN*)

Ya lo ves
el viejo sueño acabó
y tú y yo
a ambos lados del Sol.
Qué más da
quién ganó, quién perdió
si es que al final
el sueño acabó.

But know that there are others who also dream,
Because maybe one day this cursed dream,
Could come true.

The old folks pass by and laugh at the dreaming boy.
It's not that no one trusts, but it's difficult to trust.
The young man looks to the sky, while in the city
People live in fear, fear of hoping.

But know that there are others who also dream,
Because maybe one day this cursed dream,
Could come true.

I have an hourglass to measure my pain.
Sorrow falls on my heart every second.
And although it doesn't make me delusional, something has
   to change,
Although I dream songs and others prefer to keep quiet.

But know that there are others who also dream,
Because maybe one day this cursed dream,
Could come true.

Sitting on a rock on Soledad Street
Sitting as though he was Rodin's Thinker,
This is the story of a child who aged dreaming,
And continues to hope for a day that still hasn't come.

THE OLD DREAM HAS ENDED (*NO ES EL FIN*)

You see it now
The old dream has ended
And you and I
On both sides of the sun.
Who cares anymore
Who won, who lost
If in the end
The dream has ended?

Tú
tú y yo,
tú eras como el viento
y yo un campo de arroz,
pero nos quitaron
el amor y el tiempo
en nombre de Dios,
pero nos quitaron
el amor y el tiempo
en nombre de un mismo Dios.

Ya lo ves,
el viejo sueño acabó
y tú y yo
a ambos lados del Sol.
Qué más da
quién ganó, quién perdió
si es que al final
el sueño acabó.

ENIGMA DEL ÁRBOL (*MONEDAS AL AIRE*)

No había nadie en la calle, la Habana estaba vacía,
solo el guardia del barrio con su vieja linterna china.
Cuando se oyó un gran ruido debajo del asfalto
que se abrió en dos pedazos, mientras nacía un árbol.
Eran ramas enormes en espiral al cielo,
perdiéndose en las nubes como pasa en los cuentos.
Mientras el vecindario se asomaba boquiabierto,
haciendo el comentario, pensando que no era cierto.

La negra dijo que Shangó nos había mandado el castigo.
Y el viejo dijo que quizás era otro invento del enemigo.

Lo cierto es que aquel árbol causó tanta sorpresa
que nadie imaginó el final.

You,
You and I --
You were like the wind,
And me, a field of rice
But everything left us,
Love and time
In the name of God,
They left us,
Love and time
In the name of the same God.

You see it now
The old dream has ended,
And you and I,
On both sides of the sun.
Who cares anymore
Who won, who lost
If in the end
The dream has ended?

THE ENIGMA OF THE TREE (*MONEDAS AL AIRE*)

There was no one in the street, Havana was empty,
Only the neighbourhood guard with his old Chinese lantern.
When he heard a great noise under the pavement
It split in two, and a tree was born.
Huge branches spiralled to the sky,
Losing itself in the clouds, just like in the storybooks.
While the neighbourhood looked out, astonished,
Making remarks, thinking it wasn't true.

The black woman said that Shango had sent us a punishment.
The old man said that maybe it was another invention of the
    enemy.
What's certain is that the tree caused such a surprise
That no one could picture the end.

A la mañana llegaron fotógrafos y oradores,
una muchacha de quince y un matrimonio
que puso flores.
Un tipo se subió pensando que una rama llegaba a Miami,
y el barrio le gritó y puso carteles por todas partes.
La policía puso barras amarillas y luces girando
y no faltaron los turistas entre los que iban llegando.

La negra dijo que Shangó nos había mandado el castigo.
Y el viejo dijo que quizás era otro invento del enemigo.
Lo cierto es que aquel árbol causó tanta sorpresa
que nadie imaginó el final.

Llegaron los arquitectos y los científicos del museo,
mientras que los creyentes le daban vueltas por un
deseo.
Y así fue que se juntaron, políticos y santeros,
la puta y el miliciano, los hippies y los obreros.
Y cuando decidieron justo lo que iban a hacer con el árbol,
la misma tierra lo tragó y solo quedó el espacio.

La negra dijo que Shangó nos había mandado el castigo.
Y el viejo dijo que quizás era otro invento del enemigo.
Lo cierto es que aquel árbol causó tanta sorpresa
que nadie imaginó el final.

FOTO DE FAMILIA (*COMO LOS PECES*)

Detrás de todos estos años
detrás del miedo y el dolor
vivimos añorando algo,
algo que nunca más volvió.

Detrás de los que no se fueron,
detrás de los que ya no están,

The next day the photographers and speakers arrived,
A fifteen-year-old girl and a married couple
who brought flowers.
A guy climbed up, thinking that a branch would lead him to Miami,
And the neighbourhood yelled at him and put up posters everywhere.
The police put up yellow barriers and flashing lights
And among those who arrived, there were no end of tourists.

The black woman said that Shango had sent us a punishment.
The old man said that maybe it was another invention of the enemy.
What's certain is that the tree caused such a surprise
That no one could picture the end.

The architects and the scientists from the museum arrived
While the believers kept wishing over and over.
And this is how they came together,
The politicians and the *santeros**
The prostitutes and the military, the hippies and the workers.
And when they decided just what do to with the tree,
That same earth swallowed it and all that remained was the space.

The black woman said that Shango had sent us a punishment.
The old man said that maybe it was another invention of the enemy.
What's certain is that the tree caused such a surprise
That no one could picture the end.

*Santeros *are practitioners of the religion* santería.

FAMILY PHOTO (*COMO LOS PECES*)

Behind all these years,
Behind the fear and grief,
We live yearning for something,
Something that never returned.

After the ones who didn't go away,
Behind the ones who aren't with us anymore,

hay una foto de familia
donde lloramos al final.

Tratando de mirar
por el hueco de una aguja.
Tratando de vivir dentro de una misma burbuja,
Solos.

Detrás de toda la nostalgia,
de la mentira y la traición,
detrás de toda la distancia,
detrás de la separación.

Detrás de todos los gobiernos,
de las fronteras y la religión
hay una foto de familia,
hay una foto de los dos.

Tratando de mirar
por el hueco de una aguja.
Tratando de vivir dentro de una misma burbuja,
Solos.

Detrás de todos estos años
detrás del miedo y el dolor
vivimos añorando algo
y descubrimos con desilusión
que no sirvió de nada,
de nada
"o casi nada
que no es lo mismo
pero es igual."*

*De *Pequeña serenata diurna* de Silvio Rodríguez

There's a photo of a family,
Where finally, we cry.

Trying to look
Through the eye of a needle,
Trying to live in the same bubble,
Alone.

Behind all the loneliness,
The betrayals and the lies,
Behind all the distance,
Behind the separation.

Behind all governments,
Borders and religions,
There's a family picture,
There's a picture of the two of us.

Trying to look
Through the eye of a needle,
Trying to live in the same bubble,
Alone.

Behind all these years,
Behind the fear and grief,
We live yearning for something,
And we discover with disillusionment,
That it was all for nothing
Nothing
"Or that it was worth almost nothing
Which is different,
Yet really just the same."*

*From "Pequeña serenata diurnal" by Silvio Rodríguez

GRAFFITI DE AMOR (*COMO LOS PECES*)

No se supo de que barrio
pero cuando todo estaba oscuro
ella llegó bajo la luz del alba.
Y con su creyón de labios
dibujó señales en los muros,
quiso pintar lo que sintió su alma.

Y pintó y pintó por todas partes
miles de peces de un solo color
y llenó las calles con su graffiti de amor.

Cuando amaneció flotando
la ciudad inundada de dibujos
nadie entendió
quién se atrevió a tanto.
Unos la fueron buscando
y otros iban borrando los muros
y ella siguió y hasta pintó
los autos.

Y pintó y pintó por todas partes
miles de peces de un solo color
y llenó las calles con su graffiti de amor.

Por eso fue que borraron
edificios, muros y vidrieras
y hasta una Luna que un niño dibujó
en la acera.
Desde entonces prohibieron
dibujar lo que sentía el alma,
para cuidar y encadenar
la calma.

Y como no le dejaron sitios
donde dibujar su dolor,
se rayó su cuerpo
con un tatuaje de amor,
se rayó su cuerpo
con un tatuaje de amor.

GRAFFITI OF LOVE (*COMO LOS PECES*)

No one knew where she came from,
But when everything was dark,
She arrived under the light of dawn.
And with her lipstick,
She drew signs on the walls.
She wanted to paint all that she felt in her soul.

And she painted, painted everywhere,
Thousands of fish in only one colour.
And she filled the streets with her graffiti of love.

When dawn broke,
The city was flooded with drawings
No one understood:
Who could have been so daring?
Some went looking for her,
Others started erasing the walls.
And she just kept going, even painting
The cars.

And she painted and painted, everywhere,
Thousands of fish, in just one colour,
And she filled the streets with her graffiti of love.

That's why they erased
The buildings, the walls, the windows,
Erasing even the moon that a child drew
On the sidewalk.
From then on it was forbidden
To draw what one feels in the soul,
To protect and shackle
The peace.

And since they left her no place
To draw out her pain,
She scratched her body
With a tattoo of love.
She scratched her body
With a tattoo of love.

GRETTEL (*MONEDAS AL AIRE*)

Los lobos de Jim Morrison vienen hacia aquí,
las cartas del Tarot solo me hablan de tí
y es que ya no hay razón para quedarse aquí
si en todas partes todo me conduce a ti.

Grettel
cuando no estás aquí,
todo se desvanece.
Grettel
si nio estás en mí,
el día no amanece.

Esta ciudad se vuelve más difícil aún
más oscura, más sola
y es que nada es igual como cuando estás tú
por eso estoy ahora.

Grettel
cuando no estás aquí,
todo se desvanece.
Grettel
si no estás en mí,
el día no amanece.

Toda la lluvia un día puede caer,
como el dinero, como el poder,
pero tus veinte años ya lo saben muy bien
que a pesar de este mundo yo no quiero perder.

Los lobos de Jim Morrinson vienen hacia aquí,
las cartas del Tarot solo me hablan de tí
y es que ya no hay razón para quedarse aquí
cuando todo, todo, todo, me conduce a tí.

Grettel
cuando no estás aquí,
todo se desvanece.
Grettel

GRETTEL (*MONEDAS AL AIRE*)

The wolves of Jim Morrison are heading here,
the Tarot cards speak only of you
and there is no reason to stay here
if everywhere everything leads me to you.

Grettel
when you are not here,
everything disappears
Grettel
if you are not in me,
the day does not break.

This city becomes even more difficult
Even darker, more alone
and nothing is the same as when you are here
That's why I'm here now.

Grettel
when you are not here,
everything disappears
Grettel
if you are not in me
the day does not break

All the rain can fall one day,
like money, like power,
but your twenty years already know very well
that in spite of this world I do not want to lose.

The wolves of Jim Morrison are heading here,
the Tarot cards speak only of you
 and there is no reason to stay here
 if everything, everything leads me to you.

Grettel
when you are not here,
everything disappears
Grettel

Si no estás en mí,
el día no amanece.
al menos para mi
al menos para mi.

GUILLERMO TELL (*JALISCO PARK*)

Guillermo Tell no comprendió a su hijo
que un día se aburrió de la manzana en la cabeza
y echó a correr y el padre lo maldijo
pues como entonces iba probar su destreza.

Guillermo Tell, tu hijo creció
quiere tirar la flecha,
le toca a él probar su valor
usando tu ballesta.

Guillermo Tell no comprendió el empeño
pues quien se iba a arriesgar al tiro de esa flecha
y se asustó cuando dijo el pequeño
ahora le toca al padre la manzana en la cabeza.

Guillermo Tell, tu hijo creció
quiere tirar la flecha,
le toca a él probar su valor
usando tu ballesta.

A Guillermo Tell no le gustó la idea
y se negó a ponerse la manzana en la cabeza
diciendo que no era que no creyera
pero qué iba a pasar si sale mal la flecha.

Guillermo Tell tu hijo creció
quiere tirar la flecha
le toca a él probar su valor
usando tu ballesta.

Guillermo Tell no comprendió a su hijo
que un día se aburrió de la manzana en la cabeza.

if you are not in me
the day does not break.
At least not for me
At least not for me.

WILLIAM TELL (*JALISCO PARK*)

William Tell didn't understand his son
Who one day got tired of having the apple placed on his head,
And started to run away and his father cursed him.
How could he now prove his skill?

William Tell, your son has grown up.
He wants to shoot the arrow himself.
It's his turn now to show his valour,
Using your crossbow.

Yet William Tell didn't understand the challenge.
Who would ever risk having the arrow shot at them?
He became afraid when his son addressed him,
Telling William that it was now his turn
   to place the apple on his own head.

William Tell, your son has grown up.
He wants to shoot the arrow himself.
It's his turn now to show his valour,
Using your crossbow.

William Tell didn't like the idea
And refused to place the apple on his own head.
It was not that he didn't trust his son,
But what would happen if he missed?

William Tell, your son has grown up.
He wants to shoot the arrow himself.
It's his turn now to show his valour,
Using your crossbow.

William Tell didn't understand his son,
Who one day got tired of having the apple placed on his head.

HABÁNAME (*COMO LOS PECES*)

Mirando un álbum de fotos de la vieja capital,
desde los tiempos remotos de La Habana colonial.
Mi padre dejó su tierra y cuando al Morro llegó,
La Habana le abrió sus piernas y por eso nací yo.

Habana, Habana si bastara una canción
para devolverlo todo lo que el tiempo te quitó.
Habana, mi Habana si supieras el dolor
que siento cuando te canto
y no entiendes que es amor.

Escuchando a Matamoros desde un lejano lugar
La Habana guarda un tesoro que es difícil olvidar.
Y los años van pasando y miramos con dolor,
como se va derrumbando cada muro de ilusión.

Habana, Habana si bastara una canción
para devolverte todo lo que el tiempo te quitó.
Habana, mi Habana si supieras el dolor
que siento cuando te canto y no entiendes que
este llanto
es por amor.

HISTORIA DE UN DESCAPOTABLE (*NO ES EL FIN*)

En un descapotable rosado
fueron al autocine abandonado
y se desnudaron los dos
y se entregaron el alma
en silencio
y la Luna miraba en calma.

Era una noche extraña y mojada,
como si nunca fuera a pasar nada

HAVANA ME (*COMO LOS PECES*)

Looking at a photo album of the old capital,
From the distant past of colonial Havana.
My father left his land, and when he reached El Morro,
Havana opened her legs to him, and that's why I was born.

Havana, Havana, if only a song were enough
To return everything that time has taken.
Havana, my Havana,
If you only knew the pain that I feel when I sing to you,
And you don't understand that it's out of love.

Listening to Matamoros from a faraway place,
Havana holds a treasure that is difficult to forget.
And the years pass and we look on in pain,
As each wall of illusion comes tumbling down.

Havana, Havana, if only a song were enough
To return to you everything that time has taken.
Havana, my Havana, if you only knew the pain
That I feel when I sing to you and you don't understand
that this cry
is out of love.

HISTORY OF A CONVERTIBLE (*NO ES EL FIN*)

In a pink convertible,
They went to an abandoned drive-in theatre,
And they both got undressed,
Surrendering their souls to each other
In silence,
And the moon was watching calmly.

It was a strange and wet night,
As though nothing would happen,

y se durmieron los dos
y en eso fue que ocurrió
el misterio desde el aire,
desde la nada.

Se elevaron desde el suelo
como cuando el humo sube
y levitaron hacia el cielo abrazados
y se perdieron entre las nubes.

Cuando se despertaron callados
pensando que era un sueño imaginado
se descubrieron los dos
en la pantalla del cine
atrapados,
prisioneros
del otro lado.

En un descapotable rosado
se hicieron blanco y negro
como el pasado
y fueron siglos atrás
y desde entonces jamás
regresaron
a este mundo
que abandonaron.

HOMBRE DE SILICONA (*COMO LOS PECES*)

El era hombre, era hombre
pero tenía un corazón de mujer.

Estaba preso dentro de su mismo cuerpo
sin poder escapar de dolor,
su sexo que importaba si era falso o cierto
si ya vivía con la ilusión.
El era libre, era libre
pero soñaba con dejar la prisión.

They fell asleep
And this was what happened,
A mystery from out of thin air,
From nothing.

They found themselves rising
Like when smoke rises
And they were lifted, hugging, toward the heavens,
And they lost themselves in the clouds.

When they awoke quietly
Thinking that it had only been a dream,
They discovered themselves
Trapped
In the screen of the theatre,
Prisoners
Of the other side.

In the pink convertible,
They were in black and white,
Like in the past,
And they went back centuries,
And they would never
Return
To this world
That abandoned them.

SILICON MAN (*COMO LOS PECES*)

He was a man, he was a man,
But he had a heart of a woman.

He was a prisoner of his own body,
He couldn't escape his pain,
What did it matter if his sex was true or false?
If he lived with the illusion.
He was free, he was free,
But he dreamed of leaving the prison.

En el barrio lo miraban de una forma extraña
por eso apenas se asomaba a su balcón.
Sus amantes le decían: la mujer araña,
pero en la calle le gritaban: maricón.

Coleccionaba los filmes de Almodóvar
y las revistas prohíbidas por la ley,
aquella noche todo terminó en su alcoba,
la muerte le besó los labios como un gay.
El era hombre, era hombre
pero tenía un corazón de mujer.

Es duro vivir así, es duro vivir muriendo
es duro seguir viviendo, es duro vivir.
Es duro morir así, es duro morir viviendo,
es duror seguir muriendo, es duro morir.

El tipo se pinchó la dósis de silicona
sus pechos empezaron crecer
soñaba con tener los senos de Madonna,
soñaba con las piernas de Cher.
El era hombre, era hombre
pero tenía un corazón de mujer.

Estaba preso dentro de su mismo cuerpo
sin poder escapar del dolor,
su sexo que importaba si era falso o cierto
si ya moría con la ilusión.
El era libre, era libre
pero soñaba con dejar la prisión.

JALISCO PARK (*JALISCO PARK*)

Todos los domingos me iba a la ciudad
de los chocolates para ir a escalar
la Montaña Rusa, la Estrella Polar,
los carritos locos,
todo un paraíso de metal.

In the neighbourhood they looked at him funny.
That's why he hardly went onto his balcony.
His lovers called him spiderwoman
But in the streets they yelled "fag."

He collected Almodóvar's films,
And the magazines prohibited by law,
One night it all came to an end in his bedroom,
When death kissed him on the lips like a gay.
He was a man, he was a man
But he had the heart of a woman.

It's hard to live like that, it's hard to live dying
It's hard to continue to live, it's hard to live
It's hard to die like this, it's hard to die living,
It's hard to keep dying, it's hard to die.

This guy gave himself a dose of silicon,
His chest began to grow
He dreamed of having the breasts of Madonna,
He dreamed of having the legs of Cher.
He was a man, he was a man,
But he had the heart of a woman.

He was a prisoner of his own body,
He couldn't escape his pain,
What did it matter if his sex was true or false?
If he lived with the illusion.
He was free, he was free,
But he dreamed of leaving the prison.

JALISCO PARK (*JALISCO PARK*)

Every Sunday I went to the chocolate city
to climb the roller coaster,
The Polar Star,
The crazy little cars
All a paradise of metal.

Me iba a la laguna para navegar
con los botecitos en el mismo lugar.
Magos y payasos, ganas de volar
como los avioncitos del Jalisco Park.
Todo daba vueltas como el carrusel
y todos mis amigos giraban con él.

Allí pasé mi infancia en aquel rincón
y entre los aparatos buscaba una razón,
por eso la vida solo me enseñó
a través del parque lo que nos pasó.

A la Montaña Rusa la quisieron descarrilar
con todas las calumnias de la Patria Potestad
y luego a mi amiguito el padre se lo llevó
a montar el barquito y nunca regresó.

Todo daba vueltas como el carrusel
y todos sus amigos lloramos con él.
Un día jugando, no supe por qué
en el 67 mataron al Che
y así giró su historia, como el carrusel
y la soñada idea de ser como el.

Después el pelo largo, la moda y la confusión
llegaban al 70 con el sueño del millón
y así surgió aquel loco que primero nadie entendió
diciendo cosas raras como en aquella canción:
"La era está pariendo un corazón
no puede más se muere de dolor ..."

Ha pasado el tiempo y sólo quedan ya
aparatos muertos puestos a girar
y aunque no fui payaso, ni mago ni aviador
sigo dando vueltas sin pensar quien soy.

Y así tengo enemigos que me quieren descarrilar
haciéndome la guerra porque me puse a cantar.
Pero pongo la historia por encima de su razón

I went to the lagoon to sail
the little boats there.
Magicians and clowns, the urge to fly
Like the little planes in Jalisco Park.
Everything whirled around like the carousel,
And all my friends spun around with it.

I spent my childhood in that corner,
And among the attractions I looked for my purpose,
And because of that, I learned life's lessons simply
Through what happened to us in that park.

They wanted to derail the roller coaster
With the slander of the Patria Potestad
And later, my friend's father took him
To board a boat, and he never returned.

Everything spun around, like the carousel
And all his friends cried with him.
One day in 1967, I didn't know why
They killed Che
And just like that his history turned like a carousel,
And the dream to be like him was born.

After the long hair, the style and the confusion,
The 1970s arrived, with the dream of a million,
And in the midst of this that crazy guy arrived,
   who no one understood at first,
Saying weird things like in that song:
"The age is giving birth to a heart,
It can't do anything more, it's dying of pain ..."*

Now time has passed and the only thing remaining
Dead machines, made to spin,
And although I wasn't a clown, or a magician, or an aviator
I follow, spinning around, without thinking of who I am.

I have enemies who want to derail me,
Making war on me because I began to sing.
But I put history above their reasons,

y sé con qué canciones quiero hacer Revolución
aunque me quede sin voz, aunque no me
vengan a escuchar,
aunque me dejen solo como a Jalisco Park.

JAQUE MATE 1916 (*JALISCO PARK*)

El perro golpea la puerta del patio
arriba el vecino le pega a su mujer
la línea amarilla divide el asfalto
y afuera la gente no sabe qué hacer.
Veo gasolina flotando en un charco
haciendo arcoiris debajo del pie
un viejo se encuentra a su doble en un banco
y leen la prensa jugando ajedrez.

Tristán Tzara jugaba ajedrez con Lenin
en la misma calle que nació Dadá
a veces presiento que fui una pieza
y que aquel tablero era mi ciudad.
Tristán Tzara jugaba ajedrez con Lenin
en la misma calle que nació Dadá
y un año más tarde salió el fantasma
recorriendo el mundo hasta mi ciudad.

El perro se bebe a su doble en el charco
se traga el arcoiris y se echa a correr
la mujer del vecino golpea el asfalto
y la puerta de arriba no sabe qué hacer.
El vecino golpea al perro en un banco
que orina colores sobre su pie,
la prensa se pone amarilla en un charco
y afuera los dobles no sabe qué hacer.

And I know that with songs I want to make a Revolution,
Even if I'm left without a voice, even if no one comes to listen
    to me,
Even if they leave me alone
Like they did Jalisco Park.

*From "The Era" by Silvio Rodríguez

CHECKMATE 1916 (JALISCO PARK)

The dog hits the patio door
Upstairs, the neighbour hits his woman.
The yellow line divides the road,
And outside, the people don't know what to do.
I see gasoline floating in a puddle,
Making rainbows under my feet.
An old man meets his double in a bank
And they read the newspaper playing chess.

Tristan Tzara played chess with Lenin
On the same street where Dada was born.
Sometimes I have a feeling that I was a game piece
And that chessboard was my city.
Tristan Tzara played chess with Lenin
On the same street where Dada was born,
And a year later, the ghost unleashed itself,
Travelling around the world until landing in my city.

The dog drinks its reflection from the puddle.
It swallows the rainbow and starts to run.
The neighbour's woman hits the pavement,
And the upstairs door doesn't know what to do.
In the bank, the neighbour hits the dog
It urinates on his foot.
The newspaper turns yellow in a puddle,
And outside, the doubles don't know what to do.

Tristán Tzara jugaba ajedrez con Lenin
en la misma calle que nació Dadá
a veces presiento que fui una pieza
y que aquel tablero era mi ciudad.
Tristán Tzara jugaba ajedrez con Lenin
en la misma calle que nació Dadá
y un año más tarde salió el fantasma
recorriendo el mundo hasta mi ciudad.

Los viejos dividen la puerta y el banco
afuera los perros no saben qué hacer
yo leo la prensa pisando los charcos
y encuentro a mi doble en una mujer.
el perro, la puerta, el fantasma y el banco
la prensa,los dobles,el pie y la mujer
la línea amarilla, los viejos y el charco
son piezas que flotan en un ajedrez, sin saber qué hacer.

LA COMEDIA SILENTE (*NO ES EL FIN*)

Yo no quiero ser tu rana René,
ni tampoco Superman.
No me digas lo que tengo que hacer,
yo solo quiero
que me dejes un poquito en paz,
solo un poquito en paz.

Igual que toda la gente,
unos ladran y otros muerden,
yo vivo religiosamente
como en la Comedia silente.

No, no me pongas contra la pared,
yo no soy tu Peter Pan,
no me digas lo que tengo que hacer,
yo solo quiero
que me dejes un poquito en paz,
solo un poquito en paz.

Tristan Tzara played chess with Lenin
On the same street where Dada was born.
Sometimes I have a feeling that I was a game piece
And that chessboard was my city.
Tristan Tzara played chess with Lenin
On the same street where Dada was born,
And a year later, the ghost unleashed itself,
Travelling around the world until landing in my city.

The old men divide the door and the bank.
Outside the dogs don't know what to do.
And I read the newspaper, treading through puddles,
And I find my double in a woman.
The dog, the door, the phantom, and the bank
The newspaper, the doubles, the foot, and the woman
The yellow line, the old men, and the puddle
Are all pieces floating in a chess game
   without knowing what to do.

SILENT COMEDY (*NO ES EL FIN*)

I don't want to be your frog René,
Nor Superman either.
Don't tell me what I have to do.
I just want you to
Leave me in peace,
Just a little peace.

Like all people,
Some bark and some bite,
I live religiously,
Like in a silent comedy.

No, don't put me up against the wall.
I'm not your Peter Pan.
Don't tell me what I have to do.
I just want you to
Leave me in peace,
Just a little peace.

Igual que toda la gente,
unos callan y otros mienten,
yo vivo silenciosamente
como en la Comedia silente.

Cara de Globo y Soplete,
Barrilito y Barrilón
con el Gordo Matasiete
con el guardia y el ladrón.
El Conde de Luz Brillante
bailando su charlestón.
Ya no somos los de antes,
ya no me queda más mi generación.
El Hombre de las Mil Voces
no sabe como es mi voz.
Se perdieron nuestros dioses
como Armando Calderón.

LA MAREA (*NO ES EL FIN*)

No soy más, no soy menos,
no soy malo ni bueno,
no soy mar, no soy tierra,
no soy paz, ni soy la guerra.

No soy niño ni viejo,
no soy sombra ni espejo,
no soy risa ni llanto,
no te acerco, ni te espanto.

Soy más bien la marea,
tengo días malos y noches buenas,
días de gatos, días de perros,
días en que a ratos
voy a mi entierro,
pero si faltas,
mi fantasía

Like all people,
Some keep quiet and some lie.
I live silently
Like in a silent comedy.

The face of Globo and Soplete,
Barrilito and Barrilón
with the Gordo Matasiete
with the guard and the robber.
The Count of Luz Brillante
Dancing the Charleston.
Already we aren't like before.
Already I am left almost without a generation.
The Man of a Thousand Voices
Doesn't know my voice.
Our Gods are lost
Like Armando Calderón.

THE TIDE (*NO ES EL FIN*)

I'm not more, I'm not less,
I'm not bad, I'm not good,
I'm not the sea, I'm not the land,
I'm not peace, I'm not war.

I'm not a child, nor an old man,
I'm not a shadow or a mirror,
I am not a laugh or a cry,
I don't get closer to you, I don't frighten you away.

Rather, I am the tide,
I have bad days and good nights,
Days of cats, days of dogs,
Days when at times
I go to my grave,
But if you're not there,
My fantasy.

piensa que es de noche
cuando es de día.

No soy aire, ni fuego,
no soy pez, ni el anzuelo,
no soy puerto, ni barco,
no soy la flecha, ni soy el arco.

Soy más bien la marea,
tengo días malos y noches buenas,
días de gatos, días de perros,
días en que a ratos
voy a mi entierro,
pero si faltas,
mi fantasía
piensa que es de noche
cuando es de día.

LA POLÍTICA NO CABE EN LA AZUCARERA
(*COMO LOS PECES*)

Un amigo se compró un Chevrolet del 59
no le quiso cambiar algunas piezas y ahora no se mueve.
Hace mucho calor en la vieja Habana
la gente espera algo, pero aquí no pasa nada.
Un tipo gritó: ¡sálvese quien pueda!
Cada día que pasa sube más la marea.
Felipito se fue a los Estados Unidos,
allí pasa frío y aquí estaba aburrido,
en la mesa de domingo hay dos sillas vacías,
están a 90 millas de la mía.

Pero entiéndelo brother tómalo como quieras

la política no cabe en la azucarera.
"Un obrero me ve, me llama artista y noblemente me
suma su estatura,"*
anda traficando con dinero de turista,
el tiene cuatro hijos y la vida está muy dura,

Mistakes the day
For the night.

I'm not air or fire,
I'm not a fish or a hook,
I'm not a port or a boat,
I'm not the arrow, nor the bow.

Rather, I am the tide
I have bad days and good nights,
Days of cats, days of dogs,
Days when at times
I go to my grave,
But if you're not there
My fantasy
Mistakes the day
For the night.

POLITICS DOESN'T FIT IN THE SUGAR BOWL (*COMO LOS PECES*)

A friend bought a '59 Chevrolet.
He didn't want to change any parts, and now it doesn't move.
It's really hot in Old Havana.
The people are waiting for something, but here nothing happens.
A guy shouted "save yourself if you can!"
The tide gets higher with every passing day.
Feliipito left for the US.
There its cold, here it was boring.
At the table on Sunday there are two empty chairs,
They are 90 miles away from mine.

But understand it brother, take it as you'd like:

Politics doesn't fit in the sugar bowl.
"A worker sees me, he calls me an artist
and nobly I raise his status."
He goes around trading in tourist money,
He has four children and life is hard,

¡pero entiéndeme brother!
-dijo tómalo como quieras,
la política no cabe en la azucarera,

Oh Dios, que quieres de mi
Desnúdate nena que vengo por ti
Hoy seguramente que nos cortan la luz
Y no hay otra cosa que jugar al vudú

Todos quieren vivir en el noticiero
Allí no falta nada y no hace falta el dinero
Las mujeres son un buen negocio
Algunas andan solas y otras ya tienen un socio
Pero entiéndeme brother – dicen
Tómalo como quieras
La política no cabe en la azucarera

En la escuela me enseñaron que en el Apartheid
No todos son iguales y no importa la ley
Por eso me molesto con las cosas que veo
Escúchame brother: fuck your bloqueo
Pero entiéndelo man
Tómalo como quieras
La política no cabe en la azucarera

*De Llover sobre mojado de Silvio

LUCAS Y LUCÍA (*NUBES*)

Lucas y Lucía eran dos enanos
se fueron un día en un aeroplano.
Donde acaba el cielo, comienza el sky
se fueron al Norte, "donde todo lo hay."

Y buscaban y buscaban
nada más, un sitio donde
al menos poder respirar.

But understand me brother,
He said, take it as you'd like:
Politics doesn't fit in a sugar bowl.

Oh God, what do you want from me?
Get undressed, baby, I'm coming for you.
Today for sure they'll cut the lights,
And there's nothing else but to practise voodoo.

Everyone wants to live in the news.
There nothing's lacking and money isn't short.
Women are a good business.
Some work alone and some have a partner.
But understand me brother, they say
Take it as you'd like:
Politics doesn't fit in a sugar bowl.

In school they taught me that in Apartheid
Not everyone is equal and the law didn't matter.
That's why the things I see bother me.
Listen to me, brother: fuck your blockade
But understand it, man,
Take it as you'd like:
Politics doesn't fit in a sugar bowl.

LUCAS AND LUCIA (*NUBES*)

Lucas and Lucia were two kids,
Who left one day in an aeroplane.
Where the *cielo* ends, the *sky* begins.
They left for the North, "the land of everything."

And they searched and searched
For a place where, if nothing else,
At least they could breathe.

Y buscaban y buscaban
una vez más, un sitio donde
al menos poder olvidar.

Y también del Norte se escaparon
y con su aeroplano se largaron.

Entre la tormenta y el cielo nublado
llegaron a tierras de los olvidados.

Y buscaban y buscaban
nada más, un sitio donde
al menos poder respirar.

Y buscaban y buscaban
una vez más, un sitio donde
al menos poder olvidar.

Lucas y Lucía se fueron sin rumbo
a buscar un sitio en este mundo.

Dicen que aún dan vueltas en el cielo

Yo no sé donde están
yo no sé si vendrán algún día
pero cada vez más
hay más Lucas
y Lucias.

MÁS ALLÁ (*NUBES*)

Más allá del Sol,
más allá del mar,
más allá de Dios,
poco más allá.

And they searched and searched
One more time, for a place where
At least they could forget.

And they also fled the North,
With their airplane, they took off.

Between the storm and the cloudy sky
They arrived at the land of the forgotten.

And they searched and searched
For a place where, if nothing else,
At least they could breathe.

And they searched and searched
One more time, for a place where
At least they could forget.

Lucas and Lucia left without direction
To find a place in this world.

Some say that they even flew round and round in the sky,
Searching for the place of their dreams.

I don't know where they are,
And I don't know if one day they'll return,
But more and more
There are more Lucases
And Lucias.

BEYOND (*NUBES*)

Beyond the sun,
Beyond the sea,
Beyond God,
A little bit farther.

Más allá del bien,
más allá del mal,
más allá después,
poco más allá.

Ella se fue de la ciudad
y se escondió aún más allá.
Se echó a correr, se echó a volar
y se perdió aún más allá.

Más allá del Yin,
más allá del Yang,
más allá del fin,
poco más allá.

Más allá de ser o no ser,
más allá de estar o no estar,
más allá de ver,
poco más allá.

Ella se fue de la ciudad
y se escondió aun más allá.
Se echó a correr, se echó a volar
y se perdió aun más allá.

Más allá del Sol,
más allá del mar,
más allá de Dios
se fue más allá.

ESTÁS (*SIETE*)

Cada vez que me pierdo
entre la gente
y creo verte en el tímido brillo
de unos lentes
ya no sé
si estoy alucinando una vez más

Beyond good,
Beyond bad,
Beyond and then,
A little bit farther.

She left the city
And she hid even farther away.
She began to run, she began to fly
And she lost her way even farther on.

Beyond Yin,
Beyond Yang,
Beyond the end,
A little bit farther.

Beyond existing or not existing,
Beyond being there or not being there,
Beyond seeing,
A little bit farther.

She left the city
And she hid even farther away,
She began to run, she began to fly
And she lost her way even farther on.

Beyond the sun,
Beyond the sea,
Beyond God
She went even farther.

YOU ARE (*SIETE*)

Each time I lose myself
Among the people
And I think I see you in the soft shine
Of someone's glasses,
I don't know
If I'm hallucinating one more time.

o es que solo te sigo soñando
que estás donde no estás.

Cada vez que te culpo, te perdono
y te busco
y una vez que te encuentro,
te abandono
y es que no se mentir todavía
cuando creo que miento
y no dejo de hacer poesía
cuando sueño tu encuentro.

Te encuentro en los espejos
en los charcos de la acera
en los libros de un amor de colegial
en la cicatriz de un puente de madera
y en el frío ruido de la lluvia
en un portal.
Estás en los letreros de los cines
y en las vidrieras
en los bancos de los parques
sin pintar
y en la soledad de una gasolinera
y en los árboles de toda esta ciudad.

Cada vez que te miro
me olvido de la muerte
y me olvido del pasado que vendrá
yo lo dejaría todo,
solo por volver a verte
solo sé que no estoy solo
cuando sé donde estás.

Estas en los espejos
en los charcos de la acera
en los libros de un amor de colegial
en la cicatriz de un puente de madera
y en el frío ruido de la lluvia
en un portal.
Estás en los letreros de los cines

Or is it that I keep dreaming that you are
Where you are not.

Each time I blame you, I forgive you.
And I look for you,
And as soon as I find you,
I abandon you.
And it's still not a lie
When I believe I lie,
And I don't give up on writing poetry
When I dream of meeting you.

I find you in the mirrors
In the puddles on the sidewalk
In the books of a high school crush
In the scar of a wooden bridge
In the cold noise of the rain
In a doorway.
You are in the signs of the theatres
And in the shop windows
In the unpainted park benches
In the solitude of a gas station
And in all the trees of the city.

Every time I look at you
I forget death,
And I forget the past that will come.
I gave up everything,
Only to come back to see you,
Only to know that I'm not alone
When I know where you are.

You are in the mirrors
In the puddles on the sidewalk
In the books of a high school crush
In the scar of a wooden bridge
In the cold noise of the rain
In a doorway.
You are in the signs of the theatres

y en las vidrieras
en los bancos de los parques
sin pintar
y en la soledad de una gasolinera
y en los árboles de toda esta ciudad.

MI FE (*SIETE*)

Yo no sé
si perdí o si gané,
yo solo quiero que tu estés.

Una vez yo me fui y supe que,
que sin ti no sé que hacer.

Y aunque el maldito mundo
esté al revés
y hay demasiada gente
que perdió y se fue
yo nunca voy a dejar mi amor
que me arranquen mi fe.

Yo soñé y crecí sin saber
si este amor se iba a perder.
Y ahora no sé
si es el fin o si tal vez
volverá el amanecer.

Y aunque el maldito mundo
esté al revés
y hay demasiada gente
que perdió y se fue
yo nunca voy a dejar mi amor
que me arranquen mi fe.

And in the shop windows
In the unpainted park benches
In the solitude of a gas station
And in all the trees of the city.

MY FAITH (*SIETE*)

I don't know
If I won or if I lost,
I only want you here.

One time I left and I knew that
Without you I didn't know what to do.

And although this damned world
Is upside down
And there are too many people
Who have lost and left,
I'm never going to abandon my love.
They're never going to take my faith.

I dreamed and grew up without knowing
If this love would disappear.
And now I don't know
If it's the end, or if maybe
The dawn will return.

And although this damned world
Is upside down
And there are too many people
Who have lost and left.
I'm never going to abandon my love.
They're never going to take my faith.

MEMORIAS (JALISCO PARK)

Para Tomás Guitiérrez Alea

Estoy sentado en el contén del barrio
como hace un siglo atrás
a veces me pasan en la radio, a veces nada más.
y "Memorias del Subdesarrollo" sigue gustando aún
es extraño que a los 20 años
no se apagó su luz. No tengo Superman,
tengo a Elidió Valdés
y mi televiso fue ruso.
No tengo mucho más de lo que puedo hacer
y a pesar de todo lucho.
No tuve Santa Claus,
ni Árbol de Navidad
pero nada me hizo extraño
y así pude vivir teniendo que inventar
los juguetes una vez al año.

Y cuando los discos de los Beatles
no se podían tener
los chicos descubrieron que sus padres
lo escuchaban también.
Cambiamos mercenarios por compotas
cuando Playa Girón
y a las fiestas íbamos con botas
cantando una canción
de Lennon.

No tengo Superman,
tengo a Elidió Valdés
y mi televisor fue ruso.
No tengo mucho más de lo que puedo hacer
y a pesar de todo lucho.
No tuve Santa Claus,
ni Árbol de Navidad
pero nada me hizo extraño
y así pude vivir teniendo que inventar
los juguetes una vez al año.

MEMORIES (*JALISCO PARK*)

To Tomás Guitiérrez Alea

I am sitting on a curb in the neighbourhood
As though it was a century ago.
Sometimes they play me on the radio, sometimes not.
And "Memories of Underdevelopment"
   is still a favourite movie.
It's strange that how after twenty years
Its light has not gone out. I don't have Superman,
I have Elpidio Valdés,
And my television was Russian.
I don't have much more than I can do
But in spite of it all I keep struggling.
I didn't have Santa Claus,
Or a Christmas Tree.
But that didn't make me strange
I was able to make do by making up
Toys once a year.

And when they wouldn't let us have
Beatles records,
The kids discovered that their parents
Were listening to them, too.
We exchanged mercenaries for baby food
During the Bay of Pigs
And we went to parties with our boots on
Singing a Lennon song.

I don't have Superman,
I have Elpidio Valdés,
And my television was Russian.
I don't have much more I can do
But in spite of it all I keep struggling
I didn't have Santa Claus,
Or a Christmas Tree
But that didn't make me strange
I was able to make do by making up
Toys once a year.

Estoy sentado en el contén del barrio
como hace un siglo atrás
a veces me pasan en la radio
a veces no, veces nada más, a veces.

MONEDAS AL AIRE (*MONEDAS AL AIRE*)

Tiras tres monedas al aire
y le preguntas al I Ching,
sabes que no puedo salvarte
pero vienes hasta aquí
a mí,
tal vez, tal vez un milagro baje
hasta aquí.

Tienes miedo de encerrarte
y de no poder salir,
saber que no quiero escaparme
aunque sospechan de mí,
de mí,
tal vez, tal vez un milagro baje
hasta aquí.

Tiro tres monedas al aire
y le pregunto al I Ching
como será el fin.
Y aunque ya no pueda salvarte
ven y agárrate de mí,
de mí.
Tal vez, tal vez un milagro baje
hasta aquí,
tal vez.

I'm sitting on a curb in the neighbourhood
As though it was a century ago.
Sometimes they play me on the radio
Sometimes not, sometimes no more, sometimes.

COINS IN THE AIR (*MONEDAS AL AIRE*)

You throw three coins in the air
And ask the I Ching.
You know that I can't save you
But you come here
to me,
Maybe, maybe a miracle will descend
Even here.

You are afraid of being locked up,
Of not being able to leave,
Knowing that I don't want to escape
Although they suspect me,
Me.
Maybe, maybe a miracle will descend
Even here.

I throw three coins in the air
And I ask the I Ching
How will the end be.
And even though he still cannot save you,
Come and hold on to me,
Me.
Maybe, maybe a miracle will descend
Even here,
Maybe.

MUROS Y PUERTAS (*NUBES*)

Desde que existe el Mundo
hay una cosa cierta
unos hacen los muros
y otros hacen las puertas,
pero eso mi amor,
creo que eso ya lo sabes.

Unos tienen invierno
y otros las primaveras
unos encuentran suerte,
pero otros ni siquiera,
pero eso mi amor,
creo que eso ya lo sabes.

Y siempre fue así
y eso tú lo sabes,
que la libertad solo existe
cuando no es de nadie.

De que sirve la luna
si no tienes la noche,
de que sirve un molino
sino quedan Quijotes,
pero eso mi amor,
creo que eso ya lo sabes.

Y mientras se confunde
la tierra con el cielo,
unos sueñan con Dios
y otros con el dinero,
pero eso mi amor,
es lo que se ve en la calle

Y siempre fue así
y eso tú lo sabes,
que la libertad solo existe
cuando no es de nadie.

WALLS AND DOORS (*NUBES*)

Since the World began,
There's one thing certain:
Some make walls,
And some make doors.
But that, my love,
I'm sure you already know.

For some it's always winter
For others only spring.
Some find good fortune
And others never do.
But that, my love,
I think you already know.

And that's how its always been,
And you know that its true,
That freedom only exists
When it belongs to no one.

What good is the moon
If you don't have the night?
What good is the windmill
If there are no more Quixotes?
But that my love,
I think you already know.

And as the land
Dissolves into the sky,
Some dream of God
And others of wealth,
But that, my love,
Is what you see on the street.

And that's how its always been
And you know that its true,
That freedom only exists
When it belongs to no one.

Desde que existe el Mundo
hay una cosa cierta
unos hacen los muros
y otros las puertas.

MURO (*NUBES*)

Mojas el pan en el plato vacío
y apagas la televisión.
Abres la ventana y miras afuera,
la ciudad te espera en algún lugar.
Sales a la calle y te vas al muro
donde acaban todos, donde empieza el mar.
Cuentas los pasos regresando a casa
y prendes la televisión.
Te quedas dormido y cuando empieza el himno,
te vas a la cama, te vas a soñar,
mientras otro sigue recostado al muro
donde acaban todos, donde empieza el mar.

Luna
algo está sucediendo
que estoy sintiendo que esta vez me están dejando solo,
o al menos solo como la noche.

Mojas tu cara como cualquier día
y te vas sin afeitar.
Te compras la prensa y notas que al mundo
le ha cambiado el rostro para bien o mal
y sigues caminando y te vas al muro
donde acaban todos, donde empieza el mar.

Luna
algo está sucediendo
que estoy sintiendo que esta vez me están dejando solo,
o al menos solo como la noche.

Since the world began
There's one thing certain:
Some make walls
And others make doors.

WALL (*NUBES*)

You dip the bread in an empty plate
And turn off the television.
You open the windows and look outside,
The city is waiting for you somewhere.
Go out to the street and head to the wall
Where everything ends, where the sea begins.
You count the steps returning home
And turn on the television.
You feel sleepy and when the hymn begins,
You go to bed, you go to dream,
While someone else continues to hang around the wall
Where everything stops, where the sea begins.

The moon.
Something is happening
I'm feeling that this time they're leaving me alone,
Or at least as alone as the night.

You wash your face like any day,
And you go out without shaving.
You buy the newspaper and you note that the world
Has changed its face, for better or for worse,
And you keep waking to the wall
Where everything stops and the sea begins.

The moon.
Something is happening
I'm feeling that this time they're leaving me alone,
Or at least as alone as the night.

Mojas el pan en el plato vacío
y apagas la televisión.
Abres la ventana y miras afuera,
la ciudad te espera en algún lugar.
Sales a la calle y te vas al muro
donde siempre hay alguien
donde empieza el mar.

NADIE (*NO ES EL FIN*)

Ni el Sol, ni el aire
saben lo que sabe el viento.
Ni Dios, ni nadie
saben lo que tú y yo.

Una duda puede condenar ciudades,
la locura puede derribar el Sol.
Una Luna puede que te dé saudade
cuando cura todo lo que esconde el alma.

Tu amor cobarde
solo se lo lleva el viento.
Ni Dios, ni nadie
salvan lo que se perdió.

Una duda puede condenar ciudades,
la locura puede derribar el Sol.
Una Luna puede parecer mitades
cuando cura todo lo que esconde el alma.

Ni el Sol, ni el aire
saben lo que sabe el viento.
Ni Dios, ni nadie
saben lo que tú y yo.

You dip the bread in an empty plate,
And turn off the television.
You open the windows and look outside.
The city is waiting for you somewhere.
Go out to the street and head to the wall
Where there is always someone
Where the sea begins.

NO ONE (*NO ES EL FIN*)

Not the sun, not the air
Knows what the wind knows.
Not God, not anyone
Knows what you and I know.

A doubt can condemn cities,
Madness can bring down the Sun.
A moon can give you sadness
When it cures everything hidden in the soul.

Your cowardly love
Goes away with the wind.
Not God, not anyone
Can save what is lost.

A doubt can condemn cities,
Madness can bring down the Sun.
A moon can seem like halves
When it cures everything hidden in the soul.

Not the Sun, not the air
Knows what the wind knows.
Not God, not anyone
Knows what you and I know.

NO ES EL FIN (*NO ES EL FIN*)

Las oscuras aguas del Parque Almendares
brillaron cuando apareció,
ella tenía un ángel
y una nube de algodón.

Eran tan pequeños cuando en navidades
juraron para siempre amor,
pero fueron creciendo
y el hechizo se perdió.

No es el fin
muchacha no es el fin,
al final al menos no es el fin.
Si algo pudiera darte te diría
no es el fin.

Entre los espejos de los viejos bares
se esconde a ratos el dolor
y en cada copa va
dejando huellas de un amor.

Dicen que lo vieron cruzando los mares
buscando un poco de ilusión,
pero a pesar de todo
ni la Virgen lo encontró.

No es el fin
muchacha no es el fin,
al final al menos no es el fin.
Si algo pudiera darte te diría
no es el fin,
muchacha no es el fin,
al final al menos para ti.
Si algo pudiera darte te diría,
si tal vez podría aliviarte te diría
no es el fin.

IT'S NOT THE END (*NO ES EL FIN*)

The dark waters of Almendares Park
Shone when she appeared,
She had an angel
And a cloud of cotton.

They were so little when at Christmas
They swore their love forever,
But as they grew up
The magic wore off.

It's not the end,
muchacha, it's not the end.
In the end, at least it's not the end.
If I could tell you something I would tell you
It's not the end.

Pain hides from time to time,
Among the mirrors of old bars.
And leaves behind faint traces
Of a love in every cup.
It leaves footprints of love.

They say they saw him crossing the seas,
Looking for a little hope.
But in spite of everything,
Not even the Virgin found him.

It's not the end,
muchacha, it's not the end.
At the end, at least it's not the end.
If I could tell you something I would tell you
It's not the end,
Muchacha, it's not the end
At the end, at least for you.
If I could tell you something, I would tell you,
If perhaps I could help you I would tell you
It's not the end.

NUBES (*NUBES*)

No le abras la puerta
a tu soledad,
la ciudad está muerta,
pero que más da.

No jures por la tempestad
aunque tu Luna se esté apagando,
las nubes no se irán, no se irán, no se irán, no se irán
solo se quedan adentro y llorando.

Y ahora por qué rezas
en el viejo altar.
No bajes la cabeza,
y no mires atrás.

No jures por la tempestad
aunque tu Luna se esté apagando,
las nubes no se irán, no se irán, no se irán, no se irán
solo se quedan adentro y llorando.
Adentro y llorando.

PEQUEÑOS SUEÑOS (*COMO LOS PECES*)

El camionero enciende el radio
y cae la noche,
las luces en la carretera son como los sueños,
se acercan lentamente y cuando llegan
se vuelven a ir.
En la cabina la fotografía, la chica de la Playboy,
ella lo mira fijamente, no lo deja dormir,
el sabe que eso no son grandes cosas,
pero son sus sueños,
esos pequeños sueños que también ayudan a vivir.

CLOUDS (*NUBES*)

Don't open the doors
To your loneliness.
The city is dead,
But what does it matter?

Don't swear by the storm
Although your moon is burning out,
The clouds won't go away, won't go away, won't go away
   won't go away.
They only stay inside and cry.

And now, why do you pray
At the old altar?
Don't bow your head,
Don't look back.

Don't swear by the storm
Although your moon is burning out,
The clouds won't go away, won't go away, won't go away
   won't go away.
They only stay inside and cry.
Inside, crying.

LITTLE DREAMS (*COMO LOS PECES*)

The truck driver turns on the radio
And night falls,
The lights on the highway are like dreams,
They approach slowly and when they arrive,
They turn around and leave.
In the cabin, the photo, the girl from Playboy,
She stares at him intently, and it doesn't let him sleep.
He knows that these aren't big things,
But they are his dreams,
These little dreams that also help him live.

Ella colgó una foto mía encima de la cama,
yo sé que al padre no le gusta, pero yo sigo allí,
crucificado en la pared sin poder hacer nada,
solo la miro fijamente cuando se va a dormir.
Ella sabe muy bien que esas no son las grandes cosas,
pero son sus sueños
esos pequeños sueños que también ayudan a vivir.

Mi madre le ponía flores a la foto del viejo
y lo miraba fijamente antes de dormir,
ella sabía que eso no eran grandes cosas,
pero era su sueño,
esos pequeños sueños que también ayudan a vivir.

Tengo un sombrero, un par de botas,
mi amor y mi guitarra,
ella me mira fijamente y no quiero dormir,
yo sé que no son grandes cosas, pero son mis sueños
esos pequeños sueños que también
me ayudan a vivir.

Y así me pierdo caminando
cuando cae la noche,
las luces en la carretera son como los sueños,
se acercan lentamente y cuando llegan
se vuelven a ir,
son los pequeños sueños que también
ayudan a vivir
ayudan a vivir.

ROBINSON (SOLO EN UNA ISLA) (*MONEDAS AL AIRE*)

Cuando Robinson abrió los ojos
y vio que estaba solo en una isla.
En su pequeño y solitario pedazo de tierra,
abrió los brazos hacia Dios
y se quedó mirando al cielo

She hung my photo over the bed,
I know that her father doesn't like it, but I'm still there,
Crucified on the wall, unable to do anything,
I only stare at her when she goes to sleep.
She knows very well that these aren't big things,
But they are her dreams
These little dreams that also help her live.

My mother put flowers by the photo of the old man
And stares at it before sleeping,
She knew that these were not big things,
But it was her dream,
These little dreams that also help her live.

I have a hat, a pair of boots,
My love and my guitar.
She stares at me and I don't want to sleep,
I know that these aren't big things, but they are my dreams
These little dreams that also
Help me live.

And in this way, I lose myself while walking
When night falls,
The lights on the highway are like dreams,
They approach slowly and when they arrive
They turn around and leave,
They are little dreams that also
Help me to live,
Help me to live.

ROBINSON (ALONE ON AN ISLAND) (*MONEDAS AL AIRE*)

When Robinson opened his eyes,
And saw that he was alone on an island
On his solitary little piece of land,
He opened his arms to God
And remained looking at the sky

La religión empieza en los murales de la escuela,
en una foto, en un altar y en un montón de velas.
Están tumbando las estatuas del osito Misha
y en este juego de la historia
solo pasamos ficha.

Algunos prefieren decir:
¡Recuerda la Revolución ahora!
Pero otros quisieran decir:
¡Remember the Revolution now!

Cuando Robinson abrió los ojos
y vio que estaba solo en una isla.
En su pequeño y solitario pedazo de tierra,
abrió los brazos hacia Dios
y se quedó mirando al cielo.

Algunos hablan de la crisis del marxismo
algunos lloran, ríen y a otros les da lo mismo.
Están tumbando las estatuas del osito Misha
y en este juego de la historia
solo pasamos ficha.

Algunos prefieren decir:
¡Recuerda la Revolución ahora!
Pero otros quisieran decir:
¡Remember de Revolution Now!

Cuando Robinson abrió los ojos
y vio que estaba solo en una isla,
solo en una isla
como tú y yo.

Religion starts within the walls of the school,
In a photo, in an altar, in a heap of candles.
They are knocking down the statues of the little bear Misha,
And in this game of history
We are only playing dominos.

Some prefer to say:
Remember the Revolution now!
But others want to say:
"Remember the Revolution now!"*

When Robinson opened his eyes,
And saw that he was alone on an island
In his solitary little piece of land,
He opened his arms unto God
And remained looking at the sky.

Some speak of the crisis of Marxism,
Some cry, laugh, and to others it doesn't matter.
They are knocking down the statues of the little bear Misha,
And in this game of history
We are only playing dominoes.

Some prefer to say:
Remember the Revolution now!
But others want to say:
Remember the Revolution now!

When Robinson opened his eyes,
And saw that he was alone on an island,
Alone on an island
Like you and I.

in English

SEQUÍA DEL ALMA (*NUBES*)

Le tiro tantas piedras a tus fantasmas
que a ratos sueño con irme de aquí,
pero hay tanta sequía sembrada en mi alma
y es que hace tanta lluvia que no sé de ti.

Se puso viejo el árbol y las manzanas
y hay quien por el dinero le cuesta sonreír
ya lo dijo un amigo que se fue de La Habana
hay gente que se muere de ganas de vivir.

Solamente quisiera que no te olvides
que entre tanta penuria y tanto dolor,
hay quien carga su herida y sobrevive
dándole puñetazos a su corazón.

Se puso viejo el árbol y la semilla
y hay quien por el dinero le cuesta sonreír,
ya lo dijo un amigo que se fue de mi vida:
hay gente que se muere de ganas de vivir.

SERÁ SOL (*NUBES*)

En vano fue cerrar los ojos
y no saber dónde mirar.

En vano fue quedarnos solos
frente a la colina de los tontos
viendo pasar el mundo
en silencio.

Mirando como caen las hojas
tratando de encontrar a Dios,
lo que hoy es luz, mañana es sombra,
lo que fue lluvia será Sol,
será Sol.

LONGING OF THE SOUL (*NUBES*)

I throw so many stones at your ghosts
That sometimes I dream of getting away from here.
But there is such longing throughout my soul,
And there is so much rain and I don't hear from you.

The tree and the apples grew old,
And there is someone whose money problems cost him his smile.
As I've already told my friend who left Havana
There are people who die from yearning to live.

I don't want you to forget
That amidst the poverty and the pain,
Someone shoulders his burden
And survives by hitting his own heart.

The tree and the seed grew old
And there is someone whose money problems cost him his smile.
As I've already told a friend who left my life:
There are people who die from yearning to live.

IT WILL BE SUN (*NUBES*)

In vain we closed our eyes,
Not knowing where to look.

In vain we remained on our own,
Facing a hill of fools,
Watching the world go by
In silence.

Looking at how the leaves fall,
Trying to find God,
What is light today is shadow tomorrow.
What was rain will be sun.
It will be sun.

En vano fue soltar las riendas
y no saber cómo parar.
En vano fue vivir en vano
solo en la colina de los tontos
viendo pasar el mundo
en silencio.

Mirando como caen las hojas
tratando de encontrar a Dios,
lo que hoy es luz, mañana es sombra,
lo que fue lluvia será Sol,
será Sol,
será Sol.

SIETE (*SIETE*)

Siete vidas, siete mares
siete maravillas y siete ciudades.
Siete notas musicales
siete cielos y pecados capitales.
Siete potencias, siete colores
Siete lunas y siete soles.

Cuando tenía siete
me llegó el setenta
la calle era un juguete
y no nos dábamos cuenta
que diez años más tarde
con los diecisiete
nos dividió el ochenta
entre el quédate y vete.

Y todo por aquello de las dos orillas
y todo por la duda de la sombrilla
porque es que aunque lo traten
de esconder
la gente siempre sueña
porque saben que
existen:

In vain we loosen the reins,
Not knowing how to stop,
In vain we live in vain,
Alone in the hill of fools.
Watching the world go by
In silence.

Looking at how the leaves fall,
Trying to find God,
What is light today is shadow tomorrow.
What was rain will be sun.
It will be sun.
It will be sun.

SEVEN (*SIETE*)

Seven lives, seven seas
Seven marvels and seven cities.
Seven musical notes
Seven heavens and capital sins.
Seven powers, seven colours,
Seven moons and seven suns.

When I was seven,
The '70s arrived.
The street was a playground,
And we didn't realize
That ten years later,
When I was seventeen,
The eighties would divide us
Into those who stayed and those who left.

And because of the matter of "the other shore,"
And all for the doubt of the darkness,
Because although they try
To hide it,
The people always dream
Because they know
That there are:

Siete vidas, siete mares
siete maravillas y siete ciudades.
Siete notas musicales
siete cielos y pecados capitales.
Siete potencias, siete colores
Siete lunas y siete soles.
Siete enanos de blancanieves
diecisiete instantes de una primavera
y siete amaneceres.

Cuando a los veintisiete
se moría mi madre
yo descubrí que el tiempo
no fue más que un cobarde.

Y aun siguen los abuelos
de las dos orillas
echándose el anzuelo, la culpa
y la semilla.

Porque es que aunque lo traten de esconder
la gente siempre sueña
porque saben que
existen:

Siete vidas, siete mares
siete maravillas y siete ciudades.
Siete notas musicales
siete cielos y pecados capitales.
Siete potencias, siete colores
Siete lunas y siete soles.
Siete santos en siete altares
y las iglesias siguen siendo
iguales a los bares
que tienen:

Siete vidas ,siete mares
siete maravillas y siete ciudades.
Siete notas musicales
siete cielos y pecados capitales.

Seven lives, seven seas,
Seven marvels and seven cities.
Seven musical notes,
Seven skies and capital sins.
Seven powers, seven colours,
Seven moons and seven suns.
Seven dwarves of Snow White,
"Seventeen moments of spring,"*
And seven dawns.

When I was seventeen,
My mother died.
I found out that time
Was no more than a coward.

And from their opposite shores,
Our grandparents
Keep on casting blame,
Bait and seeds.

Because even though they try to hide
People always dream,
Because they know
That there are:

Seven lives, seven seas,
Seven marvels and seven cities.
Seven musical notes,
Seven skies and capital sins.
Seven powers, seven colours,
Seven moons and seven suns.
Seven saints on seven altars,
And the churches continue
Just like bars
That have:

Seven lives, seven seas,
Seven marvels and seven cities.
Seven musical notes,
Seven skies and capital sins.

Siete potencias, siete colores
Siete lunas y siete soles.
Siete enanos de blancanieves
diecisiete instantes de una primavera
y siete amaneceres.

Siete vidas, siete mares
siete notas musicales.

SOLO TÚ (PUEDES TRAER EL SOL) (*COMO LOS PECES*)

Cuando el viento pegue fuerte en tus ojos,
trata de no ponerte a llorar,
yo sé que este invierno fue más duro que otros,
pero ya está llegando el final.

Salva tu alma de la tempestad
se está acercando el ciclón
Solo si tú quieres nos podemos salvar,
solo tú puedes traer el Sol.

SOMBRAS EN LA PARED (*NUBES*)

Se ve una luz en la ciudad,
la Luna cae en cenital,
y solo con la música
te empiezas a desnudar.

Un nuevo día va a empezar,
me besas y aparece el Sol,
la gente sale a trabajar,
mientras hacemos el amor.

Seven powers, seven colours,
Seven moons and seven suns.
Seven dwarves of Snow White,
Seventeen moments of spring
And seven dawns.

Seven lives, seven seas,
Seven musical notes.

*"Seventeen Moments of Spring" was a popular Soviet-era TV program, broadcast on Cuban TV in the 1970s.

ONLY YOU (CAN BRING THE SUN) (*COMO LOS PECES*)

When the wind hits your eyes,
Try not to cry.
I know that this winter is more severe than others,
But the end is coming.

Save your soul from the storm,
The hurricane is nearing
Only if it's what you want can we save ourselves,
Only you can bring the sun.

SHADOWS ON THE WALL (*NUBES*)

There's a light in the city,
Moonlight falls from above,
And with nothing but music,
You begin to get undressed.

A new day is about to begin,
You kiss me and the sun appears,
People are going out to work,
While we make love.

Y a contraluz por el cristal,
se ve tu sombra en la pared,
pintada en la claridad.

Se escuchan los ruidos de un bar,
despierto y ya no estás,
y en la ventana la ciudad,
no deja de parpadear.

Se ve una luz en el cristal,
y cuando en la calle anochece,
solo me queda en la pared,
tu sombra volando
en la oscuridad,
tu sombra volando
en la oscuridad.

SOY UN GNOMO (JALISCO PARK)

Cada vez me parezco más a mi caricatura
Soy un gnomo y salgo a cantar vestido como un cura
Una vez te quise salvar
Pero aquí me dijeron que ya todo está hecho
Lo que no entiendo es por qué.

Cada vez me parezco más a mi caricatura
En la calle me siento mal cuando veo basura
Creo que nada va a cambiar
Mientras sigan diciendo que ya todo está hecho
Lo que no entiendo es por qué.

Cada vez, cada vez
Soy un gnomo, soy un gnomo
Soy un gnomo en este mundo
Y quiero ver algo mejor
Aunque me llenen de mierda
Yo siempre estoy de buen humor.

And against the light pouring through the glass,
Your shadow can be seen on the wall,
Painted so distinctly.

Noise from a bar can be heard,
I awake and you're not there,
And through the window,
the city doesn't even blink an eye.

There is a light through the glass,
And when night falls,
I remain alone by the wall,
Your shadow vanishing
Into the darkness,
Your shadow vanishing
Into the darkness.

I AM A GNOME (JALISCO PARK)

Each time I look more like my caricature.
I am a gnome and I go out to sing dressed as a priest.
Once I wanted to save you,
But here they told me that they've already done what they
    can.
What I don't understand is why.

Each time I look more like my caricature.
In the street I feel badly when I see trash.
I believe that nothing is going to change,
While they keep saying that everything has been done.
What I do not understand is why.

Each time, each time
I am a gnome, I am a gnome
I am a gnome in this world,
And I want to see something better,
Although they fill me with crap
I am always good-natured.

Cada vez me parezco más a mi caricatura
En un árbol de esta ciudad quiero mi sepultura
Una vez yo quise opinar
Pero aquí me dijeron que ya todo está dicho
Lo que no entiendo es por qué.

Cada vez me parezco más a mi caricatura
Desde el bosque salgo a buscar quien necesita ayuda
Una vez vine a esta ciudad
Pero aquí me dijeron que ya todo está hecho
Lo que no entiendo es por qué.

Cada vez, cada vez
Soy un gnomo, soy un gnomo
Soy un gnomo en este mundo
Y quiero ver algo mejor
Aunque me llenen de mierda
Yo siempre estoy de buen humor.

TARDE GRIS (*NUBES*)

Ni el secreto de las piedras
que caen en Jerusalén.
Ni los templos de la tierra,
ni la Torre de Babel.

Nada es más grande que tu amor deshojado,
nada es igual que cuando estoy a tu lado,
a pesar de la gente, a pesar del dolor,
nada es más grande que tu amor.

Ni las Siete Maravillas
ni el viejo Mago de Oz.
Ni el Titanic, ni la orilla
ni el misterio de algún Dios.

Nada es más grande que tu amor deshojado,
nada es igual que cuando estoy a tu lado,

Each time I look more like my caricature.
I want my grave to lie in a tree of this city.
Once I wanted to share my opinion,
But here they told me that everything has already been said.
What I do not understand is why.

Each time I look more like my caricature.
I leave the forest to look for someone in need of help.
Once I came to this city,
But here they told me that everything has been done.
What I do not understand is why.

Each time, each time
I am a gnome, I am a gnome
I am a gnome in this world,
And I want to see something better.
Although they fill me with crap,
I am always good-natured.

GREY AFTERNOON (*NUBES*)

Neither the secret of the stones
That fell in Jerusalem,
Nor the temples of the earth,
Nor the Tower of Babel.

Nothing is greater than your pure love,
Nothing is the same when I am at your side,
Despite all the people, despite all the pain,
Nothing is greater than your love.

Not the Seven Marvels,
Nor the Wizard of Oz.
Not the Titanic, nor the seashore,
Not the mystery of some god.

Nothing is greater than your pure love,
Nothing is the same when I am at your side,

a pesar de la gente, a pesar del dolor,
nada es más grande que tu amor.

Dicen que los años dejan cicatrices,
pero es que te extraño
cuando hay tardes grises,
a pesar de los años,
a pesar del dolor
nada es más grande
que tu amor.

TELÓN DE FONDO (*NO ES EL FIN*)

Yo te di mi ilusión,
mi niñez, mi país y mi corazón.
Yo te di mi bendición,
mis guerreros, mi fe y mi religión.

Y a cambio solo tú me diste un mundo
lleno de escenarios y payasos tontos,
para descubrir que solo al final
no somos más que un telón de fondo.

Yo te di mi ilusión,
mi niñez, mi país y mi corazón.
Yo te di mi pasión
y la suerte perdida de una generación.

Y a cambio solo tú me diste un mundo
lleno de escenarios y payasos tontos
y es que siempre es igual, lo mismo aquí o allá,
no somos más que un telón de fondo.

Demasiada brillantina en la radio,
demasiado verde en la TV,
demasiada sangre en los diarios
y demasiada falta de fe.

Despite all the people, despite all the pain,
Nothing is greater than your love.

They say that time leaves its scars,
But it's just that I miss you
When the afternoons are grey,
Despite all the years,
Despite all the pain
Nothing is greater
Than your love.

BACKDROP (*NO ES EL FIN*)

I gave you my dream,
My childhood, my country, my heart.
I gave you my blessing,
My fighters, my faith, and my religion.

And in return all you gave me was a world
Full of stages and silly clowns,
Only to find out at the end
We are no more than a backdrop.

I gave you my dream,
My childhood, my country, and my heart.
I gave you my passion
And the lost luck of a generation.

And in return all you gave me was a world
Full of stages and silly clowns,
And it's always the same, here or there,
We are no more than a backdrop.

Too much glitter on the radio,
Too much green on the TV,
Too much blood in the newspapers
And not enough faith.

Todo el mundo quiere ser igual que tú,
mundo en blanco y negro como Betty Boop
Pu pu ru pu pí !! Pi rú pi rú !!!

TODO SERÁ DISTINTO (*NO ES EL FIN*)

Prefieres mirar al Norte
a las canciones de Silvio
y un crucifijo entre los senos
a un libro de marxismo.

Quizás mañana salga el Sol
y todo será distinto,
lo triste será que entonces
ya no seremos lo mismo.

Hay una lluvia que va a caer,
lo dijo el viejo Bob Dylan,
a nadie le gusta perder
digan lo que digan.

Y nos pasamos el tiempo
mirando solo el pasado,
viviendo sin darnos cuenta
todo lo que hemos callado.

Prefieres mirar al Norte
a las canciones de Silvio
y un crucifijo entre los senos
a un libro de lo mismo.

Quizás mañana salga el Sol
y todo será distinto,
lo triste será que entonces
ya no seremos lo mismo,
lo triste será que entonces
ya no pensemos los mismo,
lo triste será que entonces
ya no estaremos ...

Everyone wants to be the same as you,
A world in black and white like Betty Boop

EVERYTHING WILL BE DIFFERENT (*NO ES EL FIN*)

You prefer to look to the North
Rather than to the songs of Silvio
And a crucifix around your neck
To a book of Marxism.

Maybe tomorrow the sun will come out
And everything will be different.
The sad thing will be that then
We won't be the same.

There's a rain that's going to fall,
Says the old Bob Dylan,
And no one likes to lose
Say what they may.

And we spend our time
Looking only at the past,
Living without realizing
Everything we've silenced.

You prefer to look to the North
Rather than to the songs of Silvio
And a crucifix around your neck
To a book about the same thing.

Maybe tomorrow the sun will come out
And everything will be different.
The sad thing is that then
We won't be the same.
The sad thing will be that then
We won't think the same.
The sad thing will be that then
We won't be ...

TODOS SE ROBAN (*EN VIVO*)

A tu padre le robaron la radio del auto
tú le robas los cigarros cuando está llegando el sábado
y a ti te roban cuando estás frente al televisor,
a ti te roban las ganas, te roban las ganas de amor.

Al vecino le robaron la ropa del patio,
él se robaba el dinero de la caja donde trabajó
y a ti te roban cuando estás en un mostrador
a ti te roban las ganas, te roban las ganas de amor.

A tu padre le robaron las piezas del auto
él las compra a sobreprecio al mismo tipo que se las robó
y a ti te roban los porteros y el cobrador
a ti te roban las ganas, te roban las ganas de amor.

Hay ladrones que se esconden dentro de tu cuarto,
y se esconden en los libros, en el diario y la televisión
y te roban la cabeza y el corazón
y así te roban las ganas, te roban las ganas de amor.

No me preguntes más
por los condenados a vivir en la prisión.

no me preguntes más por los que robaron
y ahora esconden su mansión
si todos se roban
todos se roban.

TROPICOLLAGE (*JALISCO PARK*)

Se fue en Havanautos
rumbo hasta Varadero
apanado en la arena

EVERYBODY STEALS (*EN VIVO*)

They stole your father's car radio.
You'll steal his cigarettes when he comes on Saturday.
And they steal from you when you are watching TV,
They steal your desire, they steal your desire for love.

They robbed your neighbour's clothes from the patio.
He robbed money from the cash register where he worked.
And they rob you when you are at the counter,
They steal your desire, they steal your desire for love.

They robbed parts of your father's car.
He bought them, at a surcharge, from the same guy who
    robbed him.
And from you they rob the doormen and the rent collector.
They steal your desire, they steal your desire for love.

There are robbers that hide inside your room,
And they hide themselves in books, in the newspapers,
    and in the television.
They rob your head and your heart,
And this is how they steal your desire, they steal your
    desire for love.

Don't ask me more
About those condemned to a life in prison.

Don't ask me more about those who stole
And now hide in their mansions.
Yes, everybody steals
Everybody steals.

TROPICOLLAGE (*JALISCO PARK*)

He left in a Havanautos rented car,
Heading to the beach at Varadero
Covered in sand

fumándose un Habano,
se tiró algunas fotos
recostado a una palma.

Volvió al Habana Libre
alquiló un Turistaxi
para ir a Tropicana
después al aeropuerto y
así se fue creyendo
que conoció La Habana.

Ese tipo pagó la cuenta
que me estaba sacando,
pero en la polaroide
y en su cabeza lleva
tropicollage, collage, collage ...

No fue a la Habana Vieja
no conoció los barrios
de obreros y creyentes.
No se tiró unas fotos
sobre los arrecifes
donde hay un mar de gente.

No vió a los constructores
ladrillo y aguardiente
cementando el futuro.
No tropezó en la calle
con uno de esos tipos
que dan cinco por uno.

Eso también es mi país
y no puedo olvidarlo
y el que quiera negarlo
en su cabeza lleva tropicollage,
collage, collage ...
Tropicollage, tropicollage,
collage, collage ...

Y a los refutadores
que me están escuchando

Smoking a cigar,
He took some photos,
Leaning against a palm tree.

He returned to the Habana Libre Hotel.
He hired a Turistaxi
To take him to the Tropicana nightclub
And then to the airport.
He left like this, believing
That he really understood Havana.

This guy paid the cheque
That supported me,
But both his photos
And his head were full of
Tropicollage, collage, collage.

He never went to Habana Vieja.
He never visited any neighbourhoods
Where the working people and the believers live.
He took no photos
On the city reefs
Amid the sea of people.

He never saw the construction workers,
Cementing the future
With bricks and cheap rum.
Nor did he have to face those guys
Changing money five for one.

That too is my country,
And I can't forget that,
And anyone who denies it
Has their heads full of
Tropicollage ...

And to those who refute this,
If you are listening to me,

piensen en lo que digo
yo sé que la divisa
hace la economía
como hace al pan el trigo.

Pero lo que no entiendo
es que por el dinero
confundan a la gente
si vas a los hoteles
por no ser extranjero
te tratan diferente.

Eso ya está pasando aquí
y yo quiero cambiarlo
cómo no, y el que quiera negarlo
en su cabeza lleva tropicollage.
collage, collage ...
Tropicollage, collage,
tropicollage, collage ...

Quieren llevarse a mi país
en una bolsa de Cubalse
de esas que dicen en inglés
que se compra fácil
esta ciudad no cabe en una foto
de almanaque de París.

La gente está inventando antenas
para ver Canal del Sol,
es que a tropicollage
le gusta salir en la televisión.
"Easy shopping", tropicollage ...
"Easy shopping", tropicollage ...

Think about what I'm saying.
I know that dollars
Make the economy go around
Just like flour makes bread.

But what I don't understand
Is that because of money
They confuse people.
If you go to hotels
And you are not a foreigner,
They treat you differently.

This is what is happening here,
And I want to change it.
And anybody who denies it
Has their head full of
Tropicollage, collage,
Tropicollage, collage ...

They want to take my country with them
In a Cubalse shopping bag,
Carried by those who say in English
That it's easy shopping.
This city doesn't fit in a photo
Of a Parisian calendar.

People are making antennas
To watch the Sun Channel.
It's because they like to appear on TV.
As tropicollage
"Easy shopping," tropicollage ...
"Easy shopping," tropicollage ...

UNA PALABRA (*NUBES*)

Una palabra no dice nada
y al mismo tiempo lo esconde todo
igual que el viento que esconde el agua
como las flores que esconde el lodo.

Una mirada no dice nada
y al mismo tiempo lo dice todo
como la lluvia sobre tu cara
o el viejo mapa de algún tesoro.

Una verdad no dice nada
y al mismo tiempo lo esconde todo
como una hoguera que no se apaga
como una piedra que nace polvo.

Si un día me faltas no seré nada
y al mismo tiempo lo seré todo
porque en tus ojos están mis alas
y está la orilla donde me ahogo,
porque en tus ojos están mis alas
y está la orilla donde me ahogo.

ONE WORD (*NUBES*)

One word says nothing,
And at the same time it hides everything,
Just like the winds that hide the water
Just like the flowers that hide the mud.

One glance says nothing,
But at the same time it says everything,
Like the rain upon your face
Or some old treasure map.

One truth says nothing,
And at the same time it hides everything,
Like a bonfire that wouldn't burn out,
Like a stone that turns to dust.

If one day I am left without you, I will be nothing,
And at the same time I will be everything
Because in your eyes are my wings
And the shore where I drown,
Because in your eyes are my wings
And the shore where I drown.

Bibliography

Alexis. Interview with Carlos Varela. Accessed 25 November 2011. http://los2musicales.blogspot.com/2011/06/alexis-carlos-varela-entrevista-y.html.

Arango, Arturo. "Con tantos palos que te dio la vida: poesía, censura y persistencia." Conferencia del Ciclo "La política cultural de la Revolución: memoria y reflexión." *Criterios* (website of the Centro Teórico-Cultural Criterios). Accessed 18 June 2007. http://www.criterios.es/pdf/arangotantospalos.pdf.

Augé, Marc. *Non-Places: An Introduction to Supermodernity*. London: Verso, 1995.

Baker, Geoffrey. *Buena Vista in the Club: Rap, Reggaetón, and Revolution in Havana*. Durham, NC: Duke University Press, 2011.

Behar, Ruth, and Lucía M. Suárez, eds. *The Portable Island: Cubans at Home in the World*. New York: Palgrave Macmillan, 2008.

Benjamin, Walter. "From the Arcades Project." In *The Blackwell City Reader*, ed. Gary Bridge and Sophie Watson, 393–400. Malden, MA: Blackwell Publishing, 2002.

Bengelsdorf, Carollee. *The Problem of Democracy in Cuba: Between Vision and Reality*. New York: Oxford University Press, 1994.

Birkenmaier, Anke, and Esther Whitfield. *Havana beyond the Ruins: Cultural Mappings after 1989*. Durham, NC: Duke University Press, 2011.

Bobes, Velia Cecilia. *Los laberintos de la imaginación: Repertorio simbólico, identidades y actores del cambio social en Cuba*. Mexico City: El Colegio de México, 2000.

Borges-Triana, Joaquín. "La generación de los topos." *Juventud Rebelde*, 28 August 1988.

— *La luz, bróder, la luz: Canción Cubana contemporánea*. La Habana: Centro Cultural Pablo de la Torriente Brau, 2009.

- "Músicos de Cuba y del mundo: Nadie se va del todo." *Temas* 47 (July–September 2006).
Burton, Richard D.E. *The Flaneur and His City: Patterns of Daily Life in Paris, 1815–1851*. Durham, UK: University of Durham, 1994.
Camnitzer, Luis. *New Art of Cuba*. Austin: University of Texas Press, 2003.
Castellanos, Ernesto Juan. *John Lennon en la Habana: With a little help from my friends*. La Habana: Ediciones Union 2005.
Chávez Negrín, Ernesto. "Población y crisis económica en Cuba: la familia y la dinámica demográfica del Período Especial." Paper presented at the Symposium "Población y pobreza en América Latina," Buenos Aires, 9–11 November 2000. Accessed 25 March 2010. 168.96.200.17/ar/libros/cuba/negrin3.rtf.
Collazo, Bobby. *La última noche que pasé contigo. 40 años de la farándula cubana*. San Juan, Puerto Rico: Editorial Cubanacán, 1987
Contee, Cheryl. "Jay-Z's Open Letter on Cuba Trip Kicks a Brick Out of a Cold War Wall." *The Guardian*, 12 April 2013, accessed 17 April 2013. http://www.theguardian.com/uk.
Coyula, Mario. "El Trinquenio Amargo y la ciudad distópica: autopsia de una utopía." Conferencia del Ciclo "La política cultural de la Revolución: memoria y reflexión." *Criterios* (website of the Centro Teórico-Cultural Criterios). Accessed 3 April 2007. http://www.criterios.es/pdf/coyulatrinquenio.pdf.
Cumaná, María Caridad, and Karen Dubinsky. "Beginning a New Cuban Dream: An Interview with Carlos Varela." *Latin American Music Review* 34, no. 2 (2013): 196–222.
de la Grange, Bertrand. "Los hijos de Guillermo Tell." *Diario de Cuba*, 26 May 2010.
de la Torre, Miguel. *La Lucha for Cuba: Religion and Politics on the Streets of Miami*. Berkeley: University of California Press, 2003.
de León, Carmela. *Sindo Garay: Memorias de un trovador*. La Habana: Letras Cubanas, 1990.
Díaz, Ariel. *La primera piedra*. La Habana: Ediciones La Memoria, 2009.
Díaz Ayala, Cristóbal. *Del areyto al rap cubano*, 4th ed. San Juan, Puerto Rico: Fundación Musicalia, 2003.
Diaz, Fidel. "A Famous Cuban Singer Is Sure of That." *Juventud Cubana*, 29 September 2004.
Díaz Tenorio, Mareelén. "La familia cubana ante la crisis de los 90." Accessed 25 March 2010. http://bibliotecavirtual.clacso.org/ar/ar/libros/cuba/cips/caudales05/Caudales/ARTICULOS/ArticulosPDF/118D019.pdf.

Donas, Ernesto. "Problematizando la canción popular: un abordaje comparativo (y sonoro) de la canción latinoamericana comprometida desde los años 1960." *Actas del V Congreso Latinoamericano de la Asociación Internacional para el Estudio de la Música Popular (IASPM-AL)*. Accessed 20 May 2008. http://www.hist.puc.cl/iaspm/rio/Anais2004%20(PDF)/Ernesto Donas.pdf.

Dubinsky Karen. *Babies without Borders: Adoption and Migration across the Americas*. New York: NYU Press and Toronto: University of Toronto Press, 2010.

Dunn, Christopher. *Brutality Garden: Tropicália and the Emergence of a Brazilian Counterculture*. Chapell Hill: University of North Carolina Press, 2001.

Echarry, Irina. "Cuba's Children of William Tell." *Havana Times.org*, 24 April 2011.

– "Three Kings Day in Cuba," *Havana Times*, January 2009.

Erickson, Daniel P. *The Cuba Wars*. New York: Bloomsbury Press, 2008.

Fernandes, Sujatha. *Cuba, Represent! Cuban Arts, State Power, and the Making of New Revolutionary Cultures*. Durham, NC: Duke University Press, 2007.

Fernández, Antonio Eligio. "Ending the Century with *Memories* ...: Paper Money, Videos, and an *X-Acto* Knife for Cuban Art," in *Cuba in the Special Period: Culture and Ideology in the 1990s*, ed. Ariana Hernandez-Reguant, 179–96. New York: Palgrave Macmillan, 2009.

Fernández, Ariel, and Pablo Herrera (prod.). *The Cuban Hip Hop All-Stars*, vol. 1. Madrid: Papaya Records, 2001.

Fornet, Ambrosio. "A propósito de Las iniciales de la tierra." *Casa de las Américas* 164 (1987): 148–53.

– "El Quinquenio Gris: Revisitando el término." Conferencia del Ciclo «La política cultural de la Revolución: memoria y reflexión». Criterios (website of the Centro Teórico-Cultural Criterios). 30 January 2007. Accessed 7 February 2007. http://www.criterios.es/pdf/fornetquinqueniogris.pdf.

Fowler Calzada, Víctor. "Limones partido." *Cubista Magazine* 5 (Summer 2006). Accessed 11 November 2006. http://www.cubistamagazine.com/050108.html.

Frith, Simon. *Performing Rites: On the Value of Popular Music*. Cambridge, MA: Harvard University Press, 1996.

Garcia, Maria Christina. *Havana USA: Cuban Exiles and Cuban-Americans in South Florida, 1959–1994*. Berkeley: University of California Press, 1996.

García Borrero, Juan Antonio. "La utopía confiscada. De la gravedad del sueño a la ligereza del realismo." *Temas* 27 (October–December 2001).

Garofalo, Reebee, ed. *Rockin' the Boat: Mass Music and Mass Movements*. Boston: South End Press, 1992.

Gil, Cristina. "La música puede cambiar ideas." *El Periódico*, 24 October 1995.

Giro, Radamés, and Isabel Gonzáles Sauto. *Cincuenta canciones en años de Revolución*. La Habana: Editorial José Martí, 2008.
Gleber, Anke. *The Art of Taking a Walk: Flanerie, Literature, and Film in Weimar Culture*. Princeton, NJ: Princeton University Press, 1999.
Grenet, Elise. "Lamento cubano." *Esther Borja con la Orquesta Numidia y Luis Carbonell*. CBMF radio station recording #E636.
Guerra, Wendy. "Llamada local: Carlos Varela." *Habaname*, 22 September 2008. Accessed 23 October 2009. http://www.elmundo.es/blogs/elmundo/habaname.
Guevara, Ernesto. "El socialismo y el hombre en Cuba." In *Obras*, t. II, 367–86. La Habana: Casa de las Américas, 1970.
Gutiérrez, Pedro Juan. *Dirty Havana Trilogy*. New York: HarperCollins, 2002.
Heras León, Eduardo. "El Quinquenio Gris: testimonio de una lealtad." Conferencia del Ciclo "La política cultural de la Revolución: memoria y reflexión." *Criterios* (website of the Centro Teórico-Cultural Criterios). Accessed 18 May 2007. http://www.criterios.es/pdf/erasleonquinquenio.pdf.
Hernández Busto, Ernesto. "Recuerdos (cubanos) de una vida dañada." *Cubista Magazine* 1 (Spring 2004). Accessed 7 October 2005. http://www.cubistamagazine.com/a1/010101.html.
Hernández, Michel. "Carlos Varela: The Return of the Woodcutter." *Cuba Now. Net*, 16 January 2007. Accessed 23 August 2010. http://www.cubanow.net/pages/articulo.php?sec=17&t=2&item=1901.
Hernández, Rafael, et al. "La música popular como espejo social." *Temas* 29 (April–June 2002): 61–80.
Hernández Reguant, Ariana, ed. *Cuba in the Special Period: Culture and Ideology in the 1990s*. New York: Palgrave Macmillan, 2010.
James, Ian Michael. *Ninety Miles: Cuban Journeys in the Age of Castro*. Lanham, MD: Rowman and Littlefield, 2006.
Jameson, Fredric. "Nostalgia for the Present." *South Atlantic Quarterly* 18, no. 2 (1989): 517–37.
Jowett, S.D. "Quebec's Not So Quiet Revolution: A Sonic History of Montreal, 1965–1975." PhD Diss., in progress, Queen's University, Kingston.
Kirk, John M., and Leonardo Padura Fuentes. *Culture and the Cuban Revolution: Conversations in Havana*. Gainesville: University Press of Florida, 2001.
Kreitz, Kelly. "On the Beat in the Modern City: The Crónica Modernista and Nineteenth-Century News." Paper presented at the 2009 Congress of the Latin American Studies Association, Rio de Janeiro, Brazil, 11–14 June 2009, p. 5. Accessed 25 November 2011. http://lasa.international.pitt.edu/members/congress.../files/KreitzKelley.pdf.

Krull, Catherine, and Jean Stubbs. "Commodification, Cityscapes, and Cultural Negotiations of Belonging in Post-1989 Cuban Diasporas." In *The Cuban Diaspora: Post-Soviet Migrations and Exiles*, ed. Nadine Fernández and Ariana Hernández-Reguant. Gainesville: University Press of Florida, forthcoming.

La O Toleano, Eyder. "Entrevistas: Un gnomo contra los leones." *La Ventana*, 3 October 2007. Accessed 2 January 2009. http://laventana.casa.cult.cu/modules.php?name=News&file=article&sid=3867.

Landau French, Anya. "Carlos Varela Unplugged at New America." *The Havana Note.com*, 18 December 2009. Accessed 5 January 2010. http://www.thehavananote.com.

Lefebvre, Henri, and Eleonore Kofman, eds. *Writings on Cities*. Malden, MA, and Oxford, UK: Blackwell Publishers, 1997.

Levin, Jordan. "Carlos Varela's Music Speaks to the Audience." *Miami Herald*, 17 May 2010.

– "Cuban's Songs Bring Message." *Miami Herald*, 6 March 1998.

Lipsitz, George. *Footsteps in the Dark: The Hidden Histories of Popular Music*. Minneapolis: University of Minnesota Press, 2007.

Lopez Sánchez, Antonio. *La canción de la nueva trova*. La Habana: Ediciones Musicales Atril, 2001.

Luis, Leopoldo. "Café G, Sueño y pesadilla del arte." *El Caimán Barbudo*, May–June, 2010.

Maasud-Piloto, Felix. *From Welcomed Exiles to Illegal Immigrants*. New York: Rowman and Littlefield, 1995.

Machado, Mabel. "Conectado con la memoria y los corazones de los cubanos." *La Jiribilla* 9 (12–18 March 2011). Accessed 15 November 2011. http://www.lajiribilla.cu/2011/n514_03/514_25.html.

Mañach, Jorge. *Indagación del choteo*. La Habana: La Verónica, 1940.

Manduley, Humberto. *El Rock en Cuba*. Bogotá: Atril Ediciones Musicales (Producciones Abdala), 2001.

Manuel, Peter. *Essays on Cuban Music: North American and Cuban Perspectives*. Lanham, MD: University Press of America, 1991.

Marañón, Gregorio. "Frases y pensamientos." *Revista Cultura* 1 (2005), Centro Bibliográfico y Cultural de la ONCE, Madrid.

Martín, Juan Luis. "Las investigaciones sociales en relación con la juventud." Intervención en la sexta reunión de investigadores de la juventud, La Habana, 28 March 1989.

Martín Fernández, Consuelo, Maricela Perera Pérez, and Maiky Díaz Pérez. "La vida cotidiana en Cuba. Una mirada psicosocial." *Temas* 7 (July–September 1996).

Matamoros, Miguel. "Bomba lacrimosa." 78 RPM LP, Victor 46691-B, 1928.
Mateo Palmer, Margarita. *Del bardo que te canta*. La Habana: Letras Cubanas, 1988.
Moore, Robin D. *Music and Revolution: Cultural Change in Socialist Cuba*. Berkeley: University of California Press, 2006.
Nasatir, Robert. "El Hijo de Guillermo Tell: Carlos Varela Confronts the Special Period." Cuban Studies 39 (2008): 44–59.
Navaarro, Desiderio. "Introducción al ciclo." «La política cultural de la Revolución: memoria y reflexión». *Criterios* (website of the Centro Teórico-Cultural Criterios). 30 January 2007. http://www.criterios.es/cicloquin queniogris.htm.
Nuez Carrillo, Iván de la. "El cóndor pasa." *La Gaceta de Cuba*, June 1989, 11–12.
– "La canción como laberinto hacia una totalidad otra." *La Gaceta de Cuba*, July 1989, 5.
Pacini Hernandez, Deborah, and Reebee Garofalo. "Between Rock and a Hard Place: Negotiating Rock in Revolutionary Cuba, 1960–1980." In *Rockin' Las Américas: The Global Politics of Rock in Latin/o America*, ed. Deborah Pacini Hernandez, Héctor Fernández L'Hoeste, and Eric Zolov, 43–67. Pittsburgh: University of Pittsburgh Press, 2004.
Padrón, Frank. "Aunque sea gris la tarde." *Revolución y Cultura* 1 (2002): 64–5.
– "El cronista del asfalto." *Encuentro en la Red*, 20 March 2006, reprinted in *Los Que Soñamos* 16 (March 2006).
Perna, Vincenzo. *Timba: The Sound of the Cuban Crisis*. London: Ashgate, 2005.
Perrone, Charles A. "Dissonance and Dissent: The Musical Dramatics of Chico Buarque." *Latin American Theatre Review* (Spring 1989): 81–94.
– *Masters of Contemporary Brazilian Song, 1965–1985*. Austin: University of Texas Press, 1989.
Quiroga, José. *Cuban Palimpsests*. Minneapolis: University of Minnesota Press, 2005.
Ramirez, Marta Maria. "Carlos Varela: Un hijo de Guillermo Tell." *La Ventana* 9 (November 2004).
Ramos, Julio. *Desencuentros de la modernidad en América Latina: Literatura y política en el siglo XIX*. Mexico City: Editorial Cuarto Propio, 2003.
Reed, T.V. *The Art of Protest: Culture and Activism from the Civil Rights Movement to the Streets of Seattle*. Minneapolis: University of Minnesota Press, 2005
Richey, Lisa Ann, and Stefano Ponte. *Brand Air: Shopping Well to Save the World*. Minneapolis: University of Minnesota Press, 2011.

Rodríguez Domínguez, Ezequiel. *Trío Matamoros: treinta y cinco años de música popular*. La Habana: Arte y Literatura, 1978.
Rother, Larry. "MTV Worker Dismissed over Cuba Concert." *New York Times*, 9 June 1994
Sanz, Joseba. *Silvio: Memoria trovada de una revolución*. Bilbao: Guazapa Liburuak, 1992.
Sarusky, Jaime. *Una leyenda de la música cubana. Grupo de experimentación sonora del ICAIC*. La Habana: Editorial Letras Cubanas, 2005.
Shaw, Lauren E. "Los Novísimos and Cultural Institutions." In *A Changing Cuba in a Changing World*, ed. Mauricio Font, 578–89. New York: Bildner Centre for Western Hemispheric Studies Graduate Centre, 2008.
Stock, Ann Marie. *On Location in Cuba: Street Filmmaking during Times of Transition*. Chapel Hill: University of North Carolina Press, 2009.
Sublette, Ned. *Cuba and Its Music from the First Drums to the Mambo*. Chicago: Chicago Review Press, 2004.
Tester, Keith. *The Flâneur*. London: Routledge, 1994.
Thomas, Susan. "Did Nobody Pass the Girls the Guitar? Queer Appropriations in Contemporary Cuban Popular Song." *Journal of Popular Music Studies* 18, no. 2 (2006): 124–43.
– "Musical Cartographies of the Transnational City: Mapping Havana in Song." *Latin American Music Review* 31, no. 2 (Fall–Winter 2010): 222–6.
Valiño, Omar. "Trazados en el agua. Para una geografía ideológica del teatro cubano de los años noventa." *Temas* 15 (July–September 1998): 116.
Varela, Carlos. Personal correspondence files.
Venegas, Christina. *Digital Dilemmas: The State, the Individual, and Digital Media in Cuba*. New Brunswick: Rutgers University Press, 2010.
Vilar, Juan "Pin." *Carlos Varela*. Madrid: Fundación Autor, 2004.
Vizcaíno Serrat, Mario. "Carlos Varela: el gnomo y el guerrero." *La Gaceta de Cuba* 1 (January–February 1994): 20–2.
– "Entrevistas: Le toca a Carlos Varela la manzana en la cabeza?" *La Ventana*, 30 July 2005. Accessed 23 October 2009. http://laventana.casa.cult.cu/modules.php?name=News&file=article&sid=2667.
von Eschen, Penny. *Satchmo Blows Up the World: Jazz Ambassadors Play the Cold War*. Cambridge: Harvard University Press, 2004.
Weiss Rachel, ed. *To and From Utopia in the New Cuban Art*. Minneapolis: University of Minnesota Press, 2011.
Wilson, Elizabeth. "From the Sphinx in the City." In *The Blackwell City Reader*, ed. Gary Bridge and Sophie Watson, 419–29. Malden, MA, and Oxford, UK: Blackwell Publishing, 2002.

Zamora, Bladimir. "Carlos Varela. Una huella en el asfalto." *El Caimán Barbudo* 22, no. 255 (1989): 20–1.
- "La gente siempre sueña." *La Jiribilla* 107 (2003). Accessed 20 June 2003. http://www.lajiribilla.cu/2003/n107_05/aprende.html.
- "Los más pegados al pantalón." *La Jiribilla* 182 (2004). Accessed 15 January 2005. http://www.lajiribilla.cu/2004/n182_10/aprende.html.

Zamora, Bladimir, and Fidel Díaz. *Trovadores de la herejía*. La Habana: Casa Editorial, 2012.

Zolov, Eric. *Refried Elvis: The Rise of the Mexican Counterculture*. Berkeley: University of California Press, 1999.

Zurbano, Roberto. "La música popular como espejo social." Sección Controversia. *Temas* 29, April–June 2002.
- . "El Rap Cubano: Can't Stop, Won't Stop the Movement!" In *Cuba in the Special Period: Culture and Ideology in the 1990s*, ed. Ariana Hernandez-Reguant, 143–59. New York: Palgrave Macmillan, 2009.

Contributors' Biographies

Joaquín Borges-Triana received his PhD at the Instituto Superior de Arte (ISA) in Havana and is the author of numerous books and articles about contemporary Cuban song. His most recent books include *Músicos de Cuba y del mundo: Nadie se va del todo* (Spain, 2013) and *La luz, bróder, la luz, Canción Cubana Contemporánea* (Havana 2009). He is a journalist for *El Caimán Barbudo* in Havana and regularly teaches Cuban and visiting students.

Jackson Browne is a US-based singer-songwriter. His debut album came out on David Geffen's Asylum Records in 1972. Since then, he has released thirteen studio albums and three collections of live performances. He was honoured with induction into the Rock and Roll Hall of Fame in 2004 and the Songwriter's Hall of Fame in 2007. Beyond his music, Browne is known for his advocacy on behalf of the environment, human rights, and arts education.

María Caridad Cumaná received her Masters in Art History at the University of Havana in 2010, and was, from 2006 to 2011, Coordinator of the Portal del cine y el audio-visual latinoamericano y caribeño at the Fundación del Nuevo Cine Latinoamericano in Havana. In 2009, she coordinated the production of a multimedia Encyclopedia of Latin American and Caribbean films on DVD. She is the co-author of two books on Cuban cinema: *Pletóricas latitudes del margen: el cine latinoamericano ante el tercer milenio* (2005) and *Mirada al cine cubano* (1999).

Karen Dubinsky is a professor in the Global Development Studies and History departments at Queen's University in Kingston, Ontario. She is the author of a number of books, most recently *Babies without Borders: Adoption and Migration across the Americas* (2010) and co-editor of *New World Coming: The Sixties and the Shaping of Global Consciousness* (2009). At Queen's she co-teaches a course on Cuban Culture and Society that brings Canadian students to the University of Havana annually.

Paul Webster Hare was a British diplomat for thirty years and from 2001 to 2004 the British Ambassador to Cuba. He now teaches International Relations at Boston University. Professor Hare is a Fellow of the Weatherhead Center for International Affairs at Harvard University and the author of articles on Cuba published by the Brookings Institution and the University of Miami. His novel set in contemporary Cuba – "Moncada – A Cuban Story" – was published in 2010.

Robin Moore is a Professor of Ethnomusicology at the University of Texas in Austin. His publications include *Nationalizing Blackness: Afrocubanismo and Artistic Revolution in Havana, 1920–1940* (1997), *Music and Revolution: Cultural Change in Socialist Cuba* (2006), *The Music of the Hispanic Caribbean* (2010), and *Musics of Latin America* (2012). Since 2005, he has served as editor of the *Latin American Music Review*.

Robert Nasatir received his PhD from Vanderbilt University and is Chair of the Department of World Languages and Cultures at Father Ryan High School in Nashville, Tennessee. He has published several articles on Cuban music, including "El Hijo de Guillermo Tell: Carlos Varela Confronts the Special Period," in *Cuban Studies* 39 (2008).

Xenia Reloba de la Cruz graduated from the Department of Journalism at the University of Havana in 1994. She has worked as an editor at various organizations in Havana, including the Martin Luther King Memorial Centre and the Centro Cultural Pablo de la Torriente Brau. In 2011 she became the editor of the journal *Casa de las Américas*, published by the Casa de las Américas in Havana.

Susan Thomas is an Associate Professor in Musicology and Women's Studies at the University of Georgia. Her book, *Cuban Zarzuela: Performing Race and Gender on Havana's Lyric Stage* (University of Illinois Press, 2008), was awarded the Pauline Alderman and Robert M. Stevenson book awards. She has contributed chapters to a number of books, including Moore, ed., *Musics of Latin America* (W.W. Norton, 2012) and Shaw and Stone, eds., *Screening Songs in Hispanic and Lusophone Cinema* (Manchester University Press, 2012), and has published in a variety of journals, including *Journal of Popular Music* and *Latin American Music Review*.

Index

"25 mil mientras sobre la verdad," 71, 89, 115

A guitarra limpia, 27
Adorno, Theodor, 8
aesthetics, 17
African culture, xii, 93–4
Afro-Cuban culture, 99
"Ahora que los mapas cambian de color," 55, 59 73, 80, 84
Los Aldeanos, xx, 86, 116–17
Alfonso, Gerardo, xviii, 5, 6, 7, 9, 18, 27, 39, 80, 109
allegory, Havana as, 84
Almodóvar, Pedro, 118
Amores perros, 116
"Apenas abro los ojos," xx, 108
Arango, Arturo, 18
Arte Vivo, 97
Asociación hermanos Saíz, 26

El B, xx
Bajo presión, 71
Baker, Geoffrey, xvi, 86, 100
Barba, Eugenio, 8
Barbería, Luis Alberto, 27
Batista, Fulgencio, 96

Baudrillard, Jean, 8
Bay of Pigs, 31, 53, 70, 96
Beat Magazine, xxv, 79
Beatles, xxv, 6, 19, 22, 32, 53, 62, 70, 101–3
Bécquer, Fernando, 27
"Bendita lluvia," 13, 56
Bengelsdorf, Carollee, 63
Berazaín, Adrián, 57
Berlin wall, 36, 63
Beuys, Joseph, 7
Birkenmaier, Anke, 86
Bobes, Marilyn, 18
Bola de Nieve, 19, 59, 69
"Bomba lacrimosa," 94, 95
Bono, 61
Bosé, Miguel, xv
Brum, Julio, 10
Buarque, Chico, 74, 109, 114
Buena Fe, 27
Buena Vista in the Club, 86
Buena Vista Social Club, 26
"Bulevar," 13, 55, 69, 82
Burton, Richard, 84

Los Cabecipelaos, 6
El Caimán Barbudo, 3, 9

276 Index

Calabrese, Omar, 8
Calderón, Armando, 60
"La calle," 109
"Callejón sin luz," 80, 88
Camnitzer, Luis, 4
Canción Cubana contemporánea, 17, 26
"La canción de las sillas," 16
Candelita, 6
Carlos Varela en vivo, 11, 25, 72, 88
Carlos Varela, All His Greatest Hits, 30
Carpentier, Alejo, 87
Carrillo, Nuez, 3, 68, 69
Carter administration, 98
Casa de las Américas, 20
Casa del Joven Creador, 6
Casa vieja, 71
Casaus, Victor, 71
Castellanos, Ernesto Juan, 62
"Castillos de area," 77
Castro, Fidel, xi, 53, 63–4, 102–3
Castro, Raul, 102
catharsis, 61, 111, 113–14, 122
censorship, xvi, xx, xxii, 60, 63, 64, 74, 98, 107, 117–18
Centro Cultural Pablo de la Torriente Brau, 26, 27
Centro de la Canción Protesta, 1967, 20
Ceredo Seso, Sergio, 3
Chaplin concert, 1989, 9, 10
Chaplin, Charlie, 60
Charles Chaplin Theatre, 9, 63, 64, 107
Cher, 70
childhood, 18, 76, 85, 89, 96, 121
Chinese cemetery, 80, 84
cinema, xiv, 38, 69
"Circulo de tiza," 57
Clash, The, 19

Cold War, xxiii, xxv, 53, 57, 120
"Colgando del cielo," 55, 115
"La comedia silente," 57, 60, 77
Communist Party of Cuba, 38
Como los peces (album), xxiii, 11, 12, 19, 25, 26, 28, 35, 36, 40–2, 45–8, 74–5, 87, 115
"Como los peces" (song), 25, 115
"Como me hicieron a mí," 56, 74, 99
"Como un angel," 11–12, 41–2, 75, 90, 122
Los Compadres, 96
Concierto por la paz, 2009, xv, 55, 104
Condesa de Merlin, 86
Cooder, Ry, 26
corruption, 35
Council for Mutual Economic Assistance, 36
Crespo, Mario, 70
Cristina Venegas, xviii
Cronista moderna, modern chronicler, 82–3, 89
Cruz, Celia, 57, 59
Cubadisco festival, 27
CubaLlama, 62
Cuban Institute of Cinematographic Art and Industry (ICAIC), 9, 20
Cuban missile crisis, 31, 96
Cuban nationalism, 83
Cubans in Cuba, those who stayed, xi, xii, 76
Cubans who left, those who left, xi, xii, 84, 111
"Cuchilla en la acera," 72, 98
Culture Department of the Union of Communist Youth, 6

Dadaist movement, 70
de la Grange, Bertrand, 63

Index 277

De vuelta a casa", 13, 71
del Casal, Julián, 82
del Llano, Eduardo, 6
del Valle, Pepe, 27
Deleuze, Gilles, 8
Delgado, Frank, xviii, 5, 6, 9, 12, 18, 27, 32, 39, 46, 57, 80
Derrida, Jacques, 8
"Desde ningún lugar," 58
"Detrás del cristal," 57, 82, 83, 85, 87, 89
diaspora, vx, xx, 62, 113–4
Díaz, Ariel, 27
disadvantages to Cuban music production, 118–9
Doble Filjo, xx
Don Quixote, 70
Donas, Ernesto, 10
Doors, The, 70, 75
Dylan, Bob, xv, 19, 70, 74, 90, 97, 109, 116

Echarry, Irina, 61, 64
"Échate a corer," 58
EGREM, 6, 10
Elpidio Valdés, 32, 53, 70, 85, 105
embargo, 63, 96
emigration, xvi, 12, 37, 45
"El enigma del árbol," 53, 73
"En una tempestad," 29
Espinosa, Norge, 4
"Estás," 29, 30, 57, 81–2

family relations, 31, 45
Feliú, Santiago, xvii, 4–5, 6, 9, 18, 24, 25, 39, 47, 109
Feliú, Vicente, 19
Fenández-Larrea, Ramón, 12
Ferrer, Pedro Luis, 5
Festival de la Nueva Trova, 16

Flâneur, 81–84
Fleites, Alex, 18
Formell, Juan, 12, 97, 111
"Foto de familia," 25, 45, 57, 62, 71, 85, 86, 99, 113
Foucault, Michel, 7, 8, 10
Fourteen Sons of William Tell, 64
Fowler Calzada, Victor, 7
Francisco, René, 64
Frith, Simon, 60
Fromm, Erich, 8
Fuentes, Diana, 89
future, v, 59

Galileo, 70
García, Charly, 19
Gema y Pavel, 26
generation of moles, xxii, 4, 39, 47
generations, xiv, xix, xxi, 16–18, 25–6, 93
Gieco, León, 19
Gil, Gilberto, 97
Gonzáles Ochoa, Julio Cesar, 89
González Iñárritu, Alejandro, 12, 116
González, Sara, 20
Gorbachev, 63
"Graffiti de amor," 43, 114
Gramsci, Antonio, 8
Grenet, Eliseo, 94
"Grettel," 45
Grey Years, Quinquenio Gris, 24, 31, 61
Grotowski, Jerzy, 8
Grupo de experimentación Sonora (GES), 20
Guattari, Félix, 8
Guerra, Wendy, 113
Guevara, Alfredo, 20
Guevara, Che, 4, 21, 31, 53, 101, 111

278   Index

"Guillermo Tell," xx, 10, 25–26, 52, 54, 62, 63, 64, 72, 88–9, 98, 114, 121
Gutiérres Alea, Tomás, 31, 38, 53, 70, 71
Gutiérrez, Diego, 27
Gutiérrez, Pedro Juan, 86, 87

Habana Abierta, 27
Habana Oculta, 26
"Habáname," 13, 47, 71, 86, 87, 89
Habanastation, 56
Hamlet, Lester, 71
Havana Beyond the Ruins, 86
Havana, City, xiv, xxiv, xxv, 45, 47, 53, 54, 57, 61, 68, 72, 74, 76, 79–91, 104, 108
Heredia, José María, 29
Hernandex-Reguant, Ariana, xx
Hernández Busto, Ernesto, 7, 10
"Hijo del fuego," 16–17, 31
Los hijos de Guillermo Tell, 13, 30, 57, 63
Hip Hop, xvi, xix, xx, 86, 116–7
Hire, Powder Keg, The, 12, 115, 116
"Historia de un descapotable," 77
"Hombre de silicona," 44
Hotel Nacional, 6, 108
"El humo del tren," 56, 85
Hussein, Saddam, 70

identity (National), xviii, xx, 7, 80, 83, 85
identity (personal), 19
Iglesias, Julio, 119
"Imagine," 102, 103
immigration, 35, 56–58, 62, 71, 76
individualism, 35, 42, 43, 44
influences, 5, 11–12, 19, 70, 80, 84, 109–10, 120–2
Instituto Cubano de Arte e Industria Cinematográficos (ICAIC), 9, 20

Instituto Superior de Arte (ISA), xv, 5, 68, 71, 77, 102, 108, 112
Interactivo, 27
internet, xvi
iron curtain, 84
Isla de la Juventud, 16

Jacinto Villa, Ignacio, 60, 69
Jalisco Park (album), 11, 25, 72, 83, 111
"Jalisco Park" (song), xxiii, xxv, 6, 10, 20, 24, 53, 57, 72, 80, 84–6, 88, 112
"Jaque mate 1916," 55, 70–1
Jara, Victor, 97
Jay Z and Beyoncé, xvii
Los jóvenes de la Nueva Trova, the youth of Nueva Trova, 16
Juventud Rebelde, 4

Los Kent, 97
Kermit the Frog, 70
Kirk, John, xviii

"Lágrimas negras," 19, 41
Larramendi, Boris, 27
Latin American bolero, 94
Latin Grammys, xviii
Laugart, Xiomara, 6, 18
Laurel and Hardy, 60
Lenin, Vladimir, 8, 55, 59, 70–71
"El leñador sin bosque", xix, 46, 55
Lennon, John, xxv, 9, 70, 102, 103
Levin, Jordan, 61
Lezama Lima, José, 87
Lins, Ivan, xv
Lipsitz, George, 52, 60
Literacy campaign, 54
El lobo, el bosque and el hombre Nuevo, 38
Love, 60, 77

Lukács, György, 8
Lyotard, Jean-Francois, 7, 8

Machado, Gerardo, 94
Madagascar, 38
Madonna, 70
"Madrugué," 6
Malécon, xxiv, 54, 74, 77
Man on Fire, 12, 116
Mañach, Jorge, 95
Manduley, Humberto, 97
Manteca, 38
Marañón, Gregorio, 10
"La marea," 30
Mariel Boatlift, 31, 37
Martí, José, 27, 82
Marx, xxii, 8
Matamoros, Miguel, 19, 70, 94, 95
McCartney, Paul, 68
media, 37, 74
Medina, Amed, 12
Memorias del subdesarrollo, Memories of Underdevelopment (film), 31
"Memorias," xx, xxiii, 19, 31–2, 53, 54, 70, 81, 85, 86, 111, 114
Metal Oscuro, 97
Meza, Ramón, 82
Miami Herald, 61
Miami, xxi, 62, 114
Milanés, Pablo, xv, xvi, 19, 20, 22, 30, 46, 57, 97, 107–9, 115
military coup, 96
"Mis amigos se estan yendo," 57
Misha the Bear, 70
modernization, 83
Monedas al aire, 11, 25, 73, 74, 84, 122
Morales, Adrián, 18
Morrison, Jim, 45, 70
Movimiento de la Nueva Trova (MNT), 20, 26

Mujer transparente, 70
"Muro," 74
"Muros y puertas," 76, 115
music production, 119–20

"Nadie," 56, 77
National Museum of Fine Arts, 3
Nicola, Noel, 19, 20, 30, 97
Nietzsche, 8
"El niño, los sueños y el reloj de arena", 45
No es el fin (album), 13, 30, 76, 86, 89, 90, 121–2
"No es el fin" (song), 77
nostalgia, 10, 30, 31, 80, 82, 84, 86–90
Novísima Trova, 26, 30
Nubes (album), 12, 27–29, 58, 75–6, 87, 88, 115, 116
"Nubes" (song), 29
Nueva Trova, xv, 4, 6, 16–21, 30, 39, 80, 96–7, 107

ocean, 37, 41, 57, 74
Ochoa, Kelvis, 27
"Oda a mi generación," 22–4, 25, 28
Operation Peter Pan, 53, 70, 111
Orozco, Yaima, 27
Ortega y Gasset, 8
"La otra orilla," 18, 57

Padrón Nodarse, Frank, 12, 52
Padrón, Humberto, 45, 71
Padura Fuentes, Leonardo, xviii
"Una Palabra," 12, 87, 115, 116
Palacio del Salsa, 120
"Para Bábara," 6, 18
Paris, 81–2
Patria Potestad, 111
Paz, Senel, 38
Pedro, Alberto, 38

Peña de 13 y 8, 26
Peña, Umberto, 3
"Pequeña serenata diurnal," 45
"Pequeños sueños," 25, 42
Pérez, Amaury, 19
Pérez, Fernando, 38
Perna, Vincenzo, 68
Pink Floyd, 110
"La polítca no cabe en la azucarera," xxiii, 25, 35, 37, 54, 58, 59
political citizenship (Cuban), xxiv, 63
Ponjuan, Eduard, 64
¿Por que Ilora Lesie Caron?, 4
post-Soviet Cuba, 59, 73, 84
post-structuralism, xxii, 7, 10
Poveda, Donato, 5
Prieto, Abel, 99
Las profecías de Amanda, 71
prostitution and pimping, 35
Proyecto del Castillo de la Fuerza, 63
Puebla, Carlos, 96

Quiroga, José, xxi, 79, 81, 86

Radio Ciudad de la Habana, 9
rafters' crisis of 1994, 73
Raitt, Bonnie, xv, 12
Ramirez, Marta Maria, 52
Ramos, Eduardo, 20
reggaeton, 117
Reich, Wilhelm, 8
religion/faith, xiii, 41, 42, 43, 104
renaissance in Cuban art, 4
Revolution Square, 114–5
revolution, xiv, xix, 4, 9, 10, 16, 18–20, 25, 31, 53, 63, 72, 84, 96, 101–2
Revuelta, Vicente, 8
Robinson Crusoe, 55, 70, 73
"Robinson," 11, 55, 55, 73
rock and roll, 97

Rodriguez, Silvio, xxiii, 16, 19–22, 24–6, 28, 30, 45, 46, 53, 57, 59, 70, 97, 98, 103, 107–9, 111–12, 115
Rodríguez, Tony, 89
Rolling Stones, The, 19
Romeo and Juliet, 70

Sabina, Joaquin, xv, 109, 118, 121
Saborit, Eduardo, 96
Sanchez, José, 94
Sanchez, Yoani, 61, 117
Santa-María, Haydée, 20
Santos, Carlos, 27
Schaffer, R. Murray, 60
Schopenhauer, 8
Scott, Tony, 12, 116
Señal en el Asfalto, 9, 11
"Sequía del alma," 12
"Será sol," 28, 75
Serrat, Joan Manuel, 19, 25, 109, 118
"Siete," 12, 29, 30, 76, 82, 83, 85, 87, 116
Simon, Paul, 19
Sintesis, xxv
Sloterdijk, Peter, 8
Snow White, 70
"Solo tú puedes traer el sol," 11, 42, 90
"Sombras en la pared," 82, 90
"Son de de la suerte," 6
Sondheim, Steven, 87
Sonido X, 97
Soviet economic model, 24
Soviet Union, xix, 11, 25, 54–55, 63, 81, 84, 102
"Soy un gnomo," 56
Special period/economic crisis, xix, xx, xxii, 11, 25–6, 35–7, 40, 41, 47, 53, 55, 61, 74–5, 98

Springsteen, Bruce, 53
Stalin, 8
Stock, Anne Marie, xviii
Strawberry and Chocolate, 38, 71
sugar, 35
Superávit, 27
survival, struggle for, 35–7, 40

Tabío, Juan Carlos, 38
Tagore, 114
Teatro Carlos Marx, 88, 104
Teatro Nacional de Guiñol, 6
"Telón de fondo," 13, 55, 77, 121
Temas, 39
"El temba", 99
theatre, xxiv, 5, 38, 61, 68, 110
theatricality in song (thesis), 68, 71, 77
"Tijeras," 6
timba, 99
"Todo será distinto," 13, 19, 30, 59, 77, 101
"Todos se roban," 55, 72
Tomás, Ángel, 4
Tosca, Alberto, 5, 18, 109
tourism, 86
Trilogía sucia de La Habana, 86
trobar, 6
Tropa Cósmica y Trovaclub, 27
"Tropicollage," 7, 10, 72, 80, 90, 98, 114
trovadores, xix, xxii, 13, 16–18, 22, 25, 29, 33, 68, 81–2, 94
Trovatur, 12
Tzara, Tristan, 55, 70–1

Unión de jóvenes comunistas, 20
University of Havana, 5
Urías, Roberto, 4
US occupation, 94
US-Cuba relations, xi, xiii, xiv, xvi, 62–63, 102

Valiño, Omar, 38
Los Van Van, xvii, 12, 85, 97
Varela, Victor, 4
Vedado, xxv, 4, 61, 79
Vega, Pastor, 71
Veloso, Caetano, 97
Vestido de Novia, 4
Video de familia, 45, 57, 71
vieja trova, 18
"El Viejo sueño acabó", xv, 13, 30, 59, 77, 87, 90, 105, 122
Vilasís, Mayra, 69
Villalón, Andy, 27
Vitier, Sergio, 20
Vivanco, William, 27
Vizcaíno Serrat, Mario, 6, 62

Warhol, Andy, 68
Whitfield, Esther, 86
William Tell, 3, 25, 30, 64, 70, 102

"Yo soy la canción que canto," 69
Young, Neil, 19

Zafra de los diez millones/Harvest of ten million, 24, 31, 53, 101
Zamora, Bladimir, 9, 12, 13
Zurbano, Roberto, xxvi, 40

www.ingramcontent.com/pod-product-compliance
Lightning Source LLC
Chambersburg PA
CBHW030305080526
44584CB00012B/451